Physical Education Framework for California Public Schools

Kindergarten Through Grade Twelve

Developed by the
Curriculum Development and
Supplemental Materials Commission

Adopted by the
California State Board of Education

Published by the
California Department of Education

Publishing Information

When the *Physical Education Framework for California Public Schools* was adopted by the California State Board of Education on September 11, 2008, the members of the State Board were Ted Mitchell, President; Ruth Bloom, Vice President; James Aschwanden; Alan Bersin; Yvonne Chan; Don Fisher; Gregory Jones; David Lopez; Kenneth Noonan; and Johnathan Williams.

The California State Board of Education approved edits to the *Physical Education Framework for California Public Schools* on May 6, 2009. The members of the State Board on that date were Ted Mitchell, President; Ruth Bloom, Vice President; Sophia Angelis; James Aschwanden; Rae Belisle; Yvonne Chan; Gregory Jones; David Lopez; Jorge Lopez; and Johnathan Williams.

This publication was edited by Faye Ong, working in cooperation with Deborah Franklin, Education Programs Consultant, Curriculum Frameworks and Instructional Resources Division. It was designed and prepared for printing by the staff of CDE Press, with the cover and interior design created and prepared by Cheryl McDonald. Typesetting was done by Jeannette Reyes. It was published by the Department of Education, 1430 N Street, Sacramento, CA 95814-5901. It was distributed under the provisions of the Library Distribution Act and *Government Code* Section 11096.

ISBN 978-0-8011-1696-4

Ordering Information

Copies of this publication are available for sale from the California Department of Education. For prices and ordering information, please visit the Department Web site at http://www.cde.ca.gov/re/pn or call the CDE Press Sales Office at 1-800-995-4099. An illustrated *Educational Resources Catalog* describing publications, videos, and other instructional media available from the Department can be obtained without charge by writing to the CDE Press Sales Office, California Department of Education, 1430 N Street, Suite 3207, Sacramento, CA 95814-5901; faxing to 916-323-0823; or calling the CDE Press Sales Office at the telephone number listed above.

Notice

The guidance *Physical Education Framework for California Public Schools* is not binding on local educational agencies or other entities. Except for the statutes, regulations, and court decisions that are referenced herein, the document is exemplary, and compliance with it is not mandatory. (See *Education Code* Section 33308.5.)

Contents

Foreword

With the adoption of the *Physical Education Model Content Standards for California Schools* in January 2005, California raised the bar for physical education instruction. High-quality, standards-based physical education instruction helps students learn not only the skills and knowledge to be physically fit and active, it also gives them the confidence and positive attitude necessary to participate in physical activities.

The Superintendent's Task Force on Childhood Obesity, Type 2 Diabetes, and Cardiovascular Disease recommends increasing the quality and quantity of instruction in physical education to provide more physical activity and enhance student achievement of California's *Physical Education Model Content Standards;* including physical education as core curriculum; and treating physical activity as essential to all students' education and health.

The *Physical Education Framework for California Public Schools: Kindergarten Through Grade Twelve*, adopted by the State Board of Education on September 11, 2008, is an essential resource for the development, implementation, and evaluation of standards-based physical education programs and instruction to meet the recommendations of the task force. Its adoption reinforces the importance of physical education as a vital component of our students' educational experience and its contribution to each student's health and well-being, social development, and readiness to learn.

The framework charges administrators and teachers with instituting standards-based physical education instruction and programs that are effective for every student. Focused on the model content standards and supported by current research, the framework emphasizes student learning with the goal of helping every student adopt a physically active lifestyle. Developed and reviewed by teachers, administrators, and physical education experts, the framework features practical examples and scenarios of student learning to assist teachers in planning instruction. The framework describes the why, when, and how of assessing student learning and presents detailed examples of different types of assessment. It provides guidance on creating a physically and emotionally safe learning environment. Based on the premise that every student can be successful in physical education with good instruction and appropriate resources, the framework also offers suggestions for adaptations to meet the instructional needs of students with disabilities or other challenges to learning.

Recognizing that effective standards-based physical education programs require administrative leadership and support, the framework addresses topics of interest to school-site and district-level administrators, including professional development, curriculum design, instructional and program evaluation, and the selection and maintenance of high-quality instructional resources.

Most important at a time when more children than ever before are obese and inactive, the framework is a call to action. It maps out a path to a physically active, healthy lifestyle for all students. Open the framework and we'll start down the path together.

JACK O'CONNELL
State Superintendent of Public Instruction

THEODORE R. MITCHELL
President, State Board of Education

Acknowledgments

The 2009 edition of the *Physical Education Framework for California Public Schools* was adopted by the State Board of Education on September 11, 2008. When the framework was adopted, the following persons were serving on the State Board:

Ted Mitchell, President
Ruth Bloom, Vice President
James Aschwanden
Alan Bersin
Yvonne Chan
Don Fisher
Gregory Jones
David Lopez
Kenneth Noonan
Johnathan Williams

Members of the Curriculum Development and Supplemental Resources Commission serving in May 2008, when the framework was recommended for adoption by the State Board, were:

Katherine Crawford, Chair, Alameda Unified School District
Constance (Connie) Tate, Vice Chair, San Joaquin County Office of Education
Hope Bjerke, Tehama County Office of Education
John Brooks, Oceanside Unified School District
Linda Childress, Riverside County Office of Education
Patricia Dixon, Palomar College
Martha Hernandez, Ventura County Office of Education
Glee Johnson
Christine Lanphere, Natomas Unified School District
Lucy Medina, Palm Springs Unified School District
Bama Medley, Santa Maria-Bonita Elementary School District
Assembly Member **Gene Mullin,** Assembly Education Committee
Dr. **RoseMary Parga-Duran,** Merced City Elementary School District
Senator **Jack Scott**
Becky Sullivan, Sacramento County Office of Education
Richard Wagoner, Los Angeles Unified School District
Monica Ward, Riverside Unified School District
Kevin Wooldridge, Education for Change Charter Management Organization

Note: Names and affiliations of individuals were current as of the time this publication was developed.

Participating directly in the development and approval process for the framework were the following members of the Physical Education Subject Matter Committee from 2005 through 2008:

Katherine Crawford (Member 2005, 2007)
Patricia Dixon (Member 2005, 2006, 2007, 2008)
Martha Hernandez (Member 2008)
Mary-Alicia McRae (Vice Chair 2005)
Assembly Member **Gene Mullin** (Member 2008)
Dr. **Charles Munger, Jr.** (Vice Chair 2006, 2007)
Dr. **Armida Ornelas** (Member 2005, 2006, 2007)
Richard Wagoner (Chair 2005, 2006)
Monica Ward (Vice Chair 2008)
Kevin Wooldridge (Chair 2007, 2008; Member 2006)

The initial draft of the framework was developed by the Physical Education Curriculum Framework and Criteria Committee (CFCC) between September 2006 and April 2007. The State Board of Education and the Curriculum Development and Supplemental Materials Commission commend the following members of the CFCC and extend great appreciation to them. (The affiliations listed were current at the time of appointment to the committee.)

Milissa Glen-Lambert, CFCC Chair, Los Angeles Unified School District
Deonna Armijo, Moorpark Unified School District
Mary Blackman, San Diego County Office of Education
Melissa Bossenmeyer (Retired), California State University, San Marcos
Daniel DeJager, San Juan Unified School District
Carrie Flint, Lawndale Elementary School District
Candace Hashimoto, Pomona Unified School District
Darcy Kelly, Manteca Unified School District
Kara Martin, Mattole Unified School District
Stacey Mounce, Woodland Joint Unified School District
Amanda Parker, Riverside Unified School District
Michael Riggs, Bonita Unified School District
Timothy Salvino, Newport-Mesa Unified School District
Susan Wilkinson, San Jose State University
Wilhelmina (Willie) Wilson, San Juan Unified School District

Special appreciation is extended to **Janet A. Seaman,** P.E.D., Professor Emerita, California State University, Los Angeles.

Gratitude is expressed to the primary writer of the 2009 edition, **Bonnie Mohnsen,** Ph.D.

For the 2009 edition of the framework, the following managers at the California Department of Education coordinated the overall process for development and publication of the document:

Thomas Adams, Director, Curriculum Frameworks and Instructional Resources Division; and Executive Director, Curriculum Development and Supplemental Materials Commission

Susan Martimo, Administrator, Curriculum Frameworks Unit

The following staff members from the Curriculum Frameworks and Instructional Resources Division contributed to the development of the 2009 edition of the framework:

Deborah Franklin, Lead Consultant, Physical Education Framework
Kenneth McDonald, Education Programs Consultant
Terri Yan, Analyst

The California Department of Education staff members who contributed to the development of the 2009 framework were:

Linda Hooper, Education Research and Evaluation Consultant, Standards and Assessment Division
Walden Williams, Special Education Consultant, Special Education Division
Dianne Wilson-Graham, Physical Education Consultant, Professional Development and Curriculum Support Division

Appreciation is expressed to the California State Library staff for assistance in locating research materials cited in the 2009 framework.

Introduction

California is a land of almost limitless opportunity for physical activity. The ocean, lakes, and rivers offer opportunities for swimming and boating; the warm climate offers year-round access to individual, dual, and team sports; the mountains provide opportunities for hiking, orienteering, and snowboarding; and public recreation programs and private businesses offer opportunities for self-defense, martial arts, fitness, dance, and other physical activities. With this diverse climate and geography, Californians can snow ski in the morning and surf in the afternoon. Because of the richness of the opportunities for physical activities, California is often viewed as a leader in the number of adults who live healthy lifestyles. Yet California children are at risk of developing hypokinetic diseases. This trend must be reversed, and one important step in that direction is the development of this framework to support implementation of standards-based physical education.

What's New?

The most important new feature of this *Physical Education Framework for California Public Schools* is its focus on the content knowledge and skills in the *Physical Education Model Content Standards for California Public Schools.* The framework supports the alignment of curriculum, instruction, assessment, and instructional resources to the state-adopted model content standards. Specific examples for implementing and assessing the standards are provided along with guidance for understanding the standards. Finally, the importance of every student achieving grade-level and course-level standards in preparation for the next level is emphasized.

When compared with the 1994 *Physical Education Framework*, this new framework provides:

- A stronger focus on student learning and the needs of the learner
- Current research references
- A standards-based lesson structure
- A more user-friendly display with charts, graphs, and illustrations
- Examples of standards-based report cards
- A greater emphasis on time spent in moderate to vigorous physical activity

Organization of the Framework

This framework is organized to assist educators with implementing standards-based physical education instruction.

For teachers, the framework supports instruction for student mastery of the physical education model content standards. Focusing on the tools for standards-based instruction, the framework highlights the instructional content of the model content standards, student assessments, instructional considerations, universal access, support, and instructional resources.

The framework defines administrators' roles and the responsibilities that are unique to physical education. In Chapter 8 the framework delineates the administrative roles and support crucial to a successful physical education program. Some topics of interest to administrators include hiring practices, supervision of teachers, professional development in physical education, the importance of a safe learning environment, and program development and evaluation in physical education.

Chapter 1 presents a new vision for physical education instruction; explains the purpose of the framework; identifies goals for administrators, teachers, and students; and examines the challenges to implementing the new vision for physical education instruction.

Chapters 2 through 4 highlight the standards-based curriculum content for the grade-level spans (kindergarten through grade five, six through eight, and nine through twelve). The chapters include an overview of the grade level or course level, standards at a glance, learning "snapshots," and a list of the state-adopted model content standards. Each grade-span section begins with a look at students' developmental capabilities. This section introduces some of the grade- and course-level knowledge and skills contained within the standards. "At a Glance" sections contain the five overarching standards for elementary and middle school and three overarching standards for high school. "Learning Snapshots" each provide a window into the teaching of a grade- or course-level standard, illustrate the standard in action, and offer instructional suggestions. Throughout the framework, examples and suggestions are provided. They are not requirements; they are intended as beginning points to help educators develop physical education lessons, assessments, policies, and procedures.

Chapter 5 guides the development of appropriate assessment tools and methods to ensure that instruction is effective and every student's progress toward achieving specific knowledge and skills is measured. Chapter 6 provides suggestions on effective classroom practices and instructional strategies. Chapter 7 suggests specific strategies to promote access to appropriate standards-based curriculum for every student. Chapter 8 describes the systems of support that should be in place for effective implementation of a rigorous and coherent physical education curriculum. Chapter 9 provides specific guidelines for the selection of instructional resources, including instructional materials, equipment and supplies, technology, and facilities.

1

Vision and Goals for Standards-Based Physical Education

Fast-forward to the year 2020. A generation of students in California is benefiting from standards-based physical education instruction. As young adults these individuals are physically active and fit. They understand the benefits of regular physical activity and know how to plan and implement their own fitness-and-wellness programs. Having mastered the necessary movement skills to participate confidently in many different forms of physical activity, they are ready to challenge themselves by pursuing new forms of movement. These young adults analyze their own movement performance on the basis of bio-mechanics principles. They develop their own learning plans for improving their motor skills and learning new ones. With an understanding of developmentally appropriate activities, they can plan and implement physical activities for young children and children with special needs. They also enjoy the social interactions that arise out of their involvement in physical activity and take responsibility for their interactions with others. They will maintain an active and healthy lifestyle throughout their lives.

Looking at physical education classes across the state in 2020, educators envision students running, jumping, and leaping, exhibiting the joy derived from movement as they participate in challenging standards-based physical activities. Physical education is a time that students look forward to each day. It is a time to move, interact with classmates, and feel good about themselves. Every student comes to class ready to be active and to learn. The teacher provides standards-based instruction designed to ensure a successful learning experience for all students. Every student has equipment so that he or she can practice throughout the instructional period. The class size allows the teacher to provide individual feedback to every student every day.[1] The physical education environment is safe and clean. Every student is getting what he or she needs to become a physically educated adult.

Focus on the Physical Education Model Content Standards

In January 2005, the State Board of Education adopted the physical education model content standards, which serve as the foundation for instruction at all grade and course levels. These model content standards represent the essential skills and knowledge that all students need to maintain physically active, healthy lifestyles. These standards focus on the content of physical education and incorporate the detail required to guide the development of consistent, high-quality physical education instructional programs aimed at student learning and achievement. The standards provide a comprehensive vision of what students need to know and be able to do at each grade and course level. In addition, the standards provide a model for high-quality course design.

With the adoption of the model content standards, physical education instruction now moves to a standards-based approach. Teachers need to shift from using

---

[1]Feedback is most effective when it is specific and positive or specific and corrective.

established instructional design models to a standards-based approach. Standards-based instructional design is based on practices and decisions that focus on student learning and includes each of these essential steps (as noted in Figure 1.1):

- Select the standard, or portion of the standard, students will learn.
- Determine the evidence that best demonstrates that students have learned the content.
- Select or create the assessment tool that is best suited to collect the evidence of student learning.
- Plan instruction.
- Create multiple opportunities for students to learn the content.
- Deliver effective instruction.
- Assess student learning of the content.
- Evaluate assessment data and make decisions about next steps (to reteach the material or move on to new material).

Figure 1.1 Standards-Based Instructional Design Process

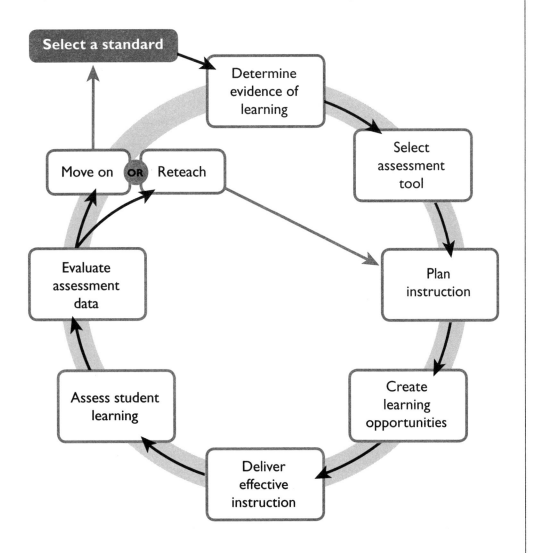

The *Physical Education Model Content Standards for California Public Schools* affirms the standing of physical education as an academic content area. The standards highlight the fact that *participation* in physical activity is not the same as learning the content in physical education. Every grade- and course-level standard should be taught and assessed for student learning. With adequate instruction and sustained effort, every student should be able to achieve the standards; however, some students with special needs may require appropriate accommodations, adaptations, or modifications to meet the standards. Decisions about how students achieve mastery of the model content standards are best left to teachers, schools, and local educational agencies.

Overarching Standards for Kindergarten Through Grade Eight

The five overarching model content standards for elementary and middle school students are as follows:

Overarching Standard 1: Students demonstrate the motor skills and movement patterns needed to perform a variety of physical activities.

Overarching Standard 2: Students demonstrate knowledge of movement concepts, principles, and strategies that apply to the learning and performance of physical activities.

Overarching Standard 3: Students assess and maintain a level of physical fitness to improve health and performance.

Overarching Standard 4: Students demonstrate knowledge of physical fitness concepts, principles, and strategies to improve health and performance.

Overarching Standard 5: Students demonstrate and utilize knowledge of psychological and sociological concepts, principles, and strategies that apply to the learning and performance of physical activity.

Overarching Standards for High School

When students reach ninth grade, they are ready to integrate all that they know with all that they can do. For high school youths, the five overarching standards for kindergarten through grade eight are consolidated into three overarching standards. Essentially, Overarching Standard 1 incorporates Standards 1 and 2 from kindergarten through eighth grade; Overarching Standard 2 incorporates Standards 3 and 4; and Overarching Standard 3 incorporates Standard 5.

Overarching Standard 1: Students demonstrate knowledge of and competency in motor skills, movement patterns, and strategies needed to perform a variety of physical activities.

Overarching Standard 2: Students achieve a level of physical fitness for health and performance while demonstrating knowledge of fitness concepts, principles, and strategies.

Overarching Standard 3: Students demonstrate knowledge of psychological and sociological concepts, principles, and strategies that apply to the learning and performance of physical activity.

Grade-Level and Course-Level Standards

Numerous grade- or course-level standards are associated with each overarching standard. Although it is important to address the grade- or course-level standards, there may be times when remediation is necessary to ensure that students can demonstrate achievement of grade- or course-level standards of previous grade levels or courses. The standards are sequential, building from grade level to grade level, from course to course. Therefore, skills and knowledge from previous grade and course levels serve as important foundations for attaining the standards at the current grade or course level.

Purpose of the Framework

The adoption of physical education model content standards raised the bar for student achievement in physical education. The purpose of this framework is to provide the necessary support so that every student can meet or exceed those standards. The framework provides guidance for effective assessment practices and high-quality instruction, establishing a supportive and safe environment, support for the teacher, and program development. The document serves as a resource for all school stakeholders in developing a quality physical education program. It is important to note, however, that the framework is not a curriculum or a how-to manual. There are many how-to manuals and curricula on the market, and Chapter 9 will assist with the selection of appropriate instructional resources for each school's program.

The framework serves as the blueprint for reform of physical education in California. It is designed to help schools transform their physical education programs into exciting and effective standards-based instructional programs. The framework outlines the implementation of the physical education model content standards and describes a comprehensive physical education system that will prepare every student for a lifelong commitment to physical activity, health, and well-being. The framework is based on two premises:

- The quality and productivity of every individual's life can be enhanced through participation in a comprehensive, inclusive, and sequential physical education program.
- Every student can learn when provided with high-quality instruction by a credentialed teacher along with the appropriate instructional resources and sufficient time.

To achieve the benefits of a comprehensive physical education program, all students must be given sufficient opportunities to attain the physical education learning standards at each grade and course level. California law clearly establishes the priority of physical education instruction. *Education Code* Section 51210 requires schools to provide a minimum of 200 minutes of physical education every 10 school days for students in grades one through six. *Education Code* Section 51222 requires schools to provide a minimum of 400 minutes of physical education every 10 school days for students in grades seven through twelve. (Please see Appendix A for selected statutes and regulations related to physical education.)

Audience

This framework is intended for a variety of audiences. One of the primary audiences is the teacher who is responsible for implementing the physical education model content standards. These teachers are typically elementary teachers with multiple-subject credentials or elementary, middle, and high school teachers with single-subject credentials in physical education. The framework is designed to provide valuable insights to both novice and expert physical education teachers.

For designers of physical education instructional materials, the framework may serve as a guide to the teaching of the physical education model content standards and provide examples of quality assessments, of program evaluation, and of high-quality instruction. Publishers will find information regarding the alignment of instructional materials with the standards as well as the expectations for instructional resources that fully support standards-based physical education instruction.

The organizers of both preservice professional-preparation and in-service professional development programs will find this framework helpful. Considerable skill and knowledge are needed to teach physical education well, and training programs for teachers need to be especially mindful of the expectations placed on K–12 students.

The framework communicates to the physical education/kinesiology faculty at all California institutions of higher education what is expected of entering students who have completed their K–12 education under the model content standards. In addition, it provides guidance for the preparation of the next generation of teachers.

Administrators will find a clearly articulated set of concepts and strategies that form the foundation of a comprehensive physical education system for kindergarten through grade twelve. Administrators are the ones who must set high expectations for the teaching of physical education and provide resources to guide program improvement in physical education. This framework will provide them with the information they need to monitor teaching and guide program improvement in physical education.

Teachers from other subject areas will benefit from the examples of cross-curricular connections. Interdisciplinary instruction can be an efficient method for using instructional time and providing students with a more holistic and deeper understanding of the material.

Community members often seek ways to help improve their local schools, and this framework will help by focusing their efforts on a common set of curricular goals. By providing ideas and resources aligned with grade- and course-level

standards, members of the community ensure their outreach efforts and dona-
tions to classrooms will be put to best use. Finally, parents, guardians, and other
caregivers of students will find the framework useful as they seek to help children
lead healthy lives and complete homework assignments. In addition, the community will gain an understanding of what children are learning in school.

Why Teach Physical Education?

Physical education contributes significantly to every student's health and
well-being. Physical education is an instructional priority for California schools.
Every student—regardless of disability, ethnicity, gender, native language, race,
religion, or sexual orientation—is entitled to a high-quality physical education
program. Physical education is an integral part of the overall education program
for every student and provides one of the few opportunities for every student to
develop the skills, knowledge, and confidence necessary to lead a physically active
lifestyle. A high-quality physical education program promotes an active lifestyle
and improved health, motor skill development, and better cognitive performance
(Etnier and Sibley 2003; Etnier et al. 1997).

Daily physical education for all students is recommended by numerous
national associations, including the Centers for Disease Control and Prevention,
the National Association for Sport and Physical Education, the National Association for State Boards of Education, the American Academy of Pediatrics, and the
American Heart Association, and is noted in *Healthy People 2010.*

Active Lifestyles and Improved Health

Concern about childhood obesity is sweeping the nation. The American Heart
Association's report *A Nation at Risk: Obesity in the United States* (2005, i), discusses the rapidly increasing incidence of obesity in the United States and notes
"if childhood obesity continues to increase, it could . . . cause our current generation of children to become the first generation in American history to live shorter
lives than their parents." According to the Centers for Disease Control, between
1976–80 and 1999–2002, the prevalence of overweight children six to eleven
years of age more than doubled from 7 to 16 percent, and the prevalence of
overweight adolescents twelve to nineteen years of age more than tripled from
5 to 16 percent (*Health, United States, 2005 with Chartbook on Trends* 2005, 9).

A student who becomes skilled and knowledgeable in physical education is
more likely to become a healthy adult who is motivated to remain healthy and
physically active throughout his/her life. The health benefits of physical activity
in adults are well documented in the U.S. Surgeon General's report titled
Physical Activity and Health (U.S. Department of Health and Human Services
1996). Among the benefits outlined in the report were reduced risk of premature
death, lower risk of heart disease, colon cancer, hypertension, diabetes, osteoporosis, as well as improved mental health and physical fitness. In addition, physical
activity improves strength and endurance; helps build healthy bones and muscles;

helps control weight; reduces anxiety and stress; increases self-esteem, mood, and concentration; and may improve blood pressure and cholesterol levels. More recent reports have confirmed the health benefits of active living and the health costs of sedentary living (Booth and Chakravarthy 2002; *Surgeon General's Call to Action to Prevent and Decrease Overweight and Obesity* 2001).

Physical education is a part of a coordinated school health program. It is the component that addresses the student's fundamental need for planned, sequential instruction that promotes lifelong physical activity and attitudes and behaviors that reduce health risks. Other components of a coordinated school health program include health education, nutrition services, health services, healthy school environment, counseling services, psychological and social services, health promotion for staff, and family and community involvement. When the eight components are planned and implemented in a supportive and consistent manner, they achieve far more in promoting health literacy and physical activity than is possible without a coherent, integrated system. A standards-based physical education program also provides an excellent opportunity to ensure that students develop positive social skills and learn to cooperate with others and accept responsibility for their own actions.

Motor Skill Development

The proper development of movement and motor skills requires instruction, practice, and appropriate feedback. Most students do not develop the proper technique or understanding of movement and motor skills on their own. Proficiency in movement and motor skills allows greater enjoyment when one participates in individual and dual sports, combatives, aquatics, tumbling and gymnastics, rhythms and dance, and team sports. In addition, this proficiency carries over to life skills, such as safely walking and climbing and avoiding falls.

Academic Performance

Over 200 studies (Etnier and Sibley 2003) have addressed the relationship between physical activity and cognitive function. Meta-analyses have been applied to the studies in general (Etnier et al. 1997) and, more specifically, to children from elementary to high school age (Etnier and Sibley 2003). According to Etnier and associates (1997), the evidence consistently shows that despite study design, student health, or type of activity, exercise improves the cognitive performance of children. One study found that "devoting substantially increased school time to health-related physical education does not have detrimental effects on students' academic achievement" (Sallis et al. 1999). Further, "students participating in daily physical education exhibit better attendance, a more positive attitude towards school and superior academic performance" (California School Boards Association 2006).

A *Study of the Relationship Between Physical Fitness and Academic Achievement in California Using 2004 Test Results* (2005) reports that while there is little research on the relationship between physical fitness and academic achievement, the research that has been conducted indicates a positive correlation between physical fitness and academic achievement. As one rises, so does the other (*A Study of the Relationship Between Physical Fitness and Academic Achievement* 2005, 1). Comparing student test results from the 2004 Physical Fitness Test (PFT), the FITNESSGRAM®, and the California Standards Tests in mathematics and English-language arts, the study found that a strong, positive relationship exists between physical fitness and academic achievement and that the relationship between the two is stronger for females than for males. The study did not address causality; therefore, "it cannot be inferred from these data that improved physical fitness caused an increase or improvement in academic achievement or vice versa (*A Study of the Relationship Between Physical Fitness and Academic Achievement* 2005, 6). The study's author noted that research has shown that as socioeconomic status improves, so do overall health and academic achievement. The conclusion was, "Cumulative evidence indicates that conditions that improve general health promote both a healthy body and improved intellectual capacity" (*A Study of the Relationship Between Physical Fitness and Academic Achievement* 2005, 6).

In the *Getting Results: Developing Safe and Healthy Kids* series, *Update 5: Student Health, Supportive Schools, and Academic Success* (2005), researchers explored the relationship between school Academic Performance Index (API) scores and physical exercise, as well as other health-related behaviors. In the study, researchers controlled for the racial/ethnic, socioeconomic, and grade-level composition of schools. The researchers found that the API scores of schools went up as physical activity went up, but it was not a strong correlation. The researchers note that the relationship between API scores and physical activity is correlational and does not explain why the API scores are related to physical activity (*Getting Results Update 5* 2005). The results do suggest that "increased physical activity for students may have beneficial consequences in low-performing schools" (*Getting Results Update* 5 2005, 30).

Additional Opportunities for Physical Activity

In addition to physical education instruction, schools offer students a variety of opportunities for physical activity throughout the school day. Physical activity is any bodily movement that is produced by the contraction of skeletal muscle and that substantially increases energy expenditure. Physical activity includes exercise, sport, dance, and other forms of movement. Physical education programs, recess, intramural sports programs, and athletic programs involve physical activity, but each serves a different purpose. Intramural sports and athletic programs provide opportunities for student learning but may not constitute high-quality, standards-based physical education instruction.

The recess period provides students with the opportunity for unstructured time during the school day. These breaks from classroom activities may enhance participation and learning in the classroom aside from the benefits gained from additional physical activity. Research shows that students work more and fidget less on recess days (Jarrett et al. 1998). Recess also provides opportunities for student decision making and contributes to creativity and social learning. California *Education Code* Section 33350(c) states the California Department of Education shall:

> . . . encourage school districts offering instruction in kindergarten and any of grades 1 to 12, inclusive, to the extent that resources are available . . . to provide daily recess periods for elementary school pupils, featuring time for unstructured but supervised play; to provide extracurricular physical activity and fitness programs and physical activity and fitness clubs. . . .

One of the recommendations of the Superintendent's Task Force on Obesity, Type 2 Diabetes, and Cardiovascular Disease (2006) is to "require that schools provide kindergarten and grades 1–6 students with opportunities for physical activity breaks (recess) at least once per 120 minutes of instruction."

Intramural programs provide opportunities for students to be physically active and apply physical education learning outside the curricular program. In addition, intramural programs give students an opportunity to implement the skills and knowledge gained in physical education and to participate in a competitive situation without being subjected to the selection processes used in athletics. A wide variety of activities (e.g., sport, dance, exercise) meet the needs, experiences, interests, and ability levels of every student.

Athletic programs are essentially designed for youths who have special skills and would like to specialize in one or more sports. They provide students with the opportunity to refine their skills and compete with others of similar interests and abilities. Athletic programs typically serve the more highly skilled and motivated students on a selective basis. Because of the emphasis on competition, performance is the primary goal. And, although athletic programs are extremely demanding physically, they are not a substitute for physical education. Because athletic programs focus on a particular sport, they do not address the full spectrum of skills and knowledge of the model content standards at grade or course levels.

Marching band, cheerleading, and JROTC also offer students opportunities to be physically active. These activities may not prepare students to meet grade- or course-level standards in physical education and may not follow the high school course of study established by California *Education Code* Section 33352(b)(7). If a district desires to award physical education credit for courses such as JROTC, marching band, cheerleading, and drill, it is the responsibility of the district to determine how each particular course, as conducted in its district, supports a course of study for grades nine through twelve that includes the eight content areas and substantially meets the objectives and criteria of *EC* 33352(b)(7). While it is not required that every course for which physical education course credit is given include all eight areas, the district is required to structure its course offerings such that all eight areas are included over the course of study offered to all students.

Goals

The framework sets forth goals for the three primary participants in the learning process: administrators, teachers, and students. The attainment of these goals will help to ensure that the vision for physical education at the beginning of this chapter becomes a reality.

Administrators

Administrators provide leadership to support high quality, standards-based physical education instruction. To achieve this goal, administrators:

1. Hire credentialed teachers and provide them with continuing professional development.
2. Ensure that the minimum required minutes for physical education are met for every student.
3. Provide safe well-maintained facilities.
4. Provide sufficient equipment and supplies so that students experience a high degree of time on task.
5. Set high expectations for physical education instruction and student learning.
6. Take a leadership role in ongoing physical education program evaluation.
7. Provide ongoing professional development for physical education teachers.
8. Ensure that state and federal codes and regulations are enforced.

Teachers

Teachers deliver high-quality, standards-based physical education instruction to every student. To achieve this goal, teachers:

1. Participate in ongoing professional development opportunities.
2. Provide instruction that is aligned to the physical education model content standards.
3. Provide a physically and psychologically safe learning environment.
4. Frequently assess student progress toward the achievement of the physical education model content standards and adjust instruction accordingly.
5. Provide students with challenging learning experiences that will help to maximize their individual achievement and with opportunities for students to meet or exceed the standards.
6. Provide alternative instructional strategies that address the specific needs of every student in California's diverse student population.
7. Identify the most successful and efficient approaches for each class so that learning is maximized.
8. Select appropriate instructional materials that are aligned with the physical education model content standards.

Students

The ultimate goal of high-quality, standards-based physical education instruction is to prepare every student for a lifetime of physical activity, health, and well-being. To achieve this goal, students:

1. Develop competency in movement and motor skills.
2. Develop competency in combining movement and motor skills.

3. Understand how movement and motor skills should be performed based on biomechanics principles.
4. Understand how to improve their movement and motor skills.
5. Understand game tactics and demonstrate their use in game settings.
6. Understand developmentally appropriate movement and motor skills.
7. Develop a healthy level of flexibility, muscular strength and endurance, body composition, and cardiorespiratory endurance.
8. Participate regularly in physical activity.
9. Understand the benefits of regular physical activity.
10. Understand how to create a personal fitness plan.
11. Demonstrate appropriate social skills in a physical activity setting.
12. Demonstrate appropriate skills in personal responsibility in a physical activity setting.

Overcoming Challenges

Moving to standards-based instruction and learning will require rethinking and refocusing. To increase the opportunity for students to be physically active, cognitively engaged, and proficient in motor skills, the curriculum, assessment, environment, instruction, and instructional materials will require both revision and a new vision of physical education. Educators can achieve reform by adhering to the guidance provided in this framework.

As standards-based physical education is implemented in kindergarten through grade twelve, more and more students will master the grade- and course-level standards. Teachers will have a clear idea of the content their students are expected to master at each grade level and course level. Less time will be spent on review and instruction of preliminary skills and knowledge.

The framework provides suggestions and strategies for overcoming the traditional challenges that physical educators have faced. In this way, the framework is a call to action. The framework charges administrators and teachers with instituting standards-based physical education instruction that is effective for every student. Chapters on instruction, support, and instructional resources guide administrators on the provision of facilities, equipment and supplies, professional development, and supervision necessary to support physical education instruction and suggest class sizes that facilitate high-quality instruction. These chapters, along with chapters on assessment and universal access, assist teachers with using their expertise to select the best instructional strategies and materials for their students. In addition, the framework puts forward the belief that every student can learn and improve his or her motor skills, social skills, and knowledge of physical education content and should be assessed on those skills and that knowledge.

The *Physical Education Model Content Standards for California Public Schools* and the *Physical Education Framework for California Public Schools* can provide the impetus for change—an opportunity to reassess current facilities, equipment and supplies, instructional strategies, and learning environment. Now is the time for change, and this document provides the guideposts to make necessary changes.

2

Standards-Based Physical Education: Kindergarten Through Grade Five

Chapter 2
Standards-Based
Physical Education:
Kindergarten
Through
Grade Five

The elementary school physical education program provides the skills and knowledge students will need to be successful in middle school and high school physical education classes. The emphasis is on the development of fundamental locomotor, nonlocomotor, and manipulative skills (Appendix B). The movement framework (i.e., body, space, effort, and relationship [Appendix C]), basic biomechanics and motor learning principles (Appendixes D and E), and elementary game tactics are also part of the content for elementary school students. Students practice the fundamental locomotor, nonlocomotor, and manipulative skills in a variety of age-appropriate activities. All students use a variety of age-appropriate equipment so that they have multiple opportunities to practice skills. As skill level develops, students begin to understand the relationship between correct technique and practice.

Elementary physical education programs also emphasize the importance of physical activity and personal fitness. Fitness is developed through daily lessons, which emphasize much physical activity, continuous movement, and challenges that involve overloading the major muscle groups. Students are provided with opportunities to understand the fitness components, fitness assessment, and the need for a lifetime of physical activity. Fifth-grade students have their first required experience with the statewide physical fitness test.

Participation in physical activity also can be an important venue for the social, psychological, and emotional development of children. Social skills and personal responsibility skills are taught and learned with feedback.[1] Physical education classes provide an ideal setting for students to learn and practice appropriate social interactions, suitable ways to express and control emotions, and desirable personal responsibility skills.

This chapter incorporates the physical education model content standards for kindergarten through grade five. It provides an explanation of the physical education content areas underlying the standards and outlines activities that are consistent with the standards. The activities in this chapter are examples of one way in which the standards may be approached. The examples are not to be interpreted as requirements for the physical education classroom or as the only way to approach a particular standard. The physical education model content standards set forth what students should know and can do. Therefore, mastery of an individual standard is achieved when students have learned the concept, principle, or skill. Content mastery does not occur simply because students have received a particular explanation or participated in a particular activity. Instead, content mastery comes from well-thought-out lessons that provide students with many practice opportunities in a variety of situations.

---

[1] Feedback is most effective when it is specific and positive or specific and corrective.

Chapter 2
Standards-Based
Physical Education:
Kindergarten
Through
Grade Five

Kindergarten

Kindergarten

Kindergarten students are embarking on a journey of formal physical education and a lifetime of movement. Some students come to kindergarten using the proper form for locomotor and nonlocomotor movements, while most are still learning these skills. Hand-eye coordination is showing steady improvement, but reaction time is still slow. Students enjoy moving to music, so rhythmic activity is an ideal focus of a lesson for practicing locomotor and nonlocomotor skills. Kindergarten students are experiencing moderate but steady growth in height, weight, and muscular strength and endurance. However, according to data from the Centers for Disease Control and Prevention, the prevalence of being at risk of overweight and being overweight for children younger than five years across all ethnic groups has significantly increased (Mei et al. 1998; Ogden et al. 1997; American Academy of Pediatrics 2003).

Kindergarten students are at the preoperational stage of cognitive development. They do not yet understand concrete logic or abstract thinking. They are, however, curious and eager to learn new skills. Some kindergarten students are kinesthetic learners who use their bodies to understand the world. The qualities of color, shape, texture, and space are important concepts for kindergarten students that should be taught in different subject areas. The concept of a circle, for example, can be learned by writing and drawing and through physical education activities that use circles.

Kindergarten students are "me-oriented." They prefer to play alone or in parallel play. Students are eager to feel independent and experience a sense of accomplishment. At the same time, they need clear expectations and help with understanding rules. It is important for teachers to focus on what the students can do rather than what they cannot do. In this way, kindergarten teachers set the stage for a lifetime of joyful movement.

In kindergarten language arts programs, students learn to match consonant and short-vowel sounds to appropriate letters so that in later years they can read complex narratives and essays. Similarly, in kindergarten physical education, students learn locomotor and nonlocomotor movements and how to manipulate objects so that in later years they can create and demonstrate movement sequences, dance steps, tumbling routines, specialized sport skills, and offensive and defensive strategies. The fundamental movement skills learned in kindergarten form the basis for all movement experiences and are used during a lifetime of physical activity.

Chapter 2
Standards-Based
Physical Education:
Kindergarten
Through
Grade Five

Kindergarten

At a Glance

STANDARD 1

Students demonstrate the motor skills and movement patterns needed to perform a variety of physical activities.

Kindergarten students learn about and interpret their environment by moving through space, often to a rhythmic beat. This movement includes moving side-to-side, forward-and-back, and upward-and-down using a variety of pathways (e.g., curved, straight, zigzag), and in relation to objects (e.g., over, under). Students practice locomotor movements, including walking, running, hopping, skipping, jumping, leaping, galloping, and sliding, to move in general space at both fast and slow speeds. Students also practice nonlocomotor movements (i.e., movements around their own axis), including bending, curling, stretching, swaying, swinging, turning, and twisting to move in personal space. Kindergarten students are also beginning to manipulate (e.g., strike, toss, kick, bounce) a wide variety of objects, including lightweight balls, beanbags, and balloons.

STANDARD 2

Students demonstrate knowledge of movement concepts, principles, and strategies that apply to the learning and performance of physical activities.

This standard represents the cognitive knowledge that supports the locomotor, nonlocomotor, and manipulative skills learned in kindergarten. Often, the physical education lesson is able to address Standards 1 and 2 simultaneously; the teacher explains the information to the students and then has them experience it. For example in kindergarten, Standard 2.5 states, "Identify the locomotor skills of walk, jog, run, hop, jump, slide, and gallop"; and Standard 1.16 states, "Perform locomotor and nonlocomotor movements to a steady beat." The teacher first reviews the names of the locomotor skills, and then students perform them to a steady beat.

For Standard 2, students are developing a movement vocabulary. Besides the names of the locomotor skills (e.g., hop, jump, slide), they learn the names of relationships (e.g., over, under, behind), space (e.g., general, personal, up, down), body parts (e.g., shoulder, neck, back), and balance (e.g., base of support). They are also beginning to describe the correct technique for fundamental manipulative skills (e.g., finger position during the follow-through phase of bouncing a ball).

Chapter 2
Standards-Based
Physical Education:
Kindergarten
Through
Grade Five

Kindergarten

STANDARD 3

Students assess and maintain a level of physical fitness to improve health and performance.

The kindergarten child's energy level and readiness to move contribute to a willingness to participate in enjoyable physical activities. The goal is for students to perform moderate to vigorous activities three to four days each week for increasing periods of time. Muscular strength and endurance are developed during kindergarten through activities performed on playground equipment such as horizontal ladders, horizontal bars, and climbing apparatus. Although kindergarten students typically do not lack flexibility, this is the time to have students demonstrate appropriate stretching exercises for the shoulders, legs, arms, and back while stressing the importance of slow, static movements.

STANDARD 4

Students demonstrate knowledge of physical fitness concepts, principles, and strategies to improve health and performance.

Similar to the relationship between Standards 1 and 2, Standard 4 provides the cognitive information to support the fitness activities experienced in Standard 3. Specifically, students learn about physical activities that are enjoyable and challenging, the names of internal parts of the body (e.g., bones, organs), how muscles are used for climbing and for moving bones, and the need to stretch muscles to keep them healthy. They also learn that the heart is a muscle, and it works with the lungs to send oxygen to the other muscles throughout the body. Kindergarten students learn the role of nutrition (including the importance of water) in providing energy for physical activity.

STANDARD 5

Students demonstrate and utilize knowledge of psychological and sociological concepts, principles, and strategies that apply to the learning and performance of physical activity.

Kindergarten students enjoy moving, so they are willing participants in many physical activities. It is important, however, for the teacher to help students associate the positive feelings derived from movement with the physical activity experience so that movement becomes an enjoyable lifelong habit. Kindergarten students tend to be solo learners, so the teaching and practicing of sharing are necessary. This practice can also include sharing the roles of leader and followers during locomotor practice. Again, the teacher helps students to associate sharing with enhanced feelings of joy and fun so that the skill is internalized.

Chapter 2
Standards-Based
Physical Education:
Kindergarten
Through
Grade Five

Kindergarten

Learning Snapshots

STANDARD I

1.1 Travel within a large group, without bumping into others or falling, while using locomotor skills.

Instruction on this standard comes after students have learned the locomotor skills (e.g., walk, run, hop, skip, jump, leap, gallop, slide), general space, and personal space. The teacher sets up four cones to define the boundaries of the general space in which this activity will occur. Posters of each locomotor movement decorate the walls to reinforce movement vocabulary and the eight locomotor skills. During the activity, the teacher calls out and demonstrates a locomotor skill and students respond by performing the skill. Safety is important when one is traveling in a confined space. The teacher emphasizes that students should focus on the activity, so that they do not bump into other students.

1.8 Demonstrate the relationship of under, over, behind, next to, through, right, left, up, down, forward, backward, and in front of by using the body and an object.

The teacher writes each of the relationship words on 8-inch by 5-inch cards: *under, over, behind, next to, through, right, left, up, down, forward, back,* and *in front of.* Several posters illustrating the various relationships decorate the walls. Each student is handed an object, such as a beanbag. The teacher calls out one of the relationships appropriate to the object used and holds up the word. Each student demonstrates the relationship using the object. During closure, the students are assigned to work in pairs. The teacher again calls out one of the relationships and holds up the word. This time, the students discuss what the word means and which word is its opposite (Standard 2.1). For example, the teacher holds up the word *over* and students state that the body would be above the object and that the opposite word would be *under.* After this lesson, the teacher reinforces the terms by using them in practical daily situations. For example, the teacher may ask students to stand next to another student or put the ball under the bench.

1.16 Perform locomotor and nonlocomotor movements to a steady beat.

Four locomotor skills are to be performed to a steady or even beat: walking, running, jumping, and hopping. All nonlocomotor movements can be performed to a steady or even beat, including turning, twisting, bending, and curling. The teacher starts the lesson with a review of the correct technique, demonstrating each skill. The teacher either plays music that has a steady beat or creates a steady beat by striking a drum or other musical instrument while asking the students to clap with the beat. Then, the teacher asks all the students to perform nonlocomotor and locomotor movements to a steady beat as the name of the movement is called out.

Chapter 2
Standards-Based
Physical Education:
Kindergarten
Through
Grade Five

STANDARD 2

2.4 Explain base of support.

"Base of support" refers to the body parts in contact with the ground and the distance between them during any given activity. This concept is best learned over time. During the initial lesson, the teacher defines "base of support" and provides several examples (e.g., the base of support for a bicycle is its two wheels and the distance between them; the base of support for a person standing is her or his two feet and the distance between them). The students are then instructed to find an open space on mats or the grass. The teacher calls out directions: "Show me how you can balance on two body parts," "show me how you can balance on four body parts," "show me how you balance at a high level," and "show me how you balance at a low level." The teacher asks students to stand with feet close together and then with feet apart. Finally, the teacher asks, "In which position did you have a more stable base of support?" During follow-up lessons, the teacher continually refers to the student's base of support when discussing the body parts in contact with the ground.

Kindergarten

STANDARD 3

3.5 Stretch shoulders, legs, arms, and back without bouncing.

Lesson closure is the appropriate time for students to perform stretching exercises. Students need to learn safe stretching exercises and the importance of performing static stretches without bouncing. There are four safe stretches.[2]

ACROSS-ARM STRETCH

Reach right arm across the chest with upper arm
    parallel to the ground.
Place left hand on right upper arm.
Gently push on right arm toward chest.
Repeat with the other arm.

SHOULDER SHRUGS

Stand.
Raise right shoulder toward earlobe.
Lower shoulder.
Raise left shoulder toward earlobe.
Lower shoulder.

ILLUSTRATION CREDITS

ACROSS-ARM STRETCH
Illustration reprinted
with permission from
B. S. Mohnsen, *Teaching
Middle School Physical
Education* (Champaign,
IL: Human Kinetics), 317.
©1997.

SHOULDER SHRUGS
Illustration reprinted
with permission from
©Bonnie's Fitware, Inc.

---

[2] Because there are few safe stretches, the same stretches are listed for both kindergarten and grade one students. These stretches are appropriate for young students.

Chapter 2
Standards-Based
Physical Education:
Kindergarten
Through
Grade Five

Kindergarten

LOWER BACK STRETCH

Lie on back with both knees bent and both feet on the ground.
Grab with both hands the thigh of one bent leg.
Pull thigh toward chest, keeping the knee at a 90-degree angle.
Repeat with other leg.

REVERSE HURDLE STRETCH

Sit with one leg extended and the other leg bent so that the sole of the foot
    is alongside the extended knee.
Bend the extended knee slightly.
Reach both hands toward toes of the
    extended leg.
Repeat with other leg.

The purpose of this activity is to instruct students on the correct stretching technique. A static stretch is a slow, sustained stretch that is held for 10 to 30 seconds. The student "stretches the muscle-tendon unit to the point where mild discomfort is felt and then backs off slightly, holding the stretch at a point just prior to discomfort. This is generally considered a safe stretch . . . especially at the elementary level, this type of stretching is preferred" (*Physical Education for Lifelong Fitness* 2005, 107). Posters and other visual aids can provide students with a picture of the correct technique. During the stretching exercises, students can also be asked to touch the muscle that is being stretched and chorally repeat the name aloud to support learning Standard 4.9.

STANDARD 4

4.6 Identify the location of the lungs and explain the role of the lungs in the collection of oxygen.

The teacher starts the lesson with an explanation that the lungs move oxygen in and air out of the body. The teacher then instructs students to place their hands on their chests and to take a deep breath to determine the location of their lungs. During an aerobic exercise or physical activity, the teacher again asks students to place their hands on their chests in the area of their lungs. Students are then asked about the differences in their breathing before and during exercise. Students answer that they were breathing more frequently when they were exercising to get more oxygen into their bodies.

ILLUSTRATION CREDITS

LOWER BACK STRETCH
Illustration reprinted with permission from B. S. Mohnsen, *Teaching Middle School Physical Education* (Champaign, IL: Human Kinetics), 317. ©1997.

REVERSE HURDLE STRETCH
Illustration reprinted with permission from B. S. Mohnsen, *Teaching Middle School Physical Education* (Champaign, IL: Human Kinetics), 318. ©1997.

Chapter 2
Standards-Based
Physical Education:
Kindergarten
Through
Grade Five

STANDARD 5

5.3 Demonstrate the characteristics of sharing in a physical activity.

Students must first understand the characteristics of sharing to demonstrate sharing during physical activities. The teacher starts the lesson by creating a chart for sharing. The left side of the chart is labeled "Sounds Like" and the right side of the chart is labeled "Looks Like." The teacher asks the students to brainstorm what sharing sounds like. The teacher writes or draws the responses in the left-hand column. The teacher then asks the students to brainstorm what sharing looks like. The teacher writes or draws the responses in the right-hand column. Then, the teacher reviews the students' responses making sure they are correct. The teacher asks students to demonstrate the characteristics of sharing listed on the chart during the motor skill practice part of the lesson. While the students are practicing locomotor and nonlocomotor movements, the teacher provides feedback to the students on their demonstrations of sharing.[3]

---

[3] Feedback is most effective when it is specific and positive or specific and corrective.

Chapter 2
Standards-Based
Physical Education:
Kindergarten
Through
Grade Five

Kindergarten *Physical Education*
Model Content Standards

STANDARD 1
Students demonstrate the motor skills and movement patterns needed to perform a variety of physical activities.

Movement Concepts

1.1   Travel within a large group, without bumping into others or falling, while using locomotor skills.
1.2   Travel forward and sideways while changing direction quickly in response to a signal.
1.3   Demonstrate contrasts between slow and fast speeds while using locomotor skills.
1.4   Create shapes at high, medium, and low levels by using hands, arms, torso, feet, and legs in a variety of combinations.

Body Management

1.5   Create shapes by using nonlocomotor movements.
1.6   Balance on one, two, three, four, and five body parts.
1.7   Balance while walking forward and sideways on a narrow, elevated surface.
1.8   Demonstrate the relationship of under, over, behind, next to, through, right, left, up, down, forward, backward, and in front of by using the body and an object.

Locomotor Movement

1.9   Perform a continuous log roll.
1.10   Travel in straight, curved, and zigzag pathways.
1.11   Jump over a stationary rope several times in succession, using forward-and-back and side-to-side movement patterns.

Manipulative Skills

1.12   Strike a stationary ball or balloon with the hands, arms, and feet.
1.13   Toss a ball to oneself, using the underhand throw pattern, and catch it before it bounces twice.
1.14   Kick a stationary object, using a simple kicking pattern.
1.15   Bounce a ball continuously, using two hands.

Rhythmic Skills

1.16   Perform locomotor and nonlocomotor movements to a steady beat.
1.17   Clap in time to a simple, rhythmic beat.

23

Chapter 2
Standards-Based
Physical Education:
Kindergarten
Through
Grade Five

STANDARD 2

Students demonstrate knowledge of movement concepts, principles, and strategies that apply to the learning and performance of physical activities.

Movement Concepts

2.1   Explain the difference between under and over, behind and in front of, next to and through, up and down, forward and backward, and sideways.

2.2   Identify and independently use personal space, general space, and boundaries and discuss why they are important.

Body Management

2.3   Identify and describe parts of the body: the head, shoulders, neck, back, chest, waist, hips, arms, elbows, wrists, hands, fingers, legs, knees, ankles, feet, and toes.

2.4   Explain base of support.

Locomotor Movement

2.5   Identify the locomotor skills of walk, jog, run, hop, jump, slide, and gallop.

Manipulative Skills

2.6   Explain the role of the eyes when striking objects with the hands, arms, and feet.

2.7   Identify the point of contact for kicking a ball in a straight line.

2.8   Describe the position of the fingers in the follow-through phase of bouncing a ball continuously.

STANDARD 3

Students assess and maintain a level of physical fitness to improve health and performance.

Fitness Concepts

3.1   Participate in physical activities that are enjoyable and challenging.

Aerobic Capacity

3.2   Participate three to four days each week in moderate to vigorous physical activities that increase breathing and heart rate.

Muscular Strength/Endurance

3.3   Hang from overhead bars for increasing periods of time.

3.4   Climb a ladder, jungle gym, or apparatus.

Flexibility

3.5   Stretch shoulders, legs, arms, and back without bouncing.

Body Composition

3.6   Sustain continuous movement for increasing periods of time while participating in moderate to vigorous physical activity.

Assessment

3.7   Identify indicators of increased capacity to participate in vigorous physical activity.

Chapter 2
Standards-Based
Physical Education:
Kindergarten
Through
Grade Five

Kindergarten

STANDARD 4

Students demonstrate knowledge of physical fitness concepts, principles, and strategies to improve health and performance.

Fitness Concepts

4.1   Identify physical activities that are enjoyable and challenging.

4.2   Describe the role of water as an essential nutrient for the body.

4.3   Explain that nutritious food provides energy for physical activity.

Aerobic Capacity

4.4   Identify the location of the heart and explain that it is a muscle.

4.5   Explain that physical activity increases the heart rate.

4.6   Identify the location of the lungs and explain the role of the lungs in the collection of oxygen.

Muscular Strength/Endurance

4.7   Explain that strong muscles help the body to climb, hang, push, and pull.

4.8   Describe the role of muscles in moving the bones.

Flexibility

4.9   Identify the body part involved when stretching.

Body Composition

4.10   Explain that the body is composed of bones, organs, fat, and other tissues.

STANDARD 5

Students demonstrate and utilize knowledge of psychological and sociological concepts, principles, and strategies that apply to the learning and performance of physical activity.

Self-Responsibility

5.1   Identify the feelings that result from participation in physical activity.

5.2   Participate willingly in physical activities.

Social Interaction

5.3   Demonstrate the characteristics of sharing in a physical activity.

5.4   Describe how positive social interaction can make physical activity with others more fun.

Group Dynamics

5.5   Participate as a leader and a follower during physical activities.

25

Chapter 2
Standards-Based
Physical Education:
Kindergarten
Through
Grade Five

Grade One

Grade One

First-graders continue a moderate and steady growth in height and weight. Many students at this grade can demonstrate the proper form for jumping, hopping, galloping, sliding, walking, running, leaping, and skipping. Additional practice opportunities and instruction should be provided for students who are experiencing difficulties with these skills. Hand-eye coordination and reaction time are improving, making the manipulation of objects easier. Static and dynamic balances are also improving, which allows for the learning of more advanced tumbling and dancing skills.

First-graders are experiencing an increasing number of formal demands for cognitive understanding in the classroom and in physical education. Fortunately, they are enthusiastic and receptive to most learning challenges. They love to try new things, learn new things, and discover new things simultaneously. They are hands-on learners who ask lots of questions. However, their ability to focus is usually limited, so new information should be presented in small increments. They also need a variety of experiences and creative activities to stay focused on the lesson.

A first-grader is still most concerned about himself or herself and can be impulsive. First-grade students are motivated by a strong desire to please family members and other adults. Friends are becoming increasingly important, although they may change frequently. First-graders can plan and carry out simple tasks and responsibilities. Appropriate early physical education experiences can extend, expand, and clarify social skills that students refine through experience.

First-graders are genuinely excited about learning in physical education. They anticipate the excitement and fun associated with moving and learning. The teacher can harness this energy and enthusiasm and channel it to help students develop skills and build a solid movement foundation.

At a Glance

STANDARD I
Students demonstrate the motor skills and movement patterns needed to perform a variety of physical activities.

First-grade students continue to improve their locomotor and nonloco-motor skills by practicing the skills using a variety of movement qualities. The first-grade emphasis is on the qualities of movement, especially the effort aspects of space (areas, levels, planes, pathways, directions) and time (fast, slow, the tempo of the music); see Appendix C. However, other aspects of effort, including weight (strong, light) and flow (free, bound), along with relationships (behind, in front of) to objects and people are also practiced. Students combine locomotor skills into sequences

Chapter 2
Standards-Based
Physical Education:
Kindergarten
Through
Grade Five

Grade One

and then, using various qualities of movement, create sequences to accompany selected pieces of music. Nonlocomotor skills are also practiced through balancing skills in which different bases of support are used and symmetrical and asymmetrical shapes are formed.

First-graders review log rolls learned in kindergarten and progress to forward rolls in tumbling. They extend their jump-rope skills from jumping over a stationary rope (learned in kindergarten) to jumping over a swinging rope and landing softly on both feet. First-graders continue to practice throwing, catching, kicking, and dribbling by using a variety of objects (e.g., balls, balloons) and practice striking by using various implements (e.g., arms, hands, feet, short-handle paddle). By the end of first grade, students demonstrate the correct technique for catching a gently thrown ball.

STANDARD 2
Students demonstrate knowledge of movement concepts, principles, and strategies that apply to the learning and performance of physical activities.

Standard 2 represents the cognitive knowledge that supports the loco-motor, nonlocomotor, and manipulative skills learned in first grade. Often, the physical education lesson is able to address Standards 1 and 2 simultaneously; the teacher explains the information to the students and then has them experience it. For example, Standard 2.10, states "Demonstrate and explain how to reduce the impact force while catching an object"; and Standard 1.13 states, "Catch, showing proper form, a gently thrown ball." The teacher explains what it means to reduce impact force while catching an object (e.g., bending the elbows when catching) and demonstrates the correct technique for catching a ball. Then, the teacher has the students practice catching a ball.

First-grade students also expand their movement vocabulary to describe directions (right, left), spatial relationships (e.g., over, under, behind), boundaries, and movement patterns (underhand, overhand). They can distinguish between similar locomotor skills, such as galloping and sliding. Students learn the correct technique for manipulative skills in greater detail (e.g., hand and finger position for catching a ball, position of nonstriking foot when kicking), building on what they learned in kindergarten.

Chapter 2
Standards-Based
Physical Education:
Kindergarten
Through
Grade Five

Grade One

STANDARD 3

Students assess and maintain a level of physical fitness to improve health and performance.

First-graders continue to perform moderate to vigorous physical activities three to four days each week for increasing periods of time. Muscular strength and endurance continue to be developed through activities performed on playground equipment such as horizontal ladders, horizontal bars, and climbing apparatus. However, students are expected to increase the difficulty of their activity. For example, students are now expected to traverse a horizontal ladder. They are also experimenting with different body positions, such as the v-sit, push-up, and squat (with a knee bend no greater than 90 degrees), which are used in later grade levels for more advanced exercises. Although first-graders typically do not lack flexibility, this is the time to have students demonstrate appropriate stretching exercises for the arms, shoulders, backs, and legs while stressing the importance of not hyperflexing or hyperextending the joints.

STANDARD 4

Students demonstrate knowledge of physical fitness concepts, principles, and strategies to improve health and performance.

Similar to the relationship between Standards 1 and 2, Standard 4 provides the cognitive information to support the fitness activities described in Standard 3. For example, students engage in a variety of moderate to vigorous physical activities. Through these activities, students discover that their heart beats faster and breathing accelerates during physical activity to provide oxygenated blood to the muscles. Students not only experience these physical changes, they can articulate them as well.

First-graders learn that stronger muscles produce greater force, more flexible muscles allow more range of motion, and an increase in endurance allows an individual to move for longer periods of time. They learn that to prevent injury, proper body position must be used when they are exercising and that water, oxygen, and food act as fuel for the body.

STANDARD 5

Students demonstrate and utilize knowledge of psychological and sociological concepts, principles, and strategies that apply to the learning and performance of physical activity.

First-graders participate willingly in new activities and respond in acceptable ways to challenges, successes, and failure. They are learning to share, cooperate, and work in groups without interfering with others. They understand the characteristics for sharing, working with others, and being an effective partner.

Chapter 2
Standards-Based
Physical Education:
Kindergarten
Through
Grade Five

Grade One

Learning Snapshots

STANDARD 1

1.10 Demonstrate the underhand movement (throw) pattern.

The underhand movement pattern is simpler than the overhead movement pattern and should be learned first. The underhand movement pattern is used in many sport skills: the softball pitch, bowling, and the underhand volleyball serve. The goal is for students to demonstrate the underhand throwing pattern using the proper form. The proper form for the underhand throwing pattern is as follows:

* Face the target.
* Hold the ball with the thumb and three fingers.
* Swing the arm back.*
* Turn the body back slightly.
* Step forward on the foot opposite to the throwing arm.*
* Turn the body forward slightly.
* Swing the arm forward with the palm facing forward.
* Release the ball.
* Follow through in the direction of the target.

During the lesson, the teacher demonstrates the correct technique for the underhand throw (also known as a toss), pointing out one or two cues that students should focus on first (items with an asterisk). Students, in pairs, practice the underhand throw. The teacher rotates through the class providing positive or corrective specific feedback on the one or two specific cues.[4] Students change partners frequently so that they learn sharing and cooperation (Standard 5.3) in the same lesson. As students' performances improve, the teacher focuses on additional cues. It is important for students to focus on generating force instead of accuracy so that proper throwing form remains the primary objective. Students practice the underhand throw throughout the school year. Multiple lessons and practice opportunities will be needed for most students to achieve throwing proficiency.

1.13 Catch, showing proper form, a gently thrown ball.

Catching is a common skill used in many sports and games. At the first-grade level, students learn the proper form for catching a gently thrown ball. The proper form is:

* Watch the ball.
* Move toward the ball.
* Fingers are pointed up if the ball is above the waist or pointed down if the ball is below the waist.
* Extend both arms.*

ILLUSTRATION CREDIT

Illustration reprinted with permission from B. S. Mohnsen, *Teaching Middle School Physical Education: A Standards-Based Approach for Grades 5-8*, 3rd ed. (Champaign, IL: Human Kinetics), 346. ©2008.

[4]Feedback is most effective when it is specific and positive or specific and corrective.

29

Chapter 2
Standards-Based
Physical Education:
Kindergarten
Through
Grade Five

- Grasp the ball with both hands.
- "Give" with the ball on contact.*

During the lesson, the teacher demonstrates the correct technique for catching while pointing out one or two cues that students should focus on first (items with an asterisk). Catching can be practiced simultaneously with the underhand throw. The teacher circulates through the class providing positive or corrective specific feedback on the one or two specific cues. Students continue to change partners frequently, so that they learn to share and cooperate (Standard 5.3) in the same lesson. As students' performances improve, the teacher focuses on additional cues. The teacher reviews and students practice the correct technique for catching throughout the year.

STANDARD 2

2.10 Demonstrate and explain how to reduce the impact of force while catching an object.

The term *impact force* as it applies to a child catching an object such as a ball with the hands is nothing more or less than the slap or sting to the palm and fingers as the ball is touched, slowed, and brought to rest. Bringing a ball to rest requires a force on the ball to be applied for a certain amount of time; as more time is taken, the force required becomes smaller, and so does the slap. An example of taking more time in order to reduce the force is bending an elbow when catching instead of keeping the arm straight. The slap can also be reduced by spreading the force that has to be applied over a large area of the hand, so that no one spot has to apply all of it; the slap is less if a ball is caught with two hands instead of one, because the force is spread over the area of two hands instead of the area of one. Another way to reduce the slap is to put some material between the palm of the hand and the ball. When a baseball player catches a ball in the palm of her or his glove, some of the energy of the ball's motion goes into squeezing and stretching the leather of the glove instead of into squeezing and stretching her or his hand.

This standard requires that students demonstrate and explain these concepts. When teaching the correct technique for catching (Standard 1.13), the teacher explains why it is important to bend elbows when catching and why baseball/softball players wear gloves. During throwing and catching practice, the teacher circulates through the class to provide feedback and periodically asks students to explain why bending their arms is important when catching.

STANDARD 3

3.6 Stretch arms, shoulders, back, and legs without hyperflexing or hyperextending the joints.

Hyperflexion means to bend a joint beyond its normal range. *Hyperextension* means to straighten a joint beyond its normal range. (See the Glossary.)

Chapter 2
Standards-Based
Physical Education:
Kindergarten
Through
Grade Five

Grade One

Both practices could result in injuries when one is stretching and should be avoided. One example of hyperflexion is the deep knee bend. One example of hyperextension is when a trunk lift is performed with the chin higher than 12 inches above the ground. These two exercises are unsafe stretches that should not be a part of physical education instruction.

The purpose of this activity is to instruct students on the correct stretching technique. A static stretch is a slow, sustained stretch that is held for 10 to 30 seconds. The student "stretches the muscle-tendon unit to the point where mild discomfort is felt and then backs off slightly, holding the stretch at a point just prior to discomfort" (*Physical Education for Lifelong Fitness* 2005, 107). Posters and other visual aids provide students with a picture of the correct technique. All flexibility exercises should be performed as static stretches with no bouncing. There are four safe stretches.[5]

ACROSS-ARM STRETCH

Reach right arm across the chest with upper arm
    parallel to the ground.
Place left hand on right upper arm.
Gently push on right arm toward chest.
Repeat with the other arm.

SHOULDER SHRUGS

Stand.
Raise right shoulder toward earlobe.
Lower shoulder.
Raise left shoulder toward earlobe.
Lower shoulder.

REVERSE HURDLE STRETCH

Sit with one leg extended and the other leg bent
    so that the sole of the foot is alongside the
    extended knee.
Bend the extended knee slightly.
Reach both hands toward toes of the extended leg.
Repeat with other leg.

LOWER BACK STRETCH

Lie on back with both knees bent and both feet on the ground.
Grab with both hands the thigh of one bent leg.
Pull thigh toward chest, keeping the knee at a 90-degree angle.
Repeat with other leg.

ILLUSTRATION CREDITS

**ACROSS-ARM STRETCH
LOWER BACK STRETCH**
Illustrations reprinted
with permission from B. S.
Mohnsen, *Teaching Middle
School Physical Education*
(Champaign, IL: Human
Kinetics), 317. ©1997.

REVERSE HURDLE STRETCH
Illustrations reprinted
with permission from B. S.
Mohnsen, *Teaching Middle
School Physical Education*
(Champaign, IL: Human
Kinetics), 318. ©1997.

SHOULDER SHRUGS
Illustration reprinted
with permission from
©Bonnie's Fitware, Inc.

[5]Because there are few safe stretches, the same stretches are listed for both kindergarten and grade one students. These stretches are appropriate for young students.

Chapter 2
Standards-Based
Physical Education:
Kindergarten
Through
Grade Five

STANDARD 4

4.5 Explain that increasing the heart rate during physical activity strengthens the heart muscle.

Before and during aerobic exercise, the teacher asks students to place their hands on their chests to feel their hearts beat. The teacher tells the students that the heart is the size of a fist (Standard 4.4) and is the most important muscle in the body. And, like the other muscles in the body, it needs to be exercised to remain strong. The teacher asks students whether their hearts are beating faster before or during exercise. When the students respond that their hearts beat faster during aerobic activity, the teacher explains that this increase in heart rate is what makes the heart stronger. During aerobic activity in future lessons, the teacher quizzes the students regarding the relationship between heart rate and strengthening the heart muscle.

STANDARD 5

5.3 Demonstrate the characteristics of sharing and cooperation in physical activity.

At the beginning of the lesson, the teacher presents a chart divided into three columns. The first column is labeled "Looks Like"; the second column is labeled "Sounds Like"; and the third column is headed "Feels Like." The teacher asks the students to discuss what sharing and cooperation look like, sound like, and feel like and records their responses. The students are then divided into pairs and assigned to a trolley activity, where they are supposed to walk forward and backwards. The students get on their trolley, thinking that this is going to be an easy task. As they begin walking, they realize that it is difficult to move unless they work together. After the students have tried to complete the task but failed, the teacher calls the students back to the chart. The class reviews the important components of sharing and cooperation. Then the students try the trolley again. The pairs are successful this time. During closure, the teacher asks students to discuss what helped them to be successful.

Grade One

ILLUSTRATION CREDIT

Illustration reprinted with permission from B. S. Mohnsen, *Teaching Middle School Physical Education* (Champaign, IL: Human Kinetics), 328. ©1997.

Chapter 2
Standards-Based
Physical Education:
Kindergarten
Through
Grade Five

Grade One

Grade One *Physical Education* *Model Content Standards*

STANDARD 1
Students demonstrate the motor skills and movement patterns needed to perform a variety of physical activities.

Movement Concepts

1.1   Demonstrate an awareness of personal space, general space, and boundaries while moving in different directions and at high, medium, and low levels in space.

1.2   Travel over, under, in front of, behind, and through objects and over, under, in front of, and behind partners, using locomotor skills.

1.3   Change speeds in response to tempos, rhythms, and signals while traveling in straight, curved, and zigzag pathways, using the following locomotor movements: walking, running, leaping, hopping, jumping, galloping, sliding, and skipping.

1.4   Change direction from forward and back and right and left in response to tempos, rhythms, and signals while walking, running, hopping, and jumping (i.e., locomotor skills).

1.5   Demonstrate the difference between slow and fast, heavy and light, and hard and soft while moving.

Body Management

1.6   Balance oneself, demonstrating momentary stillness, in symmetrical and asymmetrical shapes using body parts other than both feet as a base of support.

Locomotor Movement

1.7   Roll smoothly in a forward direction, without stopping or hesitating, emphasizing a rounded form.

1.8   Land on both feet after taking off on one foot and on both feet.

1.9   Jump a swinging rope held by others.

Manipulative Skills

1.10   Demonstrate the underhand movement (throw) pattern.

1.11   Demonstrate the overhand movement (throw) pattern.

1.12   Demonstrate the two-handed overhead (throw) pattern.

1.13   Catch, showing proper form, a gently thrown ball.

1.14   Catch a self-tossed ball.

1.15   Catch a self-bounced ball.

1.16   Kick a rolled ball from a stationary position.

1.17   Kick a stationary ball, using a smooth, continuous running approach.

1.18   Strike a balloon upward continuously, using arms, hands, and feet.

33

Chapter 2
Standards-Based
Physical Education:
Kindergarten
Through
Grade Five

1.19   Strike a balloon upward continuously, using a large, short-handled paddle.

1.20   Dribble a ball in a forward direction, using the inside of the foot.

1.21   Dribble a ball continuously with one hand.

Rhythmic Skills

1.22   Create or imitate movement in response to rhythms and music.

STANDARD 2

Students demonstrate knowledge of movement concepts, principles, and strategies that apply to the learning and performance of physical activities.

Movement Concepts

2.1   Identify the right and left sides of the body and movement from right to left and left to right.

2.2   Identify people/objects that are within personal space and within boundaries.

Body Management

2.3   Identify the base of support of balanced objects.

Locomotor Movement

2.4   Distinguish between a jog and a run, a hop and a jump, and a gallop and a slide and explain the key differences and similarities in those movements.

Manipulative Skills

2.5   Identify examples of underhand and overhand movement patterns.

2.6   Explain that in the underhand throw, the position of the fingers at the moment of release can influence the direction a tossed object and a thrown object travel.

2.7   Explain that the nonthrowing arm and hand provide balance and can influence the direction a tossed object and a thrown object travel.

2.8   Explain that the point of release influences the direction of a tossed object and of a thrown object.

2.9   Describe the proper hand and finger position for catching a ball.

2.10   Demonstrate and explain how to reduce the impact force while catching an object.

2.11   Identify the placement of the nonkicking foot when kicking with a smooth, running approach.

2.12   Identify the location of the contact point to strike an object upward.

2.13   Determine and analyze how much force is needed to move the ball forward while dribbling with the hand and with the foot.

Chapter 2
Standards-Based
Physical Education:
Kindergarten
Through
Grade Five

Grade One

STANDARD 3

Students assess and maintain a level of physical fitness to improve health and performance.

Fitness Concepts

3.1   Participate in physical activities that are enjoyable and challenging.

Aerobic Capacity

3.2   Participate three to four times each week, for increasing periods of time, in moderate to vigorous physical activities that increase breathing and heart rate.

Muscular Strength/Endurance

3.3   Demonstrate, for increasing periods of time, a "v" sit position, a push-up position with arms extended, and a squat position.

3.4   Move from a sitting to a standing position and from a lying to a sitting position without using arms to brace oneself while on the floor.

3.5   Travel hand-over-hand along a horizontal ladder or hang from an overhead bar.

Flexibility

3.6   Stretch arms, shoulders, back, and legs without hyperflexing or hyperextending the joints.

Body Composition

3.7   Sustain continuous movement for increasing periods of time while participating in moderate to vigorous physical activity.

Assessment

3.8   Identify and use two indicators of increased capacity for vigorous physical activity to measure a change in activity levels.

STANDARD 4

Students demonstrate knowledge of physical fitness concepts, principles, and strategies to improve health and performance.

Fitness Concepts

4.1   Identify enjoyable and challenging physical activities that one can do for increasing periods of time without stopping.

4.2   Explain the importance of drinking water during and after physical activity.

4.3   Explain that nutritious food provides energy for alertness and mental concentration.

Aerobic Capacity

4.4   Recognize that the heart is the most important muscle in the body and is approximately the size of a fist.

4.5   Explain that increasing the heart rate during physical activity strengthens the heart muscle.

35

Chapter 2
Standards-Based
Physical Education:
Kindergarten
Through
Grade Five

Grade One

4.6   Identify physical activities that cause the heart to beat faster.

4.7   Describe the role of blood in transporting oxygen from the lungs.

Muscular Strength/Endurance

4.8   Explain that strengthening muscles will help prevent injury and that strong muscles will produce more force.

4.9   Discuss how prolonged physical activity increases endurance, allowing movement to occur for longer periods of time.

Flexibility

4.10   Explain that the proper body position while stretching and strengthening will help prevent injury.

4.11   Diagram how flexible muscles allow more range of motion in physical activity.

Body Composition

4.12   Identify the body components (e.g., bones, muscles, organs, fat, and other tissues).

STANDARD 5

Students demonstrate and utilize knowledge of psychological and sociological concepts, principles, and strategies that apply to the learning and performance of physical activity.

Self-Responsibility

5.1   Participate willingly in new physical activities.

5.2   Identify and demonstrate acceptable responses to challenges, successes, and failures in physical activity.

Social Interaction

5.3   Demonstrate the characteristics of sharing and cooperation in physical activity.

5.4   Invite others to use equipment or apparatus before repeating a turn.

Group Dynamics

5.5   Identify and demonstrate the attributes of an effective partner in physical activity.

5.6   Identify and demonstrate effective practices for working with a group without interfering with others.

Chapter 2
Standards-Based
Physical Education:
Kindergarten
Through
Grade Five

Grade Two

Grade Two

Second-graders continue to maintain a high level of flexibility and a moderate but steady growth in muscular strength and endurance. They exhibit relatively high heart and breathing rates and are typically active intermittently, showing vigorous bursts of energy followed by periods of rest or recovery (Siedentop 2004). Locomotor and manipulative skills continue to improve, and students demonstrate a keen interest in practicing activities that they know how to perform. Static and dynamic balance skills also show steady improvement, and rhythmic skills show an increase in quality and complexity of movement.

Second-graders are entering the concrete stage in their cognitive development. During this time, they gain a better understanding of mental operations. They begin thinking logically about concrete events but still have difficulty understanding abstract concepts. Second-graders want to know how things work, including their own bodies. Their attention span is increasing, but it is still quite short. They are very literal and interpret new concepts in terms of their own experiences.

Second grade is the time when students begin working cooperatively with a partner, although they are still eager for adult approval and find criticism difficult to handle. Through social interactions with other students, children begin to develop a sense of pride in their accomplishments and abilities. These interactions also provide opportunities for helping students accept and respect differences in others. Second-graders are capable of exhibiting greater control over their emotions. They are developing a sense of right and wrong and are capable of understanding that actions have consequences.

At a Glance

STANDARD 1

Students demonstrate the motor skills and movement patterns needed to perform a variety of physical activities.

Second-grade students continue to improve their locomotor and nonlocomotor skills by focusing their practice time on mastering the correct technique. By the end of second grade, students can execute the correct form for skipping, leaping, and jumping rope repeatedly. They can also demonstrate smooth transitions between even-beat locomotor skills (e.g., walking, running, jumping, and hopping) and uneven-beat locomotor skills (e.g., sliding, skipping, and galloping). They use these skills in the performance of rhythmic sequences, such as simple folk dances (e.g., Children's Polka) or ribbon routines performed with and without a partner.

Second-graders review log rolls, forward rolls, and balances while learning to transfer weight from feet to hands and hands to feet with control. They begin their more formal tumbling education by creating their own routines

Chapter 2
Standards-Based
Physical Education:
Kindergarten
Through
Grade Five

Grade Two

that include body rolls and balances. They extend their jump rope skills from jumping over a swinging rope to repeatedly jumping over a turning rope.

Second-graders also continue to practice manipulative skills by throwing, catching, kicking, and dribbling (foot and hand) for control using a variety of objects (e.g., balls, balloons) and practice striking by using a variety of implements (e.g., short-handle paddle, bats). By the end of second grade, students can demonstrate the correct form for rolling and throwing a ball for distance as well as demonstrate more control using the other manipulative skills.

STANDARD 2

Students demonstrate knowledge of movement concepts, principles, and strategies that apply to the learning and performance of physical activities.

Standard 2 represents the cognitive knowledge that supports the locomotor, nonlocomotor, and manipulative skills learned in second grade. Often, the physical education lesson is able to address Standards 1 and 2 simultaneously; the teacher explains the information to the students and then has them experience it. For example, Standard 2.5 states, "Compare and contrast locomotor movements conducted to even and uneven beats"; and Standard 1.17 states, "Demonstrate a smooth transition between even-beat locomotor skills and uneven-beat locomotor skills in response to music or an external beat." The teacher discusses the similarities and differences between even-beat locomotor skills (run, hop, jump, walk) and uneven-beat locomotor skills (skip, gallop, slide). The teacher demonstrates transitional moves for connecting even-beat locomotor and uneven-beat locomotor skills together. Then the teacher asks the students to practice even-beat locomotor skills and uneven-beat locomotor skills with smooth transitions between them.

Second-graders learn to describe the correct technique for manipulative skills in greater detail (e.g., the role of body parts not directly involved in catching, timing to begin the kicking motion when kicking a slowly rolling ball). In addition, they learn to understand the purpose of using correct form (e.g., side orientation when batting). In preparation for gaining a deeper understanding of the science of movement, second-graders learn that a wider base of support is more stable than a narrow base of support; that, other things being equal, greater force must be applied to a ball that needs to travel a greater distance; and that the impact force from the catching or striking of a ball is reduced by increasing the area in which the ball is in contact, or increasing the time while the ball is in contact and is changing its motion. In preparation for game play in later grade

Chapter 2
Standards-Based
Physical Education:
Kindergarten
Through
Grade Five

levels, students learn to describe situations where underhand and overhand throwing and striking skills are used. They also learn the definition of "open space," which is the basis for offensive and defensive game strategies learned in fourth grade and beyond.

STANDARD 3

Students assess and maintain a level of physical fitness to improve health and performance.

Second-graders continue to perform moderate to vigorous physical activities three to four days each week for increasing periods of time. Muscular strength and endurance continue to be developed, but through more challenging activities such as the performance of curl-ups, modified push-ups, oblique curl-ups, forward and side lunges, squats (no lower than a 90-degree angle), triceps push-ups using a chair or bench, and traversing the overhead ladder one bar at a time. In terms of flexibility, students demonstrate the correct form for stretching the hamstrings, quadriceps, shoulders, biceps, and triceps. During second grade, students start measuring their own fitness levels and monitoring their personal improvement.

STANDARD 4

Students demonstrate knowledge of physical fitness concepts, principles, and strategies to improve health and performance.

Similar to the relationship between Standards 1 and 2, Standard 4 provides the cognitive information to support the fitness activities described in Standard 3. Students are learning the benefits of physical activity for maintaining good health. They are also learning about opportunities to participate in physical activity outside school.

Second-graders, in preparation for creating fitness plans in later grade levels, learn the purpose of increasing exercise intensity and duration as well as the reason for warming up muscles before they are stretched. They also learn the names of the muscles they are strengthening and stretching, as well as the benefits derived from good health-related fitness. The purpose of good nutrition, with a focus on nutritional choices and water intake, completes the second-graders' understanding of fitness concepts.

STANDARD 5

Students demonstrate and utilize knowledge of psychological and sociological concepts, principles, and strategies that apply to the learning and performance of physical activity.

In second grade, students participate in a variety of group settings with an emphasis on encouraging others, demonstrating cooperation, and avoiding

39

Chapter 2
Standards-Based
Physical Education:
Kindergarten
Through
Grade Five

Grade Two

interference with others. Students move from the sense of self in isolation and begin to embrace the concept of partners working together to solve movement problems. They begin to accept responsibility for their own behavior in a group activity. This is also when students' growing awareness of others can help to promote respect for people and for equipment during physical activities.

Learning Snapshots

STANDARD 1

1.16 Jump a rope turned repeatedly.

The critical features for jumping a long rope are:

- Stand with both feet together by the center of the rope.
- Jump over the rope as it comes under the feet.
- Jump with both feet, landing on balls of feet.
- Keep feet, ankles, and knees together.
- Bend knees on landing to reduce impact force.
- Keep hands close to the body.

The critical features for turning a long rope are:

- Hold the rope in one hand.
- Keep the upper arm of the rope hand stationary.
- Lock the wrist of the rope hand.
- Turn the thumb of the rope hand up.
- Rotate the elbow of the rope hand keeping it close to the body.

The teacher starts the lesson with a demonstration and explanation of how to jump a long rope held by others and turn a long rope for others to jump. The teacher then hands out one long jump rope to every three students. Some students will already be proficient at jumping a long rope, while other students may be beginners. The teacher allows students to progress at their own speed. If necessary, the teacher reteaches foundational skills from previous grade levels. Starting with the rope laying on the ground, the students jump back and forth over it. Then the teacher instructs the students to jump a long rope turned by their partners. The students jump one time, then two times, then three times, and so on until they can jump the rope continuously. As students are practicing, the teacher circulates through the class providing feedback.[6]

[6]Feedback is most effective when it is specific and positive or specific and corrective.

Chapter 2
Standards-Based
Physical Education:
Kindergarten
Through
Grade Five

Grade Two

1.17 Demonstrate a smooth transition between even-beat locomotor skills and uneven-beat locomotor skills in response to music or an external beat.

The locomotor skills of walking, running, hopping, and jumping are even-beat skills while the locomotor skills of galloping, sliding, and skipping are uneven-beat skills. This standard requires students to demonstrate both types of locomotor skills using a smooth transition or change between the skills. The teacher must first assess whether students can correctly perform each of the locomotor skills (Standard 1.6). Then the teacher explains and demonstrates that changes from one locomotor skill to the next need to be smooth rather than jerky. Finally, the teacher plays music and asks the students to move rhythmically with the music using both types of locomotor skills as well as smooth transitions.

STANDARD 2

2.3 Explain the importance of a wide rather than a narrow base of support in balance activities.

Students are assigned to work in pairs. The teacher asks one student in each pair to find a position in which he or she is least likely to fall over (i.e., be balanced). The teacher asks the second student in each pair to use chalk to draw a circle around the body parts in contact with the ground. The teacher then asks the same students to find positions in which they are likely to fall over (i.e., be out of balance). The teacher asks the second student in each pair to use a different colored piece of chalk to draw a circle around the body parts in contact with the ground. The students then switch roles and repeat the activity. During closure, both students compare the circles drawn around each of them and observe that they are more likely to fall over when they have a narrow base of support compared with a wider base of support.

2.5 Compare and contrast locomotor movements conducted to even and uneven beats.

Four locomotor skills (e.g., run, walk, hop, and jump) are to be performed to an even beat. Three locomotor skills (e.g., skip, gallop, and slide) are to be performed to an uneven beat. The teacher starts the lesson with a demonstration to review the correct technique for each skill. Then the teacher plays music that alternates between an even and uneven beat. Students perform the appropriate locomotor skill that matches the beat. During closure, the teacher presents the students with a Venn diagram and asks students to list similarities and differences between those locomotor skills performed to an even beat and those performed to an uneven beat.

Chapter 2
Standards-Based
Physical Education:
Kindergarten
Through
Grade Five

STANDARD 3

3.4   Traverse the overhead ladder one bar at a time.

Most schools have only one overhead ladder so this standard is often addressed using a station approach as described here. The teacher starts the lesson with a review of the safety rules and appropriate activities for the playground apparatus (e.g., horizontal bar, parallel bars, climbing apparatus, pull-up bars, low balance beams, climbing poles, overhead ladders). To add stations, the teacher places two jump ropes, for practicing jumping skills, between each piece of apparatus. Students, in pairs, are assigned to a starting station (piece of apparatus or jump rope station). After a few minutes at each station, the teacher signals the students to proceed to the next station. At the end of the lesson, the teacher reviews the safety rules. If applicable, the teacher reminds students that the apparatus is available to them during recess and lunch.

3.6   Engage in moderate to vigorous physical activity for increasing periods of time.

Moderate-intensity physical activity generally requires sustained rhythmic movements and refers to a level of effort a healthy individual might expend while, for example, walking briskly, dancing, swimming, or bicycling on level terrain. A person should feel some exertion but should be able to carry on a conversation comfortably during the activity. Vigorous-intensity physical activity generally requires sustained, rhythmic movements and refers to a level of effort a healthy individual might expend while, for example, jogging, participating in high-impact aerobic dancing, swimming continuous laps, or bicycling uphill. Vigorous-intensity physical activity may be intense enough to result in a significant increase in heart and respiration rate (http://www.cdc.gov/nccdphp/dnpa/physical/terms/). A popular aerobic activity for this age group is the performance of locomotor skills while moving in open space or around a circuit in which the locomotor skill is changed at each corner. This is known as the Four Corners activity. These moderate to vigorous physical activities should be conducted for increasing periods of time throughout the school year.

STANDARD 4

4.3   Identify ways to increase time for physical activity outside of school.

Students calculate the amount of time from when they arrive home from school until they go to bed. Students subtract the time they spend doing homework, performing chores, eating dinner, and getting ready for bed. Students explain what they do with the remaining time and how they can increase their amount of physical activity during this time. For example, students can go for walks with their parents and other family members,

ILLUSTRATION CREDIT

Illustration reprinted with permission from B. S. Mohnsen, *Teaching Middle School Physical Education* (Champaign, IL: Human Kinetics), 316. ©1997.

Chapter 2
Standards-Based
Physical Education:
Kindergarten
Through
Grade Five

Grade Two

play video games that require physical activity, and perform physical chores (e.g., rake leaves, sweep floors).

This standard links with two of the math standards in measurement and geometry, providing an opportunity for interdisciplinary learning:

Grade 2 Measurement and Geometry Standard 1.4: Tell time to the nearest quarter hour and know the relationships of time (e.g., minutes in an hour, days in a month, weeks in a year).

Grade 2 Measurement and Geometry Standard 1.5: Determine the duration of intervals of time in hours (e.g., 11 a.m. to 4 p.m.).

4.13 Identify the muscles being stretched during the performance of particular physical activities.

Stretching (flexibility) exercises are performed during the closure of lessons that involve physical activity. All flexibility exercises should be performed as static stretches with no bouncing. At the beginning of the school year, the teacher announces the name of the muscle being stretched during each activity. As the school year progresses, the students name the muscle being stretched.

STANDARD 5

5.6 Demonstrate how to solve a problem with another person during physical activity.

Second-graders spend most of their practice time working in pairs. Sometimes conflicts or problems arise that the students need to solve. It is best to provide students with a strategy beforehand for handling these types of problems. An appropriate problem-solving strategy consists of the following steps:

1. Define the problem.
2. List possible solutions.
3. Select and try one of the solutions.
4. Determine if the solution worked—and if not, then try another solution.
5. Continue the process until both students feel that the solution provided a win–win solution.

The teacher instructs the students on this five-step approach to solving problems and then creates simulations (e.g., a ball goes out of bounds and it is unclear who touched it last, during a tag game it is unclear whether a person was actually tagged) for the students to practice the strategy. During the simulations, the teacher circulates through the class providing feedback. When "real-life" problems arise, the teacher should provide appropriate feedback to ensure that students use the problem-solving strategy to resolve their issues.

43

Chapter 2
Standards-Based
Physical Education:
Kindergarten
Through
Grade Five

Grade Two

Grade Two *Physical Education* *Model Content Standards*

STANDARD 1
Students demonstrate the motor skills and movement patterns needed to perform a variety of physical activities.

Movement Concepts

1.1 Move to open spaces within boundaries while traveling at increasing rates of speed.

Body Management

1.2 Transfer weight from feet to hands and from hands to feet, landing with control.
1.3 Demonstrate balance on the ground and on objects, using bases of support other than both feet.
1.4 Create a routine that includes two types of body rolls (e.g., log roll, egg roll, shoulder roll, forward roll) and a stationary balance position after each roll.

Locomotor Movement

1.5 Jump for distance, landing on both feet and bending the hips, knees, and ankles to reduce the impact force.
1.6 Skip and leap, using proper form.

Manipulative Skills

1.7 Roll a ball for distance, using proper form.
1.8 Throw a ball for distance, using proper form.
1.9 Catch a gently thrown ball above the waist, reducing the impact force.
1.10 Catch a gently thrown ball below the waist, reducing the impact force.
1.11 Kick a slowly rolling ball.
1.12 Strike a balloon consistently in an upward or forward motion, using a short-handled paddle.
1.13 Strike a ball with a bat from a tee or cone, using correct grip and side orientation.
1.14 Hand-dribble, with control, a ball for a sustained period.
1.15 Foot-dribble, with control, a ball along the ground.
1.16 Jump a rope turned repeatedly.

Rhythmic Skills

1.17 Demonstrate a smooth transition between even-beat locomotor skills and uneven-beat locomotor skills in response to music or an external beat.
1.18 Perform rhythmic sequences related to simple folk dance or ribbon routines.
1.19 Perform with a partner rhythmic sequences related to simple folk dance or ribbon routines.

Chapter 2
Standards-Based
Physical Education:
Kindergarten
Through
Grade Five

Grade Two

STANDARD 2

Students demonstrate knowledge of movement concepts, principles, and strategies that apply to the learning and performance of physical activities.

Movement Concepts

2.1   Define *open space*.

2.2   Explain how to reduce the impact force of an oncoming object.

Body Management

2.3   Explain the importance of a wide rather than a narrow base of support in balance activities.

2.4   Explain why one hand or foot is often preferred when practicing movement skills.

Locomotor Movement

2.5   Compare and contrast locomotor movements conducted to even and uneven beats.

Manipulative Skills

2.6   Identify opportunities to use underhand and overhand movement (throw) patterns.

2.7   Identify different opportunities to use striking skills.

2.8   Compare the changes in force applied to a ball and the ball speed when rolling a ball for various distances.

2.9   Explain key elements of throwing for distance.

2.10   Identify the roles of body parts not directly involved in catching objects.

2.11   Identify when to begin the kicking motion when kicking a slowly rolling ball.

2.12   Identify the different points of contact when striking a balloon upward and striking a balloon forward.

2.13   Explain the purpose of using a side orientation when striking a ball from a batting tee.

2.14   Differentiate the effects of varying arm and hand speeds when hand-dribbling a ball.

STANDARD 3

Students assess and maintain a level of physical fitness to improve health and performance.

Fitness Concepts

3.1   Participate in enjoyable and challenging physical activities for increasing periods of time.

Aerobic Capacity

3.2   Participate three to four times each week, for increasing periods of time, in moderate to vigorous physical activities that increase breathing and heart rate.

Chapter 2
Standards-Based
Physical Education:
Kindergarten
Through
Grade Five

Grade Two

Muscular Strength/Endurance

3.3   Perform abdominal curl-ups, modified push-ups, oblique curl-ups, forward and side lunges, squats, and triceps push-ups from a chair or bench to enhance endurance and increase muscle efficiency.

3.4   Traverse the overhead ladder one bar at a time.

Flexibility

3.5   Demonstrate the proper form for stretching the hamstrings, quadriceps, shoulders, biceps, and triceps.

Body Composition

3.6   Engage in moderate to vigorous physical activity for increasing periods of time.

Assessment

3.7   Measure improvements in individual fitness levels.

STANDARD 4
Students demonstrate knowledge of physical fitness concepts, principles, and strategies to improve health and performance.

Fitness Concepts

4.1   Explain the fuel requirements of the body during physical activity and inactivity.

4.2   Describe the role of moderate to vigorous physical activity in achieving or maintaining good health.

4.3   Identify ways to increase time for physical activity outside of school.

4.4   Discuss how body temperature and blood volume are maintained during physical activity when an adequate amount of water is consumed.

4.5   Explain how the intensity and duration of exercise, as well as nutritional choices, affect fuel use during physical activity.

Aerobic Capacity

4.6   Compare and contrast the function of the heart during rest and during physical activity.

4.7   Describe the relationship between the heart and lungs during physical activity.

4.8   Compare and contrast changes in heart rate before, during, and after physical activity.

Muscular Strength/Endurance

4.9   Describe how muscle strength and muscle endurance enhance motor skill performance.

4.10   Identify muscles being strengthened during the performance of particular physical activities.

4.11   Identify which activities or skills would be accomplished more efficiently with stronger muscles.

4.12   Explain the role that weight-bearing activities play in bone strength.

Chapter 2
Standards-Based
Physical Education:
Kindergarten
Through
Grade Five

Grade Two

Flexibility

4.13   Identify the muscles being stretched during the performance of particular physical activities.

4.14   Explain why it is safer to stretch a warm muscle rather than a cold muscle.

Body Composition

4.15   Describe the differences in density and weight between bones, muscles, organs, and fat.

STANDARD 5

Students demonstrate and utilize knowledge of psychological and sociological concepts, principles, and strategies that apply to the learning and performance of physical activity.

Self-Responsibility

5.1   Participate in a variety of group settings (e.g., partners, small groups, large groups) without interfering with others.

5.2   Accept responsibility for one's own behavior in a group activity.

Social Interaction

5.3   Acknowledge one's opponent or partner before, during, and after an activity or game and give positive feedback on the opponent's or partner's performance.

5.4   Encourage others by using verbal and nonverbal communication.

5.5   Demonstrate respect for self, others, and equipment during physical activities.

5.6   Demonstrate how to solve a problem with another person during physical activity.

Group Dynamics

5.7   Participate positively in physical activities that rely on cooperation.

47

Chapter 2
Standards-Based
Physical Education:
Kindergarten
Through
Grade Five

Grade Three

Grade Three

Third grade is a pivotal time in the development of students' movement skills. Third-graders who demonstrate and understand the proper form for locomotor and nonlocomotor skills now shift their focus to combining those skills into new movement sequences. Students who cannot perform the skills using the proper technique are provided with additional learning and practice opportunities to improve these skills.

Third-grade students are willing to experiment with and explore alternative movements, such as tumbling, creative dance, and formal dance. Practice opportunities provide students with sufficient time to develop the proper form for manipulative skills, such as rolling, throwing, catching, dribbling, kicking, and striking. Fitness activities become increasingly important at this age. Early signs of poor posture and decreased flexibility begin to appear. Giving students opportunities to participate in moderate to vigorous physical activities for three to four days each week can increase overall health.

Third-graders, like second-graders, are at the concrete stage of cognitive development. Their attention spans are improving, and they are interested in why things occur. These students are fairly good at the use of inductive logic that involves going from a specific experience to a general experience. On the other hand, students at this age have difficulty using deductive logic, which involves using a general idea to determine the outcome of a specific event.

By now students have developed a self-image strong enough to tolerate how others react to them. They have developed a stronger sense of right and wrong, having reached the stage of development for internalization of rules and regulations. They are becoming more self-reliant and can work independently. Third grade is a good time to have students create goals for personal fitness and motor skills and monitor their own progress, because they have a strong desire for self-improvement. These students also experience an increased desire for interaction with others and should be provided with opportunities to practice and work toward common goals in pairs and trios.

At a Glance

STANDARD 1

Students demonstrate the motor skills and movement patterns needed to perform a variety of physical activities.

Third-grade students continue to improve their locomotor skills as they apply the skills to chasing, fleeing, and dodging in tag-type games; dance steps in line, circle, and folk dances; and jumping a rope turned forward and backwards. They continue to refine their nonlocomotor skills as they use these skills to perform forward rolls, straddle rolls, and tripods. They also apply nonlocomotor skills to balancing activities on ground-level balance beams.

Chapter 2
Standards-Based
Physical Education:
Kindergarten
Through
Grade Five

Grade Three

Manipulative practice takes on a greater role in third-grade physical education compared with previous grade levels. Students are honing their throwing, catching, kicking, and striking skills. They practice hand dribbling and foot dribbling while traveling and dodging obstacles.

STANDARD 2

Students demonstrate knowledge of movement concepts, principles, and strategies that apply to the learning and performance of physical activities.

Standard 2 represents the cognitive knowledge that supports the locomotor, nonlocomotor, and manipulative skills learned in third grade. Often, the physical education lesson is able to address Standards 1 and 2 simultaneously; the teacher explains the information to the students and then has them experience it. For example, Standard 2.7 states, "Compare and contrast folk dances, line dances, and circle dances"; and Standard 1.15 states, "Perform a line dance, a circle dance, and a folk dance with a partner." After students have had the opportunity to learn and perform all three types of dance, they are given the opportunity to describe the similarities and differences between them.

Third-graders can describe the correct technique for manipulative skills in greater detail (e.g., the correct hand position when catching a ball at different levels), building on knowledge gained in kindergarten through second grade. In addition, they can describe technique differences when applying manipulative skills in different situations (e.g., throwing for accuracy, dribbling a ball while changing direction, throwing to a stationary partner, throwing to a moving partner). In preparation for game play in later grades, students learn about altering speed and direction to avoid an opponent.

STANDARD 3

Students assess and maintain a level of physical fitness to improve health and performance.

Third-graders continue to perform moderate to vigorous physical activities three to four days each week for increasing periods of time. They start each exercise period with a warm-up and conclude each exercise period with a cool-down. Muscular strength and endurance continue to be developed. In addition, students are expected to perform an increasing number of abdominal curl-ups, oblique curl-ups on each side of the body, modified push-ups or traditional push-ups with hands on a bench, forward lunges, side lunges, and triceps push-ups from a chair. Students also learn how to properly lift and carry heavy objects so as not to incur injury. In terms of

Chapter 2
Standards-Based
Physical Education:
Kindergarten
Through
Grade Five

flexibility, students are expected to hold stretches for hips, shoulders, hamstrings, quadriceps, triceps, biceps, back, and neck for increasing periods of time, up to 30 seconds (*Physical Education for Lifelong Fitness* 2005, 107). To monitor their progress, third-graders continue to measure and record in a log their performance on health-related physical fitness assessments.

STANDARD 4

Students demonstrate knowledge of physical fitness concepts, principles, and strategies to improve health and performance.

Similar to the relationship between Standards 1 and 2, Standard 4 provides the cognitive information to support the fitness activities described in Standard 3. For Standard 4, students are learning about warm-up and cool-down activities and the importance of readying the body for activity and recovery. In addition, they are learning to identify the body's reaction (e.g., increased heart rate, increased breathing) to physical activity.

Third-graders, in preparation for creating a fitness plan in later grade levels, learn the five components of health-related fitness, the principle of progression (i.e., workloads must be increased to improve fitness), the names of major muscles, proper lifting techniques to prevent back injuries, and unsafe flexibility exercises that should be avoided. They also learn about the relationship between the heart, lungs, blood, and oxygen during physical activity.

STANDARD 5

Students demonstrate and utilize knowledge of psychological and sociological concepts, principles, and strategies that apply to the learning and performance of physical activity.

Third-graders enjoy assuming responsibility for setting goals, working toward goals, and monitoring progress either alone or with others. As their social interaction skills improve, students learn to use movement cues and words of encouragement when working with a partner. They learn the purpose of safety procedures and rules along with the consequences of not following those procedures and rules. This is also a time when students' increasing ability to work with others can be used to help students learn to accept and appreciate differences in themselves and others.

Grade Three

Chapter 2
Standards-Based
Physical Education:
Kindergarten
Through
Grade Five

Grade Three

Learning Snapshots

STANDARD 1

1.1 **Chase, flee, and move away from others in a constantly changing environment.**

The skills of chasing, fleeing, and moving away from others are individual defensive and offensive strategies that students will use at upper-grade levels in many sports and games. At the third-grade level, students practice these skills and use them in simple tag games. Working in pairs, defensive players chase while offensive players flee. Offensive players use fakes to convince the defense they are going in one direction but then move in a different direction. Defensive players learn to keep their eyes focused on the offensive player's torso, because most fakes occur with arms and legs. Offensive players change direction and speed constantly to evade the defensive players.

Students practice these skills frequently throughout the school year in pairs and in small groups. It is important when practicing these skills that the teacher set boundaries by placing one cone at each corner of the activity area, so that students know they must remain in a defined area. During closure, students can be asked to describe how changing speed and direction can allow one person to move away from another (Standard 2.1).

1.2 **Perform an inverted balance (tripod) by evenly distributing weight on body parts.**

A tripod involves placing the head and both hands on the ground, creating a triangle and then positioning knees on elbows and maintaining a balanced position. The most important aspect of this skill is creating a solid foundation or base of support. When demonstrating and describing the tripod, the teacher reminds students that a tricycle is more stable than a bicycle, and a triangle foundation is more stable than positioning hands and the head in a straight line. Students practice the correct head and hand position to ensure that they are creating a triangle. The teacher monitors students to determine whether they have mastered the correct position. Then the teacher has students practice balancing their knees on their elbows. This lesson should be performed on mats or on grass.

51

Chapter 2
Standards-Based
Physical Education:
Kindergarten
Through
Grade Five

Grade Three

STANDARD 2

2.2 Explain and demonstrate the correct hand position when catching a ball above the head, below the waist, near the middle of the body, and away from the body.

The teacher should demonstrate and explain the correct technique for catching a ball above the head, below the waist, near the middle of the body, and away from the body. In the explanation, the teacher should include the following points:

- Watch the ball.
- Move to the ball—if it is away from the body.
- Hands are positioned so fingers point up if the ball is at the middle of the body or above the waist.
- Hands are positioned so fingers point down if the ball is below the waist.
- Extend the arms.
- Grasp the ball with both hands.
- Give with the ball on contact.

Once the teacher has introduced the skills, students practice throwing and catching in pairs. The teacher circulates through the class, providing feedback and asking students to explain the correct hand position when the ball is above the head, below the waist, near the midsection of the body, and away from the body.[7] The teacher reteaches the information until students are able to demonstrate and explain the correct hand position.

STANDARD 3

3.1 Demonstrate warm-up and cool-down exercises.

A sound practice is to have students do a warm-up prior to vigorous physical activity at the beginning of instruction. A cool-down should be done at the end of a vigorous activity, but it may not be necessary if the physical activity is not vigorous. Therefore, a teacher should consider the lesson focus and type of physical activity in the lesson before including warm-up and cool-down activities as instructional time might be better spent in learning activities.

A warm-up consists of mild exercises (e.g., brisk walking, knee lifts, or any full-body movement that progressively warms up the muscles) performed to prepare the body for more vigorous exercise. A cool-down consists of mild exercises performed after an activity so that the body gradually returns to a resting state. Stretching exercises (also known as flexibility exercises) are best performed during the cool-down. Once they have learned the routine, students demonstrate the warm-up and cool-down exercises by assisting the teacher in leading the warm-up and cool-down phases of lessons.

---

[7] Feedback is most effective when it is specific and positive or specific and corrective.

Chapter 2
Standards-Based
Physical Education:
Kindergarten
Through
Grade Five

Grade Three

ILLUSTRATION CREDITS

ACROSS-ARM STRETCH
REVERSE HURDLE STRETCH
LOWER BACK STRETCH
Illustrations reprinted
with permission from B. S.
Mohnsen, *Teaching Middle
School Physical Education*
(Champaign, IL: Human
Kinetics), 317-18. ©1997.

SHOULDER SHRUGS
Illustration reprinted
with permission from
©Bonnie's Fitware, Inc.

NECK STRETCH
Illustration reprinted
with permission from
C. Hinton, *Fitness for
Children* (Champaign, IL:
Human Kinetics), 51.
©1995.

3.6 Hold for an increasing period of time basic stretches for hips, shoulders, hamstrings, quadriceps, triceps, biceps, back, and neck.

Stretching exercises are done during cool-down for lessons that involve physical activity. All stretching exercises (also known as flexibility exercises) should be performed as static stretches with no bouncing. At the third-grade level, each stretch should be a minimum of 10 seconds increasing to not more than 30 seconds by the end of the school year (*Physical Education for Lifelong Fitness* 2005, 107). Safe stretches are illustrated below:

ACROSS-ARM STRETCH

Reach right arm across the chest with upper arm
  parallel to the ground.
Place left hand on right upper arm.
Gently push on right arm toward chest.
Repeat with the other arm.

SHOULDER SHRUGS

Stand.
Raise right shoulder toward earlobe.
Lower shoulder.
Raise left shoulder toward earlobe.
Lower shoulder.

REVERSE HURDLE STRETCH

Sit with one leg extended and the
  other leg bent so that the sole
  of the foot is alongside the extended knee.
Bend the extended knee slightly.
Reach both hands toward toes of the extended leg.
Repeat with other leg.

LOWER BACK STRETCH

Lie on back with both knees
  bent and both feet on
  the ground.
Grab with both hands the
  thigh of one bent leg.
Pull thigh toward chest, keeping the knee at a 90-degree angle.
Repeat with other leg.

NECK STRETCH

Stand.
Tuck chin to chest.
Rotate neck so left ear is over
  left shoulder keeping
  chin tucked to chest.
Rotate neck so right ear is over right shoulder keeping chin tucked to chest.

Note: Students should not rotate the head in a circle.

Chapter 2
Standards-Based
Physical Education:
Kindergarten
Through
Grade Five

FORWARD LUNGE

Stand and extend one leg forward with the
  knee bent at a 90-degree angle.
Lean forward so weight is on the bent leg.
Keep the rear leg extended.
Repeat with the other leg.

STANDARD 4

4.14 Identify flexibility exercises that are not safe for the joints and should
be avoided.

There are several flexibility exercises that have traditionally been performed
but are dangerous to the performer. (See Appendix F for a list of contraindicated exercises and alternatives.) Some of these contraindicated exercises
are illustrated below:

CONTRAINDICATED EXERCISES

DEEP KNEE
BENDS

NECK CIRCLE
(NECK ROLL)

HURDLER'S STRETCH

STANDING TOE TOUCHES
CHERRY PICKERS
(standing toe touches
performed rapidly)

WINDMILLS

(standing toe touches where the right
hand touches the left foot and the left
hand touches the right foot in rapid
succession)

ILLUSTRATION CREDITS

FORWARD LUNGE
Illustration reprinted
with permission from B. S.
Mohnsen, *Teaching Middle
School Physical Education*
(Champaign, IL: Human
Kinetics), 318. ©1997

**DEEP KNEE BENDS
NECK CIRCLE
HURDLER'S STRETCH
STANDING TOE TOUCHES
WINDMILLS**
Illustrations reprinted
with permission from
©Bonnie's Fitware, Inc.

Chapter 2
Standards-Based
Physical Education:
Kindergarten
Through
Grade Five

Grade Three

The teacher creates a bulletin board displaying pictures of unsafe exercises with an explanation of why each exercise is dangerous. During physical education instruction, the teacher distributes a set of cards that depict safe and unsafe exercises. Students are asked to identify those that are unsafe and to select from the set of cards a safe exercise to perform.

STANDARD 5

5.1 **Set a personal goal to improve a motor skill and work toward that goal in nonschool time.**

Third-grade students are working on a variety of skills (e.g., rolling, throwing, catching, kicking, striking, dribbling with a hand, and dribbling with feet). After introducing a skill to the students, the teacher asks them to write a personal goal for improving the skill. Goals should be clear, measurable, and achievable. Students are instructed to practice the skill during nonschool time and to monitor their progress in a log. Throughout the year, the teacher reviews the logs and assesses students' performances to determine whether students are meeting their goals or need adjustments to their goals or practice plans.

Chapter 2
Standards-Based
Physical Education:
Kindergarten
Through
Grade Five

Grade Three *Physical Education*
Model Content Standards

STANDARD 1
**Students demonstrate the motor skills and movement patterns needed
to perform a variety of physical activities.**

Movement Concepts

1.1   Chase, flee, and move away from others in a constantly changing
environment.

Body Management

1.2   Perform an inverted balance (tripod) by evenly distributing weight
on body parts.

1.3   Perform a forward roll.

1.4   Perform a straddle roll.

Locomotor Movement

1.5   Jump continuously a forward-turning rope and a backward-turning rope.

Manipulative Skills

1.6   Balance while traveling and manipulating an object on a ground-level
balance beam.

1.7   Catch, while traveling, an object thrown by a stationary partner.

1.8   Roll a ball for accuracy toward a target.

1.9   Throw a ball, using the overhand movement pattern with increasing
accuracy.

1.10   Throw and catch an object with a partner, increasing the distance from
the partner and maintaining an accurate throw that can be easily caught.

1.11   Kick a ball to a stationary partner, using the inside of the foot.

1.12   Strike a ball continuously upward, using a paddle or racket.

1.13   Hand-dribble a ball continuously while moving around obstacles.

1.14   Foot-dribble a ball continuously while traveling and changing direction.

Rhythmic Skills

1.15   Perform a line dance, a circle dance, and a folk dance with a partner.

STANDARD 2
**Students demonstrate knowledge of movement concepts, principles, and
strategies that apply to the learning and performance of physical activities.**

Movement Concepts

2.1   Describe how changing speed and changing direction can allow one
person to move away from another.

Manipulative Skills

2.2   Explain and demonstrate the correct hand position when catching a ball
above the head, below the waist, near the middle of the body, and away
from the body.

Chapter 2
Standards-Based
Physical Education:
Kindergarten
Through
Grade Five

2.3   Explain the difference between throwing to a stationary partner and throwing to a moving partner.

2.4   Identify the key elements for increasing accuracy in rolling a ball and throwing a ball.

2.5   Identify the differences between dribbling a ball (with the hand and the foot, separately) while moving forward and when changing direction.

Rhythmic Skills

2.6   Define the terms folk dance, line dance, and circle dance.

2.7   Compare and contrast folk dances, line dances, and circle dances.

STANDARD 3

Students assess and maintain a level of physical fitness to improve health and performance.

Fitness Concepts

3.1   Demonstrate warm-up and cool-down exercises.

3.2   Demonstrate how to lift and carry objects correctly.

Aerobic Capacity

3.3   Participate three to four days each week, for increasing periods of time, in continuous moderate to vigorous physical activities that require sustained movement of the large-muscle groups to increase breathing and heart rate.

Muscular Strength/Endurance

3.4   Perform increasing numbers of each: abdominal curl-ups, oblique curl-ups on each side, modified push-ups or traditional push-ups with hands on a bench, forward lunges, side lunges, and triceps push-ups from a chair.

3.5   Climb a vertical pole or rope.

Flexibility

3.6   Hold for an increasing period of time basic stretches for hips, shoulders, hamstrings, quadriceps, triceps, biceps, back, and neck.

Body Composition

3.7   Sustain continuous movement for increasing periods of time while participating in moderate to vigorous physical activity.

Assessment

3.8   Measure and record improvement in individual fitness activities.

STANDARD 4

Students demonstrate knowledge of physical fitness concepts, principles, and strategies to improve health and performance.

Fitness Concepts

4.1   Identify the body's normal reactions to moderate to vigorous physical activity.

4.2   List and define the components of physical fitness.

4.3   Explain the purpose of warming up before physical activity and cooling down after physical activity.

57

Chapter 2
Standards-Based
Physical Education:
Kindergarten
Through
Grade Five

Grade Three

4.4   Recognize that the body will adapt to increased workloads.

4.5   Explain that fluid needs are linked to energy expenditure.

4.6   Discuss the need for oxygen and fuel to be available during ongoing muscle contraction so that heat and waste products are removed.

Aerobic Capacity

4.7   Describe the relationship between the heart, lungs, muscles, blood, and oxygen during physical activity.

4.8   Describe and record the changes in heart rate before, during, and after physical activity.

Muscular Strength/Endurance

4.9   Explain that a stronger heart muscle can pump more blood with each beat.

4.10   Identify which muscles are used in performing muscular endurance activities.

4.11   Name and locate the major muscles of the body.

4.12   Describe and demonstrate how to relieve a muscle cramp.

4.13   Describe the role of muscle strength and proper lifting in the prevention of back injuries.

Flexibility

4.14   Identify flexibility exercises that are not safe for the joints and should be avoided.

4.15   Explain why a particular stretch is appropriate preparation for a particular physical activity.

Body Composition

4.16   Differentiate the body's ability to consume calories and burn fat during periods of inactivity and during long periods of moderate physical activity.

STANDARD 5
Students demonstrate and utilize knowledge of psychological and sociological concepts, principles, and strategies that apply to the learning and performance of physical activity.

Self-Responsibility

5.1   Set a personal goal to improve a motor skill and work toward that goal in nonschool time.

5.2   Collect data and record progress toward mastery of a motor skill.

5.3   List the benefits of following and the risks of not following safety procedures and rules associated with physical activity.

Social Interaction

5.4   Use appropriate cues for movement and positive words of encouragement while coaching others in physical activities.

5.5   Demonstrate respect for individual differences in physical abilities.

Group Dynamics

5.6   Work in pairs or small groups to achieve an agreed-upon goal.

Chapter 2
Standards-Based
Physical Education:
Kindergarten
Through
Grade Five

Grade Four

Grade Four

Fourth-grade students are at a transitional stage between childhood and youth. There is still very little difference in motor skill performance between boys and girls, and there should be equal expectations for both in terms of physical performance. Eye-hand coordination is improving, fine-motor activities are performed with more skill, and the greatest gain in strength begins at this stage. Students are also experiencing improvements in reaction time and balance, although the center of gravity is still located in the midsection of the body, making balance a challenge. In kindergarten through third grade, students should have mastered the proper form for locomotor and nonlocomotor skills and learned to manipulate objects in a variety of ways. The focus now shifts to using the proper form for manipulating (e.g., kicking, throwing, striking) objects.

Fourth grade marks a period of increased curiosity and rapid mental growth. Attention spans increase; consequently, students can focus for longer periods of time on learning movement concepts and principles. Specific principles and concepts for this grade level include basic offensive and defensive strategies and the correct way to perform motor skills.

Fourth-graders are continuing to grow in self-confidence that leads to a new-found sense of freedom. They are likely to test rules during play and challenge how rules apply to them. Winning becomes important, so teachers will need to emphasize self-competition over team competition. Conflicts can erupt easily but are also quelled quickly. Explaining the purpose of rules is important at this stage of development and will help to eliminate many unnecessary conflicts. Belonging is still important at this stage, so learning opportunities that involve small-group activities and modified team games are appropriate.

At a Glance

STANDARD 1

Students demonstrate the motor skills and movement patterns needed to perform a variety of physical activities.

Fourth-grade students apply nonlocomotor skills to balancing stunts with a partner. They apply locomotor skills to basic square-dance steps and learn dances performed during early California times to connect with the history–social science curriculum.[8] They also apply locomotor skills to individual offensive and defensive moves (e.g., a slide in basketball defense) and to jumping a self-turned rope. Manipulative skill practice takes on a much greater role in fourth-grade physical education as students improve

---

[8] The grade four history–social science content standard 4.2.5 states: "Describe the daily lives of the people, native and nonnative, who occupied the presidos, missions, ranchos, and pueblos."

Chapter 2
Standards-Based
Physical Education:
Kindergarten
Through
Grade Five

Grade Four

their form for throwing, catching, kicking, punting, striking, serving, hand-dribbling, foot-dribbling, trapping, and volleying using a forearm pass in a variety of situations.

STANDARD 2

Students demonstrate knowledge of movement concepts, principles, and strategies that apply to the learning and performance of physical activities.

Standard 2 represents the cognitive knowledge that supports the loco-motor, nonlocomotor, and manipulative skills learned in fourth grade. Often, the physical education lesson is able to address Standards 1 and 2 simultaneously; the teacher explains the information to the students and then has them experience it. For example, Standard 2.2 states, "Describe ways to create more space between an offensive player and a defensive player"; and Standard 1.3 states, "Change direction quickly to increase the spacing between two players." The teacher explains that changing direction quickly is one way to create more space between an offensive and defensive player. Then, in partners, the students practice changing direction to create more space between players.

Fourth-graders continue to learn more about the correct technique for manipulative skills (e.g., body orientation when serving and striking a ball, body position for volleying a ball). They can describe the similarities and differences between similar skills (e.g., underhand throw and underhand serve, punting and kicking, striking with a long-handled implement and striking with a short-handled implement) as well as the correct technique for the use of skills in different situations (e.g., dribbling without a defender, dribbling with a defender). Fourth-graders also continue their rhythms education by designing routines to music that include even and uneven locomotor patterns.

STANDARD 3

Students assess and maintain a level of physical fitness to improve health and performance.

Fourth-graders continue to perform moderate to vigorous physical activities three to four days each week for increasing periods of time. The students also demonstrate warm-up and cool-down exercises before and after, respectively, the activity. Muscular strength and endurance are still developing, but students are expected to perform an increasing number of abdominal curl-ups, oblique curl-ups on each side of the body, modified push-ups or traditional push-ups, and triceps push-ups as well as hanging by the hands from an overhead bar with hips and knees at 90-degree angles. In addition, students demonstrate the correct body

Chapter 2
Standards-Based
Physical Education:
Kindergarten
Through
Grade Five

Grade Four

position for pushing and pulling large objects. In terms of flexibility, students demonstrate basic stretches using proper body alignment for the hamstrings, quadriceps, hip flexors, triceps, back, shoulders, hip adductors, hip abductors, and calves. Fourth-graders continue to measure and record individual changes in aerobic capacity and muscular strength by using scientifically based health-related physical fitness tests. By the end of the school year, students are expected to meet minimum standards on the fitness test items.

STANDARD 4

Students demonstrate knowledge of physical fitness concepts, principles, and strategies to improve health and performance.

Similar to the relationship between Standards 1 and 2, Standard 4 provides the cognitive information to support the fitness activities described in Standard 3. For Standard 4, students are learning the correct body positions for performing lower-body stretches to prevent injuries. In addition, they are setting personal short-term goals for aerobic endurance, muscular strength and endurance, and flexibility and monitoring their progress toward their goals throughout the year.

Fourth-graders, in preparation for creating a personal fitness plan in later grade levels, learn the principles of physical fitness or F.I.T.T. (frequency, intensity, time, and type); the purpose of warm-up and cool-down periods; how to calculate heart rate and the importance of a strong heart; the value of muscular endurance, muscular strength, aerobic, and flexibility exercises; and the correct form to use for pushing and pulling heavy objects properly to prevent back injuries. They also continue their nutrition education by learning the role that food (especially carbohydrates) and water play in helping to improve physical performance.

STANDARD 5

Students demonstrate and utilize knowledge of psychological and sociological concepts, principles, and strategies that apply to the learning and performance of physical activity.

Fourth-graders assume greater responsibility for setting goals, working toward the goals, and monitoring their progress during nonschool time. They accept responsibility for their performance on fitness tests and in activity settings and learn to respond to winning or losing with dignity and respect. Fourth-graders continue to include others in physical activities and respect individual differences in skill levels and motivation.

Chapter 2
Standards-Based
Physical Education:
Kindergarten
Through
Grade Five

Learning Snapshots

STANDARD 1

1.13 Strike, with a paddle or racket, a lightweight object that has been tossed by a partner.

Striking with a paddle or racket is a skill used in sports such as tennis, badminton, pickleball, and paddle tennis. The goal is for students to demonstrate the forehand, backhand, overhand, and underhand striking patterns by using the proper form. The proper form for forehand striking is:

- Use a handshake grip.
- Watch the ball.
- Turn side to the target.*
- Step forward with the foot opposite the striking hand.*
- Swing the racket or paddle back.*
- Swing the racket or paddle forward.
- Keep the arm straight as the racket or paddle contacts the ball.
- Follow through in the direction of the target.

During the lesson, the teacher demonstrates the correct technique for striking a lightweight object with a paddle or racket. The teacher also describes two or three cues that students should focus on first (items marked with an asterisk). Students work in pairs: one student tosses the ball (a skill first learned in grade one), and the second student strikes the ball. The teacher circulates through the class, providing feedback on the two or three specific cues.[9] As students' performances improve, the teacher focuses on additional cues. It is important that students focus on generating a forceful strike rather than strive for accuracy and that they perform the skill in one smooth motion rather than practice the cues separately. For example, a forceful strike calls for the paddle to travel at a high speed, which calls for not only increasing the speed of the arm relative to the body, but also the speed of the body relative to the ground, so students need to swing the arm forward and step forward at the same time. During lesson closure, the teacher asks students to name the cues for performing a strike. To link with Standard 2.4 (Describe the appropriate body orientation to strike a ball, using the forehand movement pattern), emphasis should be placed on students noting the correct body orientation when striking a ball. The teacher reviews striking skills, and students practice them throughout the school year.

---

[9] Feedback is most effective when it is specific and positive or specific and corrective.

ILLUSTRATION CREDIT

Illustration reprinted with permission from B. S. Mohnsen, *Teaching Middle School Physical Education* (Champaign, IL: Human Kinetics), 231. ©1997.

Chapter 2
Standards-Based
Physical Education:
Kindergarten
Through
Grade Five

Grade Four

1.21 Perform a series of basic square-dance steps.

During a square-dance unit the students are divided into four groups. All students in each group receive one of the four cards listed below.

CARD #1
Circle left
All students join hands, forming a circle, and walk to the left.

CARD #2
Circle right
All students join hands, forming a circle, and walk to the right.

CARD #3
Alemande left
Students turn to their corners.
Students join left hands.
Students walk counterclockwise once around their corners, returning to the starting position.

ILLUSTRATION CREDITS

CARDS #1–4
Illustrations reprinted with permission from B. S. Mohnsen, *Teaching Middle School Physical Education: A Standards-Based Approach for Grades 5–8*, 3rd ed. (Champaign, IL: Human Kinetics), 516–517. ©2008.

63

Chapter 2
Standards-Based
Physical Education:
Kindergarten
Through
Grade Five

Grade Four

CARD #4

Do-si-do

Students face their partners.

Students walk forward toward their partners passing right shoulders.

Students walk around their partners back to back.

Students walk backward away from their partners passing left shoulders.

Each group walks through the dance step on its card. Then new groups are formed with one student from each of the original groups. Students teach their new group the dance step they learned in their original group, so that everyone learns all four steps. The teacher then asks the students to perform all four steps in sequence. The teacher circulates throughout the class, providing feedback.

STANDARD 2

2.6 Distinguish between punting and kicking and describe the similarities and differences.

Kicking and punting are similar skills. Both involve striking a ball with the foot. The critical steps for a punt are as follows:

- Hold one side of the ball with each hand.
- Tip front end of the ball up (if it is a football).
- Watch the ball.
- Take a short step with the kicking foot.
- Take a long step with the nonkicking foot.
- Drop the ball.
- Use arms for balance.
- Swing the kicking foot forward and upward.
- Contact the ball with the instep of the kicking foot.
- Follow through with the kicking foot.

The critical steps for a kick are as follows:

- Place the ball on the ground.
- Stand behind the ball.
- Step forward on the nonkicking foot.
- Swing the kicking leg back.
- Use arms for balance.

Chapter 2
Standards-Based
Physical Education:
Kindergarten
Through
Grade Five

Grade Four

- Swing the kicking leg forward.
- Straighten the knee.
- Contact the ball with the instep of the foot.
- Follow through with the kicking foot.

As the teacher introduces each skill with an explanation and demonstration, the teacher also points out the differences between the two skills. After a lesson when the students practice kicking and punting, the teacher asks each student to complete a Venn diagram for class work or homework that illustrates the similarities and differences between kicking and punting.

STANDARD 3

3.4 Perform increasing numbers of each: abdominal curl-ups, oblique curl-ups on each side, modified push-ups or traditional push-ups, and triceps push-ups.

For students to perform increasing numbers of an exercise, they must increase their muscular endurance. Muscular endurance is improved by performing each exercise two to three days per week. Students perform each exercise for six to 15 repetitions. Once the students can perform the exercise for 15 repetitions, then they should work toward two sets. A set is a group of repetitions (15 for endurance) performed without rest. So, two sets mean performing 15 repetitions, resting or performing a different exercise, and performing 15 more repetitions (*Physical Education for Lifelong Fitness* 2005, 88–91). Each of the exercises in this standard is illustrated below.

ABDOMINAL CURL-UPS

OBLIQUE CURL-UPS

65

Chapter 2
Standards-Based
Physical Education:
Kindergarten
Through
Grade Five

MODIFIED PUSH-UPS

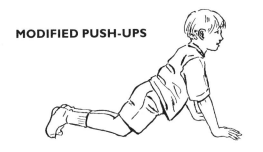

Grade Four

TRICEPS PUSH-UPS

TRADITIONAL PUSH-UPS

STANDARD 4

4.2   Explain the principles of physical fitness: frequency, intensity, time, and type.

Students must follow a protocol that includes a specific frequency, intensity, time, and type (of exercise) to improve their fitness. Table 2.1 shows the protocol for each principle of fitness (F.I.T.T.).

If students are asked to follow these protocols when exercising during physical education, they will learn the principles of physical fitness quickly. Specific learning activities can also be provided. For example, students are given 3-inch by 5-inch cards with the information that goes in each cell of the chart. Students are then asked to create a chart like Table 2.1. Students review this information throughout the year during the warm-up and cool-down.

ILLUSTRATION CREDITS

MODIFIED PUSH-UPS
TRICEPS PUSH-UPS
Illustrations reprinted
with permission from
©Bonnie's Fitware, Inc.

TRADITIONAL PUSH-UPS
Illustration reprinted with
permission from B. S.
Mohnsen, *Teaching Middle
School Physical Education*
(Champaign, IL: Human
Kinetics), 165. ©1997.

Chapter 2
Standards-Based
Physical Education:
Kindergarten
Through
Grade Five

Grade Four

Table 2.1 Protocols for the Principles of Fitness

Frequency (times per week)	Intensity	Time	Type
CARDIORESPIRATORY ENDURANCE[1]			
Developmentally appropriate physical activity on all or most days of the week. Several bouts of physical activity lasting 15 minutes or more daily.	Mixture of moderate and vigorous intermittent activity. Moderate includes low-intensity games, low-activity positions, some chores, and yard work. Vigorous includes games involving running or chasing and playing sports.	Accumulation of at least 60 minutes and up to several hours of activity. Up to 50% of accumulated minutes should be accumulated in bouts of 15 minutes or more.	Variety of activities. Activities should be selected from the first three levels of the activity pyramid. Continuous activity should not be expected for most students.
MUSCULAR STRENGTH[1]			
Two or three days per week.	Very light weight.	At least one set (may do two sets), 6–15 reps, at least 20–30 minutes.	Major muscle groups, one exercise per muscle of muscle group.
MUSCULAR ENDURANCE[1]			
Two or three days per week.	Very light weight.	At least one set (may do two sets), 6–15 reps, at least 20–30 minutes.	Major muscle groups, one exercise per muscle of muscle group.
FLEXIBILITY[1]			
Three times per week, preferably daily and after a warm-up to raise muscle temperature.	Slow elongation of the muscle to the point of mild discomfort and back off slightly.	Up to four to five stretches per muscle or muscle group. Hold each stretch 10–30 seconds. Always warm up properly prior to stretching.	The preferred stretch for the classroom is slow, static stretching for all muscles or muscle groups.
BODY COMPOSITION[2]			
Three to six days, daily preferred.	Light aerobic activity. 45–65% of maximum heart rate. "Talk test": talking should be relatively easy.	30 to 60 plus minutes.	Light aerobic exercise.

[1]Sources: *Physical Education for Lifelong Fitness: The Physical Best Teacher's Guide* (Second edition, page 69, Table 5.1; page 90, Table 6.1; and page 116, Table 7.1. © 2005 by National Association for Sport and Physical Education. Reprinted with permission from Human Kinetics, Champaign, IL).

Charles B. Corbin. Fitness for Life Physical Activity Pyramid for Children Poster. Champaign, IL: Human Kinetics, 2003

[2]Source: Charles B. Corbin et al. *Concepts of Fitness and Wellness: A Comprehensive Lifestyle Approach* (Seventh edition). New York: McGraw-Hill, 2008, page 285.

Chapter 2
Standards-Based
Physical Education:
Kindergarten
Through
Grade Five

Grade Four

STANDARD 5

5.5 Include others in physical activities and respect individual differences in skill and motivation.

Students, in groups of six, are participating in a tag game wearing football "flags." The teacher asks students to design a tag game to play with students who are in wheelchairs or who use crutches. The students determine that these students can participate in the game of tag with a few modifications: (1) each student in a wheelchair or with crutches has an able-bodied partner she or he must stay in contact with; and (2) everyone walks instead of runs. Students may suggest other modifications, such as everyone has a partner, not just the students who have to use aids to walk or move. To meet this standard, students need to actually demonstrate inclusion of others in the activities.

Chapter 2
Standards-Based
Physical Education:
Kindergarten
Through
Grade Five

Grade Four

Grade Four *Physical Education*
Model Content Standards

STANDARD 1
Students demonstrate the motor skills and movement patterns needed to perform a variety of physical activities.

Body Management

1.1 Perform simple balance stunts with a partner while sharing a common base of support.

1.2 Change direction quickly to maintain the spacing between two players.

1.3 Change direction quickly to increase the spacing between two players.

1.4 Determine the spacing between offensive and defensive players based on the speed of the players.

Locomotor Movement

1.5 Jump a self-turned rope.

Manipulative Skills

1.6 Throw and catch an object with a partner while both partners are moving.

1.7 Throw overhand at increasingly smaller targets, using proper follow-through.

1.8 Throw a flying disc for distance, using the backhand movement pattern.

1.9 Catch a fly ball above the head, below the waist, and away from the body.

1.10 Kick a ball to a moving partner, using the inside of the foot.

1.11 Kick a stationary ball from the ground into the air.

1.12 Punt a ball dropped from the hands.

1.13 Strike, with a paddle or racket, a lightweight object that has been tossed by a partner.

1.14 Serve a lightweight ball to a partner, using the underhand movement pattern.

1.15 Strike a gently tossed ball with a bat, using a side orientation.

1.16 Keep a foot-dribbled ball away from a defensive partner.

1.17 Keep a hand-dribbled ball away from a defensive partner.

1.18 Manipulate an object by using a long-handled implement.

1.19 Stop a kicked ball by trapping it with the foot while standing still.

1.20 Volley a tossed lightweight ball, using the forearm pass.

Rhythmic Skills

1.21 Perform a series of basic square-dance steps.

1.22 Perform a routine to music that includes even and uneven locomotor patterns.

69

Chapter 2
Standards-Based
Physical Education:
Kindergarten
Through
Grade Five

Grade Four

STANDARD 2

Students demonstrate knowledge of movement concepts, principles, and strategies that apply to the learning and performance of physical activities.

Movement Concepts

2.1   Explain the difference between offense and defense.

2.2   Describe ways to create more space between an offensive player and a defensive player.

Body Management

2.3   Describe the appropriate body orientation to serve a ball, using the underhand movement pattern.

2.4   Describe the appropriate body orientation to strike a ball, using the forehand movement pattern.

Manipulative Skills

2.5   Explain the similar movement elements of the underhand throw and the underhand volleyball serve.

2.6   Distinguish between punting and kicking and describe the similarities and differences.

2.7   Compare and contrast dribbling a ball without a defender and with a defender.

2.8   Explain the differences in manipulating an object when using a long-handled implement and when using a short-handled implement.

2.9   Identify key body positions used for volleying a ball.

Rhythmic Skills

2.10   Design a routine to music that includes even and uneven locomotor patterns.

STANDARD 3

Students assess and maintain a level of physical fitness to improve health and performance.

Fitness Concepts

3.1   Participate in appropriate warm-up and cool-down exercises for particular physical activities.

3.2   Demonstrate the correct body position for pushing and pulling large objects.

Aerobic Capacity

3.3   Participate three to four days each week, for increasing periods of time, in continuous moderate to vigorous physical activities at the appropriate intensity to increase aerobic capacity.

Muscular Strength/Endurance

3.4   Perform increasing numbers of each: abdominal curl-ups, oblique curl-ups on each side, modified push-ups or traditional push-ups, and triceps push-ups.

Chapter 2
Standards-Based
Physical Education:
Kindergarten
Through
Grade Five

3.5   Hang by the hands from an overhead bar with the hips and knees each at a 90-degree angle.

Flexibility

3.6   Demonstrate basic stretches using proper alignment for hamstrings, quadriceps, hip flexors, triceps, back, shoulders, hip adductors, hip abductors, and calves.

Body Composition

3.7   Sustain continuous movement for increasing periods of time while participating in moderate to vigorous physical activity.

Assessment

3.8   Measure and record changes in aerobic capacity and muscular strength, using scientifically based health-related physical fitness assessments.

3.9   Meet minimum requirements for health-related physical fitness, using scientifically based health-related physical fitness assessments.

STANDARD 4

Students demonstrate knowledge of physical fitness concepts, principles, and strategies to improve health and performance.

Fitness Concepts

4.1   Identify the correct body alignment for performing lower-body stretches.

4.2   Explain the principles of physical fitness: frequency, intensity, time, and type.

4.3   Set personal short-term goals for aerobic endurance, muscular strength and endurance, and flexibility and monitor progress by measuring and recording personal fitness scores.

4.4   Identify healthful choices for meals and snacks that help improve physical performance.

4.5   Explain why the body needs water before, during, and after physical activity.

4.6   Explain why the body uses a higher percentage of carbohydrates for fuel during high-intensity physical activity and a higher percentage of fat for fuel during low-intensity physical activity.

4.7   Explain the purpose of warm-up and cool-down periods.

Aerobic Capacity

4.8   Calculate personal heart rate per minute by recording heartbeats for ten-second intervals and 15-second intervals.

4.9   Explain why a strong heart is able to return quickly to its resting rate after exertion.

4.10   Identify two characteristics of physical activity that build aerobic capacity.

4.11   Determine the intensity of personal physical activity by using the concept of perceived exertion.

71

Chapter 2
Standards-Based
Physical Education:
Kindergarten
Through
Grade Five

Grade Four

Muscular Strength/Endurance

4.12   Describe the difference between muscular strength and muscular endurance.

4.13   Explain why muscular endurance or muscular strength activities do not increase muscle mass in preadolescent children.

4.14   Recognize how strengthening major muscles can improve performance at work and play.

4.15   Describe the correct form to push and pull heavy objects.

Flexibility

4.16   Explain the value of increased flexibility when participating in physical activity.

Body Composition

4.17   Explain the effect of regular, sustained physical activity on the body's ability to consume calories and burn fat for energy.

STANDARD 5
Students demonstrate and utilize knowledge of psychological and sociological concepts, principles, and strategies that apply to the learning and performance of physical activity.

Self-Responsibility

5.1   Set a personal goal to improve an area of health-related physical fitness and work toward that goal in nonschool time.

5.2   Collect data and record progress toward attainment of a personal fitness goal.

5.3   Accept responsibility for one's own performance without blaming others.

5.4   Respond to winning and losing with dignity and respect.

Social Interaction

5.5   Include others in physical activities and respect individual differences in skill and motivation.

Group Dynamics

5.6   Accept an opponent's outstanding skill, use of strategies, or ability to work effectively with teammates as a challenge in physical activities.

72

Chapter 2
Standards-Based
Physical Education:
Kindergarten
Through
Grade Five

Grade Five

Grade Five

Fifth-grade students are entering early adolescence and are beginning to experience many physical changes. At this age, it is not uncommon for girls to be taller than boys. Differences in strength and motor skill performance may be attributed to experience and students' practice opportunities. Flexibility continues to decrease, especially in boys, presenting the need for more stretching exercises during physical education. Students continue to manipulate a variety of objects using eye-hand and eye-foot coordination. However, the emphasis now shifts to improving accuracy and distance while efficiently manipulating objects using body parts (e.g., hand, foot) or implements (e.g., racket, bat).

Fifth-graders experience a marked increase in intellectual curiosity. They have a thirst for knowledge and a wide range of interests. They like to experiment and to investigate the world around them. Problem-solving activities and intellectual challenges are appropriate for this age group. They are especially interested in knowing about the human body and how to improve health and performance. Teachers can address this interest by teaching concepts and principles of movement related to the physical and motor skills that the students are learning.

Fifth-graders thrive in a small-group activity in which three to four students interact cooperatively. Students are showing increased control over emotions, taking pride in individual accomplishments, and enjoying their successes and achievements. They are beginning to develop an awareness of individual differences related to gender, cultural heritage, ethnicity, and physical ability, making this an ideal time to teach the positive aspects of diversity and the importance of listening to the ideas of others.

At a Glance

STANDARD 1

Students demonstrate the motor skills and movement patterns needed to perform a variety of physical activities.

Fifth-grade students apply nonlocomotor skills to small-group balancing stunts. They apply locomotor skills to creative dances and movement routines to music that also involve the manipulation of an object. The locomotor skill of jumping is the focus of practice in fifth grade, including jumping for height, jumping for distance, and jumping a rope turned by others.

The practice of manipulative skills continues to play a much greater role in fifth-grade physical education. The emphasis for fifth grade is improving distance and accuracy. Students focus on both when practicing throwing, fielding, punting, striking, serving, dribbling, passing, and volleying as well as refining their performances of trapping and catching. The practice

73

Chapter 2
Standards-Based
Physical Education:
Kindergarten
Through
Grade Five

of many of these skills takes on the added challenge of performance in an open environment (one that has variables such as a defender), thus preparing students for the lead-up games performed in sixth grade.

STANDARD 2
Students demonstrate knowledge of movement concepts, principles, and strategies that apply to the learning and performance of physical activities.

Standard 2 represents the cognitive knowledge that supports the locomotor, nonlocomotor, and manipulative skills practiced in fifth grade. The physical education lesson is often able to address Standards 1 and 2 simultaneously; the teacher explains the information to the students and then has them experience it. For example, Standard 2.5 states, "Design a routine to music, changing speed and direction while manipulating an object." Standard 1.18 states, "Design and perform a creative dance, combining locomotor patterns with intentional changes in speed and direction"; and Standard 1.19 states, "Design and perform a routine to music that involves manipulation of an object." All three standards can be learned together. The teacher explains the principles for designing a routine to music, and then students work on their creative dance or manipulative routine while applying those principles.

By the end of fifth grade, students are competent identifying the correct technique for fundamental manipulative skills (e.g., identifying the phases for striking a ball, identifying adjustments that need to be made when catching a ball thrown off center). In preparation for game play in sixth grade, students learn about the importance of open space from a strategic perspective. In preparation for gaining a deeper understanding of the science of movement, fifth-graders learn the differences in technique between applying force on liftoff and receiving force on landing when jumping for height and distance.

STANDARD 3
Students assess and maintain a level of physical fitness to improve health and performance.

Fifth-graders continue to perform moderate to vigorous physical activities three to four days each week for increasing periods of time. They start each activity period with warm-up exercises and conclude each activity period with cool-down exercises. Muscular strength and endurance continue to be developed, and students are expected to perform an increasing number of oblique curl-ups on each side of the body and triceps push-ups. In terms of flexibility, students perform exercises that stretch certain muscle areas in preparation for certain physical activities. Fifth-graders continue

Chapter 2
Standards-Based
Physical Education:
Kindergarten
Through
Grade Five

Grade Five

to measure their health-related physical fitness using a scientifically based assessment. By the end of the school year, students are expected to meet the minimum requirements on these fitness test items. In addition, they can plan a day of healthy, balanced meals and snacks designed to enhance physical activity performance.

STANDARD 4

Students demonstrate knowledge of physical fitness concepts, principles, and strategies to improve health and performance.

Similar to the relationship between Standards 1 and 2, Standard 4 provides the cognitive information to support the fitness activities described in Standard 3. For Standard 4, students record water intake, heart rates, and perceived exertion before, during, and after physical activity. Then they compare their heart rates with their perceived exertion levels so they learn what being in their target heart rate zones feels like.

Fifth-graders, in preparation for creating a personal fitness plan in sixth grade, learn the application of the principles of training to each component of health-related fitness, how to calculate target heart rate, elements of warm-up and cool-down activities, the value of strength and flexibility exercises, and the use of technology (e.g., heart monitors, pedometers) to assist in the pursuit of physical fitness. Students are given the results of their most recent health-related physical fitness assessment and instructed to identify one or more ways to improve performance in those areas where minimum standards were not met. They also continue their nutrition education by learning meal planning, the effects of dehydration, the relationship between caloric intake and expenditure, and the benefits of maintaining a healthy body composition.

STANDARD 5

Students demonstrate and utilize knowledge of psychological and sociological concepts, principles, and strategies that apply to the learning and performance of physical activity.

Fifth-graders assume greater responsibility for setting long-term goals related to personal fitness and motor skill performance, working toward their goals outside school and monitoring their progress. They also demonstrate personal responsibility by acting in a safe and healthy manner even when confronted by negative peer pressure and the temptation to act recklessly. Fifth-graders demonstrate social skills by adapting physical activities to accommodate individual differences and by showing appreciation for games and activities reflecting diverse heritages. They listen to the ideas of others and acknowledge these contributions while also contributing their own ideas during cooperative problem-solving activities.

75

Chapter 2
Standards-Based
Physical Education:
Kindergarten
Through
Grade Five

Grade Five

Learning Snapshots

STANDARD 1

1.3   Jump for distance, using proper takeoff and landing form.

This standard asks students to demonstrate the proper form when jumping for distance. The correct technique for jumping is:

- Swing arms back.
- Bend the knees halfway.
- Swing arms forward.
- Push off with the toes.
- Reach forward.
- Land on heels.
- Bend knees.
- Shift weight from heels to balls of feet.

This standard parallels Standard 1.2 that asks students to demonstrate the proper form when jumping for height. The difference between the two skills is that on takeoff the performer reaches forward when jumping for distance and reaches upward when jumping for height. Specifically, the performer jumping for distance wants to take off at a 45-degree angle for maximum distance. This standard also links to Standard 2.2. As students are learning to jump, the teacher explains the science behind applying force on takeoff and receiving force on landing. For students to learn the skill correctly, the teacher needs to circulate through the class as students are practicing and provide them with feedback on their form.[10]

1.19   Design and perform a routine to music that involves manipulation of an object.

This standard is best addressed toward the end of the school year after students have learned how to move to music and can demonstrate a variety of manipulative skills. The teacher reviews with the students how to move to the beat of the music. The teacher plays a contemporary song with a strong beat. The teacher asks the students to clap in rhythm with the music. Then students are provided with a basketball or rubber playground ball and asked to design a ball-handling routine to music. The teacher assigns students to groups of four to six, and students perform their routines for their assigned group.

STANDARD 2

2.1   Explain the importance of open space in playing sport-related games.

The concept of "open space" forms the basis of all offensive and defensive strategies. The offense tries to create open space (i.e., areas where there are no defensive players) so that the offense can move a receiver into that space

---

[10]Feedback is most effective when it is specific and positive or specific and corrective.

Chapter 2
Standards-Based
Physical Education:
Kindergarten
Through
Grade Five

Grade Five

(invasion sports—basketball, soccer) or hit the ball into that space (field sports—softball; net sports—volleyball). The defense tries to close space (cover all areas) to prevent the offense from advancing the ball down the field or scoring. The teacher can best convey this concept to students by using video clips, software simulations, or three-dimensional models. Once the students are introduced to the concept, they apply it while working on Standard 1.6 ("Throw and catch an object underhand and overhand while avoiding an opponent").

STANDARD 3

3.7 Sustain continuous movement for an increasing period of time while participating in moderate to vigorous physical activities.

Moderate-intensity physical activity generally requires sustained rhythmic movements. It refers to a level of effort that a healthy individual might expend while, for example, walking briskly, dancing, swimming, or bicycling on level terrain. A person should feel some exertion but should be able to carry on a conversation comfortably during the activity. Vigorous-intensity physical activity generally requires sustained, rhythmic movements and refers to a level of effort a healthy individual might expend while, for example, jogging, participating in high-impact aerobic dancing, swimming continuous laps, or bicycling uphill. Vigorous-intensity physical activity may be intense enough to increase heart and respiration rates significantly. Popular aerobic activities for this age group include the performance of short jump rope activities, line dances, or moving around a circuit (learning stations) during which the locomotor skill is changed at each corner (Four Corners Activity).

STANDARD 4

4.1 Record and analyze food consumption for one day and make a plan to replace foods with healthier choices and adjust quantities to enhance performance in physical activity.

Students are asked to record their food consumption for one day. Simultaneously, students work on Standard 4.6 ("Record water intake before, during, and after physical activity") for the same day. Students are given the time in class to analyze their food consumption in relation to the Food Pyramid. For independent class work or homework, students design a one-day food plan that meets the recommendations of the Food Pyramid.

STANDARD 5

5.2 Work toward a long-term physical activity goal and record data on one's progress.

Fifth-grade students are working on Standard 3.7 ("Sustain continuous movement for an increasing period of time while participating in moderate to vigorous physical activities"). Together with Standard 5.2, students

77

Chapter 2
Standards-Based
Physical Education:
Kindergarten
Through
Grade Five

write long-term goals related to increasing the time they are participating in physical activity and record their progress toward their goals. The goals should be clear, measurable, and achievable. The teacher provides feedback on the goals before the students begin to work toward them. The students are given a form or chart with columns for dates, times, and activities. Throughout the year the teacher reviews the progress sheets with students to determine whether they have met their goals or need to adjust them.

Grade Five

Chapter 2
Standards-Based
Physical Education:
Kindergarten
Through
Grade Five

Grade Five

Grade Five *Physical Education* *Model Content Standards*

STANDARD 1
Students demonstrate the motor skills and movement patterns needed to perform a variety of physical activities.

Body Management

1.1   Perform simple small-group balance stunts by distributing weight and base of support.

Locomotor Movement

1.2   Jump for height, using proper takeoff and landing form.
1.3   Jump for distance, using proper takeoff and landing form.

Manipulative Skills

1.4   Enter, jump, and leave a long rope turned by others.
1.5   Throw a flying disc accurately at a target and to a partner, using the backhand movement pattern.
1.6   Throw and catch an object underhand and overhand while avoiding an opponent.
1.7   Field a thrown ground ball.
1.8   Punt a ball, dropped from the hands, at a target.
1.9   Stop a kicked ball by trapping it with the foot while moving.
1.10   Strike a dropped ball, with a racket or paddle, toward a target by using the forehand movement pattern.
1.11   Hit a softly tossed ball backhanded with a paddle or racket.
1.12   Strike a tossed ball, with different implements, from a side orientation.
1.13   Serve a lightweight ball over a low net, using the underhand movement pattern.
1.14   Dribble a ball (by hand or foot) while preventing another person from stealing the ball.
1.15   Dribble a ball and kick it toward a goal while being guarded.
1.16   Pass a ball back and forth with a partner, using a chest pass and bounce pass.
1.17   Volley a tossed ball to an intended location.

Rhythmic Skills

1.18   Design and perform a creative dance, combining locomotor patterns with intentional changes in speed and direction.
1.19   Design and perform a routine to music that involves manipulation of an object.

Chapter 2
Standards-Based
Physical Education:
Kindergarten
Through
Grade Five

STANDARD 2

Students demonstrate knowledge of movement concepts, principles, and strategies that apply to the learning and performance of physical activities.

Movement Concepts

2.1   Explain the importance of open space in playing sport-related games.

2.2   Explain the differences in applying and receiving force when jumping for height and distance.

Body Management

2.3   Explain how to adjust body position to catch a ball thrown off-center.

Manipulative Skills

2.4   Identify the following phases for striking a ball: preparation, application of force, follow-through, and recovery.

Rhythmic Skills

2.5   Design a routine to music, changing speed and direction while manipulating an object.

STANDARD 3

Students assess and maintain a level of physical fitness to improve health and performance.

Fitness Concepts

3.1   Demonstrate how to warm up muscles and joints before running, jumping, kicking, throwing, and striking.

3.2   Plan a day of healthful balanced meals and snacks designed to enhance the performance of physical activities.

Aerobic Capacity

3.3   Participate three to four days each week, for increasing periods of time, in continuous moderate to vigorous physical activities at the appropriate intensity for increasing aerobic capacity.

Muscular Strength/Endurance

3.4   Perform an increasing number of oblique curl-ups on each side.

3.5   Perform increasing numbers of triceps push-ups.

Flexibility

3.6   Perform flexibility exercises that will stretch particular muscle areas for given physical activities.

Body Composition

3.7   Sustain continuous movement for an increasing period of time while participating in moderate to vigorous physical activities.

Assessment

3.8   Assess health-related physical fitness by using a scientifically based health-related fitness assessment.

Chapter 2
Standards-Based
Physical Education:
Kindergarten
Through
Grade Five

Grade Five

3.9   Meet age- and gender-specific fitness standards for aerobic capacity, muscular strength, flexibility, and body composition, using a scientifically based health-related fitness assessment.

STANDARD 4
Students demonstrate knowledge of physical fitness concepts, principles, and strategies to improve health and performance.

Fitness Concepts

4.1   Record and analyze food consumption for one day and make a plan to replace foods with healthier choices and adjust quantities to enhance performance in physical activity.

4.2   Explain why dehydration impairs temperature regulation and physical and mental performance.

4.3   Develop and describe three short-term and three long-term fitness goals.

4.4   Examine personal results of a scientifically based health-related physical fitness assessment and identify one or more ways to improve performance in areas that do not meet minimum standards.

4.5   Explain the elements of warm-up and cool-down activities.

4.6   Record water intake before, during, and after physical activity.

4.7   Describe the principles of training and the application to each of the components of health-related physical fitness.

Aerobic Capacity

4.8   Identify the heart rate intensity (target heart-rate range) that is necessary to increase aerobic capacity.

4.9   Determine the intensity of personal physical activity, using the concept of perceived exertion.

4.10   Compare target heart rate and perceived exertion during physical activity.

4.11   Measure and record the heart rate before, during, and after vigorous physical activity.

4.12   Explain how technology can assist in the pursuit of physical fitness.

Muscular Strength/Endurance

4.13   Explain the benefits of having strong arm, chest, and back muscles.

Flexibility

4.14   Explain the benefits of stretching after warm-up activities.

Body Composition

4.15   Explain why body weight is maintained when calorie intake is equal to the calories expended.

4.16   Describe the short- and long-term benefits of maintaining body composition within the healthy fitness zone.

Chapter 2
Standards-Based
Physical Education:
Kindergarten
Through
Grade Five

STANDARD 5

Students demonstrate and utilize knowledge of psychological and sociological concepts, principles, and strategies that apply to the learning and performance of physical activity.

Self-Responsibility

5.1   Improve the level of performance on one component of health-related physical fitness and one identified motor skill by participating in fitness and skill development activities outside school.

5.2   Work toward a long-term physical activity goal and record data on one's progress.

5.3   Distinguish between acts of physical courage and physically reckless acts and explain the key characteristics of each.

5.4   Act in a safe and healthy manner when confronted with negative peer pressure during physical activity.

Social Interaction

5.5   Contribute ideas and listen to the ideas of others in cooperative problem-solving activities.

5.6   Acknowledge orally the contributions and strengths of others.

Group Dynamics

5.7   Accommodate individual differences in others' physical abilities in small-group activities.

5.8   Appreciate physical games and activities reflecting diverse heritages.

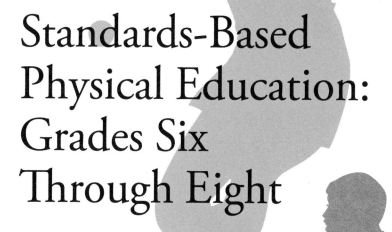

3

Standards-Based
Physical Education:
Grades Six
Through Eight

The physical education program in grades six through eight provides the opportunity to expand a student's performance and understanding of fundamental movement and motor skills to more specialized movement and motor skills used in a variety of content areas (individual and dual activities, team activities, rhythms and dance, combatives, aquatics, adventure/outdoor activities, and tumbling and gymnastics). The standards are grade-specific; therefore, the physical education classes are organized by grade level. Students may experience sixth through eighth-grade physical education in an elementary school setting, a middle school setting, or a combination of settings. Because most students in California public schools attend a middle school or junior high school for some part of grades six through eight, the terms *middle school* and *middle school student* are used throughout this chapter. Whatever the setting for physical education, students need to demonstrate mastery of the standards for their grade level.

The transition from elementary school to the middle school environment will most likely include new experiences such as dressing for physical education class, lockers, a larger school facility, and interacting with a greater number of peers. A supportive environment that provides students with opportunities to successfully interact with their new environment and peers sets the stage for a positive middle school experience. Middle school physical education programs work most effectively when they are designed for student success and emphasize learning, enjoyment, conceptual knowledge, appropriate challenges, and cooperation.

Standards-based middle school physical education provides students with experiences in a wide variety of activities (e.g., soccer, dancing, climbing). During middle school, students learn to refine, combine, and apply a variety of movement and motor skills in different physical activity settings. It is important that students have developmentally appropriate equipment and many practice opportunities throughout all their learning experiences. Pretesting will help determine whether students need instruction or remediation on the fundamental movement and motor skills from previous grade levels. The physical education model content standards provide guidance on which content areas to address in which grade levels. It may be necessary, however, for teachers to reteach or review and provide practice on fundamental skills from previous grade levels. (See Chapter 7, "Universal Access," for additional information on meeting the instructional needs of students.)

The emphasis at sixth grade is on the application of movement and motor skills in lead-up or modified games along with folk and line dancing, stunts, and tumbling. The emphasis at seventh grade is on multicultural dancing, individual and dual physical activities, track and field, combatives, and adventure/outdoor activities. The emphasis at eighth grade is on team activities, square dancing, and gymnastics/tumbling. In each area of physical education, the critical elements for each motor skill as well as concepts and principles related to biomechanics, motor development, motor learning, and game tactics are taught.

Middle school physical education programs continue to emphasize the importance of physical activity and personal fitness throughout the school year.

Students are provided with opportunities to improve their fitness as well as to understand more advanced concepts related to physical fitness and physical activity. Providing the student with the opportunity to participate in a variety of activities that are enjoyable and engaging is beneficial in increasing aerobic fitness (Wright and Karp 2006). Students should be active most of the time during physical education to experience the aerobic benefits.

Participation in physical activity can also be an important venue for the social, psychological, and emotional development of adolescents. Social skills and personal responsibility skills need to be taught and practiced and feedback given.[1] Physical education classes provide an ideal setting for adolescents to learn and practice those skills.

This chapter incorporates the physical education model content standards for grades six through eight, providing an explanation of the physical education content areas underlying the standards and outlining activities that are consistent with the intent of the standards. The activities in this chapter are examples of one way in which the standards may be approached. The examples are not to be interpreted as requirements for the physical education classroom or as the only instructional approach to a particular standard. The physical education model content standards set forth what students should know and can do. Therefore, mastery of an individual standard is achieved when students have actually learned the concept, principle, or skill. Content mastery does not occur simply because students have received a particular explanation or participated in a particular activity; students master the content through effective instruction and multiple opportunities to practice.

---

[1] Feedback is most effective when it is specific and positive or specific and corrective.

Grade Six

Sixth-grade students are rapidly entering adolescence and experiencing numerous physical changes. This is the beginning of a two- to three-year growth spurt for some students that can account for 20 percent of their eventual adult stature. The heart and lungs are also increasing in size and capacity proportionate to height and weight gains. Students enjoy being active, engaging in fitness activities, assessing their own fitness levels, and creating personal fitness plans. Students at this stage can combine various skills in cooperative activities. The focus now shifts to providing students with experiences that help them transition from using the proper form for fundamental movement skills to sport-skill learning.

Sixth-grade students are moving toward the capacity for abstract thinking. No longer satisfied with pat answers, they demand more thorough explanations. Sixth-graders experience a marked increase in attention span that allows more complex and challenging cognitive activities. However, sixth-graders can be easily distracted from learning experiences because of the mental, social, and emotional changes that they are experiencing.

Students in sixth grade are more independent in thought and action than younger students. They are also more likely to seek out new challenges in individual and group activities and to test the limits of acceptable behavior. They are, however, capable of respecting the performance of others and providing appropriate feedback.[2] Cooperation is an important social skill for this age group, including cooperation with opponents in game settings. Students also learn cooperation that facilitates development of motor skills.

Sixth-grade physical education may be taught in a variety of environments: in an elementary school, a middle school, or a junior high school, by a teacher with a multiple-subject credential or by a teacher with a single-subject credential. In the elementary setting, sixth-grade teachers may team-teach or coordinate with a physical education specialist or adapted physical education specialist to adequately address the sixth-grade standards. The elementary setting provides additional opportunities for cross-curricular instruction, smaller class sizes, and teachers who often know their students well. The challenges faced by sixth-grade teachers in the elementary setting include limited facilities, such as the lack of dressing facilities. Students must participate in physical education wearing their school clothing. Teachers communicate with parents about when students should dress for physical education and what clothing and shoes are appropriate for physical education instruction. It is important in the elementary school setting to create a schedule for physical education so that only a few classes use the facilities at one time, and each class has ample room for all students to participate safely.

In the middle school setting, physical education teachers have the support of other physical education teachers in a department setting. They may have better facilities and changing rooms, so students can be expected to change clothes for

---

[2]Feedback is most effective when it is specific and positive or specific and corrective.

Grade Six

physical education. However, middle school physical education teachers also face instructional challenges: larger class sizes, more students-per-teacher contacts, and more heterogeneous classes. These challenges are addressed throughout the framework.

At a Glance

STANDARD 1

Students demonstrate the motor skills and movement patterns needed to perform a variety of physical activities.

Sixth-grade students combine nonlocomotor, locomotor, and motor skills while incorporating qualities of movement (e.g., relationships, levels, speed, direction, and pathways) in complex physical activities. Sixth grade represents a shift from the practice of fundamental manipulative skills to specialized sport skills. The students are also given learning opportunities to develop rhythmic skills as they perform folk and line dances, as well as develop and demonstrate rhythmic routines to music. Stunts, tumbling, and rhythmic patterns are also introduced as students prepare for more advanced tumbling and gymnastics skills that will be learned in the eighth grade.

STANDARD 2

Students demonstrate knowledge of movement concepts, principles, and strategies that apply to the learning and performance of physical activities.

Standard 2 represents the cognitive knowledge that supports the loco-motor, nonlocomotor, and manipulative skills practiced in sixth grade. Often, the physical education lesson is able to address Standards 1 and 2 simultaneously; the teacher explains the information to the students and then has them experience it. For example, Standard 2.6 states, "Explain the role of the legs, shoulders, and forearm in the forearm pass"; and Standard 1.1 states, "Volley an object repeatedly with a partner, using the forearm pass." The teacher starts the lesson by describing the correct technique for the forearm pass (including the role of the legs, shoulders, and forearms) and then demonstrating the skill. As the students practice the forearm pass with a partner, the teacher asks students to explain the role of the legs, shoulders, and forearms.

By the end of sixth grade, students can identify dance steps and rhythm patterns and explain the contribution of movement qualities to the aesthetic dimension of physical activity. Sixth-graders are also expanding their understanding of biomechanics (see the Glossary) by learning the variables involved with increasing and decreasing the forces applied by the body or another object and those controlling the intended flight of an object. The students are expanding their knowledge of motor learning. Students learn the correct type of feedback (specific positive, specific corrective) to provide. They improve their understanding of offensive strategies by identifying opportunities to pass or dribble while being closely guarded. In sixth grade, students develop and teach a cooperative game that uses rules, skills, and offensive strategies.

STANDARD 3

Students assess and maintain a level of physical fitness to improve health and performance.

Sixth-graders continue to perform moderate to vigorous physical activities while monitoring their heart rates, but they increase the frequency from three to four days each week to a minimum of four days each week. They assess their own level of health-related physical fitness and compare themselves with established standards for good health. Students use this information to generate personal goals for each fitness component. As students continue to participate in fitness activities, they monitor changes in their health-related physical fitness status.

STANDARD 4

Students demonstrate knowledge of physical fitness concepts, principles, and strategies to improve health and performance.

Similar to the relationship between Standards 1 and 2, Standard 4 provides the cognitive information to support the fitness activities described in Standard 3. For Standard 4, students learn different methods of monitoring heart rate intensity. These methods include heart rate monitors and placing two fingers over the wrist.

Sixth-grade students learn the long-term benefits of regular participation in physical activity and classify activities as aerobic and anaerobic. They also distinguish between effective and ineffective warm-ups, cool-downs, and flexibility exercises (stretches). Sixth-grade students compile and analyze the effects of caloric intake and energy expenditures through physical activity. By the end of sixth grade, students have developed a one-day physical fitness plan using the F.I.T.T. (frequency, intensity, time, and type) principles and addressing each component of health-related physical fitness.

Grade Six

> **STANDARD 5**
>
> Students demonstrate and utilize knowledge of psychological and sociological concepts, principles, and strategies that apply to the learning and performance of physical activity.
>
> Sixth-grade students participate in cooperative group activities. They identify the individual roles and responsibilities necessary to make their group successful. They compare their own behavior with those roles and responsibilities to ensure that they are productive members of the group. These cooperative physical activities also allow students to develop and collaborate on common goals and agree on possible solutions to a variety of physical challenges.

Learning Snapshots

STANDARD 1

1.4　Strike an object consistently, using an implement, so that the object travels in the intended direction at the desired height.

For this standard, students practice striking skills using a variety of implements (e.g., paddles, racquets) and objects (e.g., balloons, balls, shuttlecock). As students practice their forehand striking skills, they should use the following technique:

- Watch the ball.
- Turn one side toward the target.
- Swing the implement backwards.
- Step with the opposite foot.
- Swing the racket or paddle forward.
- Contact, with a straight arm, the object.
- Follow through in the direction of the target.

The point of contact between the implement and object determines the direction and height at which the object will travel. Students work in pairs and experiment with contacting objects at different heights from the ground and at different takeoff angles. This standard can be integrated with Standard 2.8 by asking students to illustrate how the intended direction of an object is affected by the angle of the implement at the time of contact.

1.7　Perform folk and line dances.

This lesson focuses on learning the line dance Pata Pata. The students are organized into four groups. Each student in a group receives a copy of the same card, one of the four cards listed below.

ILLUSTRATION CREDIT

Illustration reprinted with permission from B. S. Mohnsen, *Teaching Middle School Physical Education* (Champaign, IL: Human Kinetics), 231. ©1997.

89

Chapter 3
Standards-Based
Physical Education:
Grades Six
Through Eight

Grade Six

CARD #1

1. Step right foot to the right.
2. Return right foot to the starting position.
3. Step left foot to the left.
4. Return left foot to the starting position.

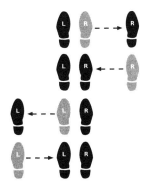

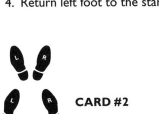

CARD #2

1. Move toes of left and right feet apart.
2. Move heels of left and right feet apart.
3. Move heels of left and right feet together.
4. Move toes of left and right feet together.

CARD #3

1. Kick right foot forward.
2. Touch toes of right foot behind the body.
3. Kick right foot forward.
4. Step back on right foot and pivot
   1/4 turn clockwise.

CARD #4

1. Kick left foot forward.
2. Step back on left foot.
3. Step back on right foot.
4. Step back on left foot.

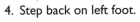

Each group walks through the dance steps on the card. Then new groups are
formed with one student from each of the original groups. Students teach
their new group the dance step, so that everyone learns all four steps. The
teacher then asks the students to perform all four steps in sequence. The
teacher circulates throughout the class providing feedback.

Grade Six

STANDARD 2

2.1 Explain how to increase force based on the principles of biomechanics.

Ways of increasing force are as follows:

- Increase the speed of the striking implement or body part.
- Use stronger muscles (e.g., hip flexors when kicking a ball).
- Use a heavier striking implement.
- Use more muscles.
- Use a longer lever.
- Increase the distance over which force is applied.
- Stretch the muscle prior to contraction (e.g., pull the arm back, then throw).
- Use sequential movement of the body's muscles.

Students are introduced to one or two ways to increase force during each instructional unit. The students experiment with each method to prove to themselves that it does increase force. For example, students throw a ball using only their wrist joint; then their wrist and elbow joints; then their wrist, elbow, and shoulder joints; and finally their entire bodies. The teacher asks the students to observe and identify in which situation the ball traveled farther. Then the students explain to a partner why the ball went farther when more body parts were involved. The different ways to increase force should be reviewed throughout the year to ensure that the students understand and remember them.

STANDARD 3

3.6 Monitor the intensity of one's heart rate during physical activity.

There are three general methods of monitoring heart rate during physical education instruction: listening to the heart beat using a stethoscope, recording the heart rate using a heart rate monitor, and feeling the heart rate at a pulse point (e.g., wrist). The teacher demonstrates each method for the students. Students select a method, depending on the equipment available, for monitoring the intensity of their heart rates during physical activity. When using a stethoscope or feeling for a pulse, students should count for 15 seconds and then multiply the number by four to determine the beats per minute.

STANDARD 4

4.2 Develop a one-day personal physical fitness plan specifying the intensity, time, and types of physical activities for each component of health-related physical fitness.

This standard requires students to identify safe exercises for each component of health-related physical fitness. The students are then asked to sequence the exercises and to determine the intensity level and duration of time for each exercise. Prior to completing this task, the teacher instructs students on the following exercise protocols:

Table 3.1 Protocols for Exercise

Frequency (times per week)	Intensity	Time	Type
CARDIORESPIRATORY ENDURANCE[1]			
Daily or nearly every day. Three or more sessions per week.	Moderate to vigorous activity. Maintaining a target heart rate is not expected at this level. A 12–16 rating of perceived exertion (RPE).	30–60 minutes daily activity. A single session of 20 minutes or more.	Play, games, sports, work, transportation, recreation, physical education, or planned exercise in the context of family, school, and community activities. Brisk walking, jogging, stair climbing, basketball, racket sports, soccer, dance, lap swimming, skating, lawn mowing, and cycling.
MUSCULAR STRENGTH[1]			
Two or three days per week.	Light weight	At least one set (may do three sets), 6–15 reps, at least 20–30 minutes.	Major muscle groups, one exercise per muscle or muscle group.
MUSCULAR ENDURANCE[1]			
Two or three days per week.	Light weight	At least one set (may do three sets), 6–15 reps, at least 20–30 minutes.	Major muscle groups, one exercise per muscle or muscle group.
FLEXIBILITY[1]			
Three times per week, preferably daily and after a warm-up to raise muscle temperature.	Slow elongation of the muscle to the point of mild discomfort and back off slightly.	Up to four to five stretches per muscle or muscle group. Hold each stretch 10–30 seconds. Always do a warm-up properly prior to stretching.	The preferred stretch for the classroom is slow static stretching for all muscles or muscle groups.
BODY COMPOSITION[2]			
Three to six days, daily preferred.	Light aerobic activity. 45–65% of maximum heart rate. "Talk test": talking should be relatively easy.	30 to 60 plus minutes.	Light aerobic exercise.

[1]Sources: *Physical Education for Lifelong Fitness: The Physical Best Teacher's Guide* (Second edition, page 69, Table 5.1; page 90, Table 6.1; and page 116, Table 7.1. © 2005 by National Association for Sport and Physical Education. Reprinted with permission from Human Kinetics, Champaign, IL).

[2]Source: Charles B. Corbin et al. *Concepts of Fitness and Wellness: A Comprehensive Lifestyle Approach* (Seventh edition). New York: McGraw-Hill, 2008, page 285.

Chapter 3
Standards-Based
Physical Education:
Grades Six
Through Eight

Grade Six

STANDARD 5

5.2 Evaluate individual responsibility in group efforts.

Students learn that each member of a group has an important role to play. And, if a member neglects his or her responsibility, then the group's performance will suffer.

Students are assigned to groups of six and asked to participate in Traffic Jam:

- Form groups of six divided into subgroups of three.
- Place seven carpet squares in a line.
- Instruct one student to stand on each carpet square, facing the middle square that is unoccupied.
- Tell students that the objective is for the students on the right side of the middle square to end up on the left side of the middle square, and *vice versa*, by stepping only on carpet squares—not the floor or ground.
- Establish the rules:

    – At all times only one person may occupy a carpet square.
    – A person can move onto an empty carpet square in front of him.
    – A person can move around a person facing her onto an empty carpet square on the other side of the person.

At the end of the activity, each group answers the following questions:

- What was each individual's role in the activity?
- Did individuals fulfill their roles?
- If individuals did not fulfill their roles, what was the result?

Each group member then evaluates his or her individual role in the group activity and whether he or she helped or hindered the group's progress.

Grade Six *Physical Education Model Content Standards*

STANDARD 1
Students demonstrate the motor skills and movement patterns needed to perform a variety of physical activities.

Manipulative Skills

1.1   Volley an object repeatedly with a partner, using the forearm pass.

1.2   Strike a ball continuously against a wall and with a partner, using a paddle for the forehand stroke and the backhand stroke.

1.3   Strike an object consistently, using a body part, so that the object travels in the intended direction at the desired height.

1.4   Strike an object consistently, using an implement, so that the object travels in the intended direction at the desired height.

1.5   Dribble and pass a ball to a partner while being guarded.

1.6   Throw an object accurately and with applied force, using the underhand, overhand, and sidearm movement (throw) patterns.

Rhythmic Skills

1.7   Perform folk and line dances.

1.8   Develop, refine, and demonstrate routines to music.

Combinations of Movement Patterns and Skills

1.9   Combine relationships, levels, speed, direction, and pathways in complex individual and group physical activities.

1.10   Combine motor skills to play a lead-up or modified game.

1.11   Design and perform smooth, flowing sequences of stunts, tumbling, and rhythmic patterns that combine traveling, rolling, balancing, and transferring weight.

STANDARD 2
Students demonstrate knowledge of movement concepts, principles, and strategies that apply to the learning and performance of physical activities.

Movement Concepts

2.1   Explain how to increase force based on the principles of biomechanics.

2.2   Explain how impact force is reduced by increasing the duration of impact.

2.3   Analyze and correct errors in movement patterns.

2.4   Provide feedback to a partner to assist in developing and improving movement skills.

2.5   Identify practices and procedures necessary for safe participation in physical activities.

Manipulative Skills

2.6   Explain the role of the legs, shoulders, and forearm in the forearm pass.

2.7   Identify the time necessary to prepare for and begin a forehand stroke and a backhand stroke.

2.8   Illustrate how the intended direction of an object is affected by the angle of the implement or body part at the time of contact.

2.9   Identify opportunities to pass or dribble while being guarded.

Rhythmic Skills

2.10   Identify steps and rhythm patterns for folk and line dances.

2.11   Explain how movement qualities contribute to the aesthetic dimension of physical activity.

Combination of Movement Patterns and Skills

2.12   Develop a cooperative movement game that uses locomotor skills, object manipulation, and an offensive strategy and teach the game to another person.

STANDARD 3

Students assess and maintain a level of physical fitness to improve health and performance.

3.1   Assess the components of health-related physical fitness (muscle strength, muscle endurance, flexibility, aerobic capacity, and body composition) by using a scientifically based health-related fitness assessment.

3.2   Compare individual physical fitness results with research-based standards for good health.

3.3   Develop individual goals for each of the components of health-related physical fitness (muscle strength, muscle endurance, flexibility, aerobic capacity, and body composition).

3.4   Participate in moderate to vigorous physical activity a minimum of four days each week.

3.5   Measure and evaluate changes in health-related physical fitness based on physical activity patterns.

3.6   Monitor the intensity of one's heart rate during physical activity.

STANDARD 4

Students demonstrate knowledge of physical fitness concepts, principles, and strategies to improve health and performance.

4.1   Distinguish between effective and ineffective warm-up and cool-down techniques.

4.2   Develop a one-day personal physical fitness plan specifying the intensity, time, and types of physical activities for each component of health-related physical fitness.

4.3   Identify contraindicated exercises and their adverse effects on the body.

4.4   Classify physical activities as aerobic or anaerobic.

4.5   Explain methods of monitoring heart rate intensity.

4.6   List the long-term benefits of participation in regular physical activity.

4.7   Compile and analyze a log noting the food intake/calories consumed and energy expended through physical activity.

STANDARD 5
Students demonstrate and utilize knowledge of psychological and sociological concepts, principles, and strategies that apply to the learning and performance of physical activity.

Self-Responsibility

5.1   Participate productively in group physical activities.

5.2   Evaluate individual responsibility in group efforts.

Social Interaction

5.3   Identify and define the role of each participant in a cooperative physical activity.

Group Dynamics

5.4   Identify and agree on a common goal when participating in a cooperative physical activity.

5.5   Analyze possible solutions to a movement problem in a cooperative physical activity and come to a consensus on the best solution.

Grade Seven

Grade Seven

Seventh-grade students are moving through a critical stage in their development as they become concerned with the changes occurring in their bodies. Accelerated physical development is marked by increases in height, weight, heart size, lung capacity, and muscular strength. The head, hands, and feet of an adolescent attain mature size before the legs, which attain their full length before arms. This uneven muscle and bone development often results in lack of coordination and awkwardness, leading to temporary disruptions or brief regressions in motor skills performance.

Seventh-grade students are beginning the transition from the concrete stage to the abstract stage in their cognitive development. This transition provides the capacity for abstract thinking and metacognition (ability to know what one knows). Students are better able to anticipate future events and to formulate goals to address those situations. They are gaining additional insight into sources of previously unquestioned attitudes, behaviors, and values. Seventh-grade students are capable of demonstrating and analyzing more complex movement patterns and strategies. They possess a greater knowledge of fitness and are capable of creating weeklong personal fitness plans designed to improve their current level of health-related physical fitness.

Seventh-grade students are becoming more independent of their parents and increasingly dependent on the approval of their peers. Some students become rebellious toward parents because they want to make decisions for themselves. They like to experience challenges and test their limits. Physical education provides these students with challenging activities in a safe and controlled environment. It is not unusual for students in this age group to display erratic and inconsistent behavior. They are experiencing chemical and hormonal imbalances, which can lead to moodiness, anger, and an acute sensitivity to criticism. However, these students are increasingly able to solve problems and resolve conflicts within a group setting. They are also more likely to express an appreciation for cooperation and fair play as they adhere to group rules. A well-planned physical education program takes into account the importance of the transition from sixth to eighth grade and the rapid physical, social, and emotional changes occurring at this level.

At a Glance

STANDARD 1
Students demonstrate the motor skills and movement patterns needed to perform a variety of physical activities.

In sixth grade students were given the opportunity to practice specialized sport skills, such as dribbling and the forearm pass. Seventh grade allows students the opportunity to refine those skills. Through individual and dual activities, adventure/outdoor activities, combative activities, and track and field activities, students have a chance to practice body management and locomotor, nonlocomotor, and specialized sport skills. Rhythm activities include dances from cultures around the world to help students develop greater understanding and acceptance of their own and others' heritages.

STANDARD 2

Students demonstrate knowledge of movement concepts, principles, and strategies that apply to the learning and performance of physical activities.

Standard 2 represents the cognitive knowledge that supports the loco-motor, nonlocomotor, and specialized sport skills taught in seventh grade. For efficient instruction, teachers develop lessons that address Standards 1 and 2 simultaneously when appropriate. For example, Standard 2.6 states, "Diagram and demonstrate basic offensive and defensive strategies for individual and dual physical activities" and links to Standard 1.4, which states, "Demonstrate body management and object-manipulation skills needed for successful participation in individual and dual physical activities." Several instructional units for this grade level focus on individual and dual physical activities. During these units, the teacher provides instruction on the basic offensive and defensive strategies. The students practice the strategies and then diagram them, thus addressing standards under both Overarching Standards 1 and 2.

By the end of seventh grade, students can identify and describe the key elements in a variety of movement patterns. They are also able to analyze movement patterns, detect and correct errors in performance, and chart their own motor skill development in specific activities. Students learn that practicing skills as a whole and practicing skills in parts are appropriate in different learning situations.

In the sixth grade, students developed a cooperative game and taught the game to another person. In grade seven students extend this knowledge by creating an individual or dual game using manipulative skills, offensive and defensive strategies, and a scoring system.

STANDARD 3

Students assess and maintain a level of physical fitness to improve health and performance.

Seventh graders continue to perform moderate to vigorous physical activities a minimum of four days each week for increasing periods of time. They also continue to assess their own health-related physical fitness and compare themselves with minimum fitness competencies. With this

Grade Seven

information they develop goals and plan and implement a weekly personal fitness program. Throughout the school year, the students, with assistance from their teacher, revise their fitness programs as their fitness needs change.

STANDARD 4

Students demonstrate knowledge of physical fitness concepts, principles, and strategies to improve health and performance.

Standard 4 provides the cognitive information to support the fitness activities described in Standard 3. For Standard 4, students create fitness plans. These fitness plans specify proper warm-up and cool-down techniques, apply the principles of exercise for each component of health-related fitness, and allow students to select activities that they prefer. Seventh-grade students also have an understanding of the effects on heart rate during exercise, immediately following exercise (recovery phase), and while at rest. They can describe the relationship between physical activity and nutrition necessary to achieve a desired level of physical fitness.

STANDARD 5

Students demonstrate and utilize knowledge of psychological and sociological concepts, principles, and strategies that apply to the learning and performance of physical activity.

Seventh-graders accept greater responsibility for their own improvement and demonstrate greater acceptance of individuals who are different. They can identify appropriate and inappropriate risks involved in the physical activities they are learning. They also understand the role and responsibilities of the leader and see the value of encouraging others during physical activity.

Learning Snapshots

STANDARD 1

1.1 Demonstrate mature techniques for the following patterns: overhand, sidearm, and underhand throwing; catching; kicking/ punting; striking; trapping; dribbling (hand and foot); and volleying.

This standard asks students to demonstrate the proper form for 11 motor skill patterns. The teacher demonstrates each skill, pointing out critical features. Students practice each skill repeatedly in a variety of closed situations (i.e., with no variables) and open situations (i.e., with variables) throughout the school year. During practice opportunities, students work in groups of three. Two of the students practice the skill, while the third provides feedback using a checklist of key elements.[3] Each student has the opportunity to both practice a skill and provide feedback. A video camera may also be used so that the students can receive visual feedback on their own performances. Their teacher circulates throughout the class, providing specific positive or specific corrective feedback to the students on their performances. This standard links with Standard 2.1, which asks students to identify and describe the key elements in the mature performance of these 11 motor skills.

STANDARD 2

2.4 Explain and demonstrate spin and rebound principles for performing manipulative skills.

To explain and demonstrate these principles, students must first be taught the biomechanics related to spin and rebound.

- Force applied below the center of gravity causes backward rotation (back spin), which results in a ball staying in the air longer, bouncing higher off the ground, then having a smaller forward velocity and a shorter roll.
- Force applied above the center of gravity causes forward rotation (top spin), which results in a ball having a quick drop, leaving the ground with a lower but longer bounce, and then having a larger forward velocity and a longer roll.
- Force to the left of the center of gravity results in counterclockwise spin (as seen from above), and force to the right of the center of gravity results in clockwise spin.
- Bouncing an object with no spin causes it to rebound at an angle from the surface equal to that at which it strikes.

Once students have learned these four concepts, they are provided with basketballs or rubber playground balls. Students demonstrate the result of spin and rebound and explain why it occurs.

STANDARD 3

3.5 Participate in moderate to vigorous physical activity a minimum of four days each week.

Moderate-intensity physical activity generally requires sustained rhythmic movements and refers to a level of effort a healthy individual might expend while, for example, walking briskly, dancing, swimming, or bicycling on level terrain. A person should feel some exertion but should be able to carry on a conversation comfortably during the activity. Vigorous-intensity physical activity generally requires sustained, rhythmic movements and refers to a level of effort a healthy individual might expend while, for

---

[3] Feedback is most effective when it is specific and positive or specific and corrective.

example, jogging, participating in high-impact aerobic dancing, swimming continuous laps, or bicycling uphill. Vigorous-intensity physical activity may be intense enough to result in a significant increase in heart and respiration rate. Although these activities can and do occur during physical education, the focus of this standard is making physical activity a regular part of an individual's daily activities. Therefore, students are encouraged to participate in physical activity on their own and to monitor their activity time and intensity.

STANDARD 4

4.2 Identify physical activities that are effective in improving each of the health-related physical fitness components.

This standard asks students to match physical activities to the health-related physical fitness component that it develops. Students have been performing exercises for each of the fitness components since early elementary school, so a brief reinforcement activity is appropriate. The teacher makes a series of cards, each with the name and a picture of an exercise. The teacher displays five posters with the following labels: cardiorespiratory endurance, muscular strength, muscular endurance, flexibility, and body composition. Students are asked to match each exercise to one of those health-related physical fitness components. In future lessons, during the warm-up and cool-down phases, the teacher asks individual students the purpose of each exercise they perform. Standard 4.3 supports this standard as the teacher follows up with questions regarding which of the exercises students prefer to do for each component.

STANDARD 5

5.1 Identify appropriate and inappropriate risks involved in adventure, individual, and dual physical activities.

Appropriate risks are those that offer a challenge to the student but have a low risk of injury. Inappropriate risks are those with a high risk of injury. It is important for students to differentiate between the two types of risks. Appropriate risks require a personal challenge, but inappropriate risks are simply dangerous. The teacher can explain the two types of risks and then provide, or ask students for, examples of each. During follow-up lessons, the teacher provides students with a list of activities and asks them to categorize the risk level of the activities as appropriate or inappropriate. Or, the teacher can ask students to create a graphic organizer and use it to represent appropriate and inappropriate activities related to risk.

101

Chapter 3
Standards-Based
Physical Education:
Grades Six
Through Eight

Grade Seven

Grade Seven *Physical Education Model Content Standards*

STANDARD 1
Students demonstrate the motor skills and movement patterns needed to perform a variety of physical activities.

Manipulative Skills

1.1   Demonstrate mature techniques for the following patterns: overhand, sidearm, and underhand throwing; catching; kicking/punting; striking; trapping; dribbling (hand and foot); and volleying.

Rhythmic Skills

1.2   Perform multicultural dances.

Combinations of Movement Patterns and Skills

1.3   Combine manipulative, locomotor, and nonlocomotor skills into movement patterns.

1.4   Demonstrate body management and object-manipulation skills needed for successful participation in individual and dual physical activities.

1.5   Demonstrate body management and locomotor skills needed for successful participation in track and field and combative activities.

1.6   Demonstrate body management and object-manipulation skills needed for successful participation in introductory adventure/outdoor activities.

STANDARD 2
Students demonstrate knowledge of movement concepts, principles, and strategies that apply to the learning and performance of physical activities.

Manipulative Skills

2.1   Identify and describe key elements in the mature performance of overhand, sidearm, and underhand throwing; catching; kicking/punting; striking; trapping; dribbling (hand and foot); and volleying.

Movement Concepts

2.2   Analyze movement patterns and correct errors.

2.3   Use principles of motor learning to establish, monitor, and meet goals for motor skill development.

2.4   Explain and demonstrate spin and rebound principles for performing manipulative skills.

2.5   Compare and contrast the effectiveness of practicing skills as a whole and practicing skills in smaller parts.

2.6   Diagram and demonstrate basic offensive and defensive strategies for individual and dual physical activities.

Chapter 3
Standards-Based
Physical Education:
Grades Six
Through Eight

Grade Seven

Combination of Movement Patterns and Skills

2.7 Develop an individual or dual game that uses a manipulative skill, two different offensive strategies, and a scoring system and teach it to another person.

STANDARD 3

Students assess and maintain a level of physical fitness to improve health and performance.

3.1 Assess one's own muscle strength, muscle endurance, aerobic capacity, flexibility, and body composition by using a scientifically based health-related fitness assessment.

3.2 Evaluate individual measures of physical fitness in relationship to patterns of physical activity.

3.3 Develop individual goals, from research-based standards, for each of the five components of health-related physical fitness.

3.4 Plan a weekly personal physical fitness program in collaboration with the teacher.

3.5 Participate in moderate to vigorous physical activity a minimum of four days each week.

3.6 Assess periodically the attainment of, or progress toward, personal physical fitness goals and make necessary adjustments to a personal physical fitness program.

STANDARD 4

Students demonstrate knowledge of physical fitness concepts, principles, and strategies to improve health and performance.

4.1 Develop a one-week personal physical fitness plan specifying the proper warm-up and cool-down activities and the principles of exercise for each component of health-related physical fitness.

4.2 Identify physical activities that are effective in improving each of the health-related physical fitness components.

4.3 Match personal preferences in physical activities with each of the five components of health-related physical fitness.

4.4 Explain the effects of physical activity on heart rate during exercise, during the recovery phase, and while the body is at rest.

4.5 Describe the role of physical activity and nutrition in achieving physical fitness.

4.6 Identify and apply the principles of overload in safe, age-appropriate activities.

4.7 Explain progression, overload, and specificity as principles of exercise.

4.8 Discuss the effect of extremity growth rates on physical fitness.

STANDARD 5

Students demonstrate and utilize knowledge of psychological and sociological concepts, principles, and strategies that apply to the learning and performance of physical activity.

Self-Responsibility

5.1   Identify appropriate and inappropriate risks involved in adventure, individual, and dual physical activities.

5.2   Accept responsibility for individual improvement.

Social Interaction

5.3   Demonstrate an acceptance of differences in physical development and personal preferences as they affect participation in physical activity.

Group Dynamics

5.4   Evaluate the effect of expressing encouragement to others while participating in a group physical activity.

5.5   Identify the responsibilities of a leader in physical activity.

Grade Eight

Eighth-grade students reflect a wide range of individual differences that are inherent to puberty, including height, weight, skill competency, and maturity. Gender differences are becoming more pronounced as males' shoulders grow larger than their hips and as females' hips grow larger than their shoulders. Despite these differences, all students are capable of attaining greater motor achievement and should be encouraged to set realistic personal goals and monitor their own progress.

Eighth-grade students are capable of abstract thinking at this stage of their cognitive development. They can understand and consider several aspects of a problem simultaneously. Skills such as logical thought, deductive reasoning, and systematic planning also emerge during this stage. With these emerging cognitive skills, students successfully engage in modified team sports and learn the complexities of offensive and defensive team strategies. Eighth-grade students also plan alternative activities for their personal fitness plan, so that they are prepared for inclement weather or injury.

Eighth-grade students are searching for their adult identity; their appearance is becoming increasingly important to them. This focus on appearance provides teachers with an opportunity to stress the importance of good health and fitness. Eighth-graders are also able to accept responsibility for their behavior, work cooperatively with a large group, resolve individual and group conflicts, and focus on long-term group goals—all important skills for participating in team activities.

At a Glance

STANDARD I
Students demonstrate the motor skills and movement patterns needed to perform a variety of physical activities.

By eighth grade students are competent in locomotor, nonlocomotor, and manipulative skills as well as offensive and defensive strategies and a number of specialized skills. In the eighth grade, students develop these skills further by applying them to team physical activities and by creating fundamental tumbling or gymnastics routines. Development of rhythmic skills also continues as students create and perform square dances.

STANDARD 2
Students demonstrate knowledge of movement concepts, principles, and strategies that apply to the learning and performance of physical activities.

Standard 2 represents the cognitive knowledge that supports the specialized motor skills learned in eighth grade. Learning experiences that address

105

Chapter 3
Standards-Based
Physical Education:
Grades Six
Through Eight

Standards 1 and 2 simultaneously provide for better use of instructional time and a more thorough understanding of the content for students. For example, Standard 2.2 ("Explain the rotation principles used in performing various manipulative skills") and Standard 1.5 ("Demonstrate fundamental gymnastic/tumbling skills") deepen student knowledge when taught together. During the gymnastics/tumbling unit, the teacher explains that an object with a shorter axis of rotation rotates more quickly. The teacher describes and demonstrates both the squat forward roll and pike forward roll, noting that the squat forward roll requires less effort because it uses a shorter axis of rotation. Students are then asked to perform both the squat and pike forward rolls to better understand this concept and to improve their motor skill performance.

By the end of the eighth grade, students have experienced a variety of physical activities. Now they can begin to see the relationships between motor skills and how the learning of one skill can be transferred to help learn a similar skill. In addition, students can identify the characteristics of highly skilled performance and apply that knowledge to improve their skills. They also understand the influence of physical characteristics on selection of developmentally appropriate physical activities (e.g., taller players may have an advantage in basketball). Students in grade eight can diagram, explain, and justify offensive and defensive strategies in team activities and use the strategies to develop and teach a game that utilizes the elements of spin or rebound, penalties, and a scoring system.

STANDARD 3

Students assess and maintain a level of physical fitness to improve health and performance.

Eighth-graders continue to perform moderate to vigorous physical activities a minimum of four days each week for increasing periods of time while making adjustments in their activities based on changes in weather and physical wellness. They also continue to assess their own health-related physical fitness and compare themselves with minimum fitness competencies. Using this information, they refine their goals then plan and implement a two-week personal fitness program. Depending on their progress, students continue to adjust their personal fitness program and refine their goals for the five components of health-related physical fitness.

STANDARD 4

Students demonstrate knowledge of physical fitness concepts, principles, and strategies to improve health and performance.

Similar to the relationship between Standards 1 and 2, Standard 4 provides the cognitive information to support the fitness activities described in Standard 3. For Standard 4, the students refine their fitness plans.

Grade Eight

Eighth-grade students are building upon their seventh-grade experience in creating a personal fitness plan by expanding it from one to two weeks. This experience is preparation for developing fitness plans throughout their lives. Students also identify appropriate substitute physical activities for times when their usual fitness program is disrupted by inclement weather, travel, or minor injury.

Eighth-graders explain different types of conditioning to support different physical activities. They identify safety procedures for, and apply basic principles in, resistance training activities. They are also able to explain how nutrition and participation in physical activity impact weight control, self-concept, and physical performance. This is a crucial time to help students apply their knowledge, so they can use it for the remainder of their lives.

STANDARD 5

Students demonstrate and utilize knowledge of psychological and sociological concepts, principles, and strategies that apply to the learning and performance of physical activity.

By eighth grade students have developed the skills necessary to recognize their need for lifelong physical activity and to accept responsibility for developing and achieving new, realistic personal goals. Group affiliation assumes added importance at this level, with emphasis on team participation, roles of group members, group loyalty, and the identification of ethical and unethical behavior in group activities. Students continue to practice supporting each member of their team and encouraging others to be inclusive of every member of their team and class. Students begin to think of themselves as members of a team and use cooperation to achieve common goals. They learn to identify and apply specific criteria for successful team participation and to lead and follow by sharing leadership positions.

Learning Snapshots

STANDARD 1

1.1 Identify and demonstrate square dance steps, positions, and patterns set to music.

This lesson occurs during a square-dance unit. The students are divided into groups of eight. In each group, two students receive Card #1, two students receive Card #2, two students receive Card #3, and two students receive Card #4.

Chapter 3
Standards-Based
Physical Education:
Grades Six
Through Eight

Grade Eight

CARD #1

Four Ladies Right-Hand Star/Four Ladies Left-Hand Star

Four dancers move toward center of square forming a small circle with their sides
to the center of circle.

Left or right arm (depending on the call) is raised.

All hands are touching, with elbows straight.

Four dancers move counterclockwise (left-hand star) or clockwise (right-hand star).

CARD #2

Right and Left Through

Couples 1 and 3 (or couples 2 and 4) walk forward and shake right hands with
their opposites.

Couples walk pass the right shoulder of their opposite.

Couples release the hands of their opposites.

Couples join left hands with their partner in front of the gentleman's body.

Ladies place right hand on their right hip.

Gentlemen place right hand over ladies' right hand.

Partners pivot to the left for four steps to face the opposite direction.

Couples end up facing their opposite.

The process is usually repeated so that couples return to their home position.

CARD #3

Ladies' Chain (call is side ladies' chain or head ladies' chain)

Two couples face each other.

Gentlemen remain in place.

Ladies walk forward.

Ladies extend right hands to each other.

Ladies continue walking, passing right shoulders.

Ladies release hands.

Ladies give left hands to opposite gentlemen.

Ladies put right hands on right hips.

Gentlemen put right arms around ladies' waists.

Gentlemen put right hands on ladies' right hands.

Gentlemen pivot around with the ladies to the left in four steps.

Couples end up facing each other.

The call is usually repeated so ladies return to their home position.

CARD #4

Grand Right and Left

Everyone faces his or her partner.

Partners join right hands.

Gentlemen walk counterclockwise passing partner's right shoulder.

Ladies walk clockwise passing partner's right shoulder.

Partners release hands.

Gentlemen continue to walk counterclockwise for the remainder of the call.

Ladies continue to walk clockwise for the remainder of the call.

Everyone joins left hands with the person approaching.

Everyone walks forward, passing left shoulders with the person whose hand they
are holding.

Everyone releases left hands.

Everyone joins right hands with the person approaching.

Everyone walks forward, passing right shoulders with the person whose hand they are holding.

Everyone releases right hands.

Everyone joins left hands with the person approaching.

Everyone walks forward, passing left shoulders with the person whose hand they are holding.

Everyone releases left hands.

Everyone joins right hand with the person approaching (their original partner).

Each pair reads its card, discusses how the call (series of movements) is performed, and practices the call. Once students have learned the call, they return to their group of eight and teach their call (step-by-step) to the rest of the group. When all students have learned the four calls, the teacher plays a song that includes the four calls. The teacher circulates through the class during the lesson, providing feedback.[4]

1.4 Apply locomotor, nonlocomotor, and manipulative skills to team activities.

This lesson is part of an invasion sports or a speed-a-way unit. The teacher begins instruction with a review of throwing, catching, passing with feet, trapping, kicking, and lifting. The students are organized into groups of four with two on offense and two on defense. The offense starts with the ball near the goal line. Using the skills reviewed at the beginning of the lesson, the offense attempts to score against the defense. The player with the ball has several options: throwing the ball to the teammate who is positioned across the goal line, dropping the ball to the ground and kicking it to score, dropping the ball and passing it to the teammate who then kicks to score, or dropping the ball and lifting it to the teammate who then runs across the goal line to score. This standard can be taught in conjunction with Standard 2.5 ("Diagram, explain, and justify offensive and defensive strategies in modified and team sports, games, and activities") by having the students diagram and explain the options they selected for scoring when playing offense.

STANDARD 2

2.6 Develop and teach a team game that uses elements of spin or rebound, designated offensive and defensive space, a penalty system, and a scoring system.

During seventh grade, the students learned the biomechanics related to spin and rebound. This standard asks students to develop their own team game that uses elements of spin or rebound. Every game has purpose, equipment, organization patterns, movements, limitations (rules and penalties), and at least one way to score. Game tactics or strategies (decisions about what to do in a competitive situation) are also a part of most team games and sports.

---

[4] Feedback is most effective when it is specific and positive or specific and corrective.

109

Chapter 3
Standards-Based
Physical Education:
Grades Six
Through Eight

For this standard, the teacher devises a work sheet listing the components of a game. Students are organized into groups of four to create their own game. The students try their game to ensure that it works. Then the students teach their game to another group of four.

STANDARD 3

3.6 Participate safely in moderate to vigorous physical activity when conditions are atypical (weather, travel, injury).

This standard asks students to participate in moderate to vigorous physical activity on atypical days. Atypical days include those when the weather is bad, travel is required, or an individual has an injury. Students brainstorm options for participating in physical activity during these times as a link to Standard 4.2. Possible solutions may include working out indoors (e.g., gymnasium, fitness lab, mall) or, if injured, discussing modifications with a doctor. After an atypical day, the students report how they participated in moderate to vigorous physical activity.

STANDARD 4

4.3 Identify ways of increasing physical activity in routine daily activities.

The teacher creates a bulletin board in the gymnasium or locker room with a heading of "Ways to Increase Physical Activity." Students are asked to post their ideas, as pictures or words, over several weeks. During each class closure, the teacher takes time to discuss new additions to the bulletin board with the students.

STANDARD 5

5.7 Model support toward individuals of all ability levels and encourage others to be supportive and inclusive of all individuals.

The teacher asks students to brainstorm ways to include individuals with different strengths and weaknesses in their current activity (e.g., team sport, gymnastics). The teacher then sets up simulations (e.g., a volleyball game in which some students are good at spiking and some are good at setting, a basketball game in which a student in a wheelchair wants to participate) so students can practice including individuals of all ability levels in their activity. Throughout the lesson, the teacher circulates through the class and provides feedback to the students. During class closure, the teacher asks students to discuss ways to encourage others to be supportive and inclusive of all individuals.

Chapter 3
Standards-Based
Physical Education:
Grades Six
Through Eight

Grade Eight

Grade Eight *Physical Education*
Model Content Standards

STANDARD 1

Students demonstrate the motor skills and movement patterns needed to perform a variety of physical activities.

Rhythmic Skills

1.1   Identify and demonstrate square dance steps, positions, and patterns set to music.

1.2   Create and perform a square dance.

Combinations of Movement Patterns and Skills

1.3   Demonstrate basic offensive and defensive skills and strategies in team physical activities.

1.4   Apply locomotor, nonlocomotor, and manipulative skills to team physical activities.

1.5   Demonstrate fundamental gymnastic/tumbling skills.

1.6   Create and perform a routine using fundamental gymnastic/tumbling skills, locomotor and nonlocomotor movement patterns, and the elements of speed, direction, and level.

STANDARD 2

Students demonstrate knowledge of movement concepts, principles, and strategies that apply to the learning and performance of physical activities.

Movement Concepts

2.1   Describe and demonstrate how movement skills learned in one physical activity can be transferred and used to help learn another physical activity.

2.2   Explain the rotation principles used in performing various manipulative skills.

2.3   Explain how growth in height and weight affects performance and influences the selection of developmentally appropriate physical activities.

Combination of Movement Patterns and Skills

2.4   Identify the characteristics of a highly skilled performance for the purpose of improving one's own performance.

2.5   Diagram, explain, and justify offensive and defensive strategies in modified and team sports, games, and activities.

2.6   Develop and teach a team game that uses elements of spin or rebound, designated offensive and defensive space, a penalty system, and a scoring system.

Chapter 3
Standards-Based
Physical Education:
Grades Six
Through Eight

Grade Eight

STANDARD 3

Students assess and maintain a level of physical fitness to improve health and performance.

3.1   Assess the components of health-related physical fitness (muscle strength, muscle endurance, aerobic capacity, flexibility, and body composition) by using a scientifically based health-related physical fitness assessment.

3.2   Refine individual personal physical fitness goals for each of the five components of health-related physical fitness, using research-based criteria.

3.3   Plan and implement a two-week personal physical fitness plan in collaboration with the teacher.

3.4   Participate in moderate to vigorous physical activity a minimum of four days each week.

3.5   Assess periodically the attainment of, or progress toward, personal physical fitness goals and make necessary adjustments to a personal physical fitness program.

3.6   Participate safely in moderate to vigorous physical activity when conditions are atypical (weather, travel, injury).

STANDARD 4

Students demonstrate knowledge of physical fitness concepts, principles, and strategies to improve health and performance.

4.1   Develop a two-week personal physical fitness plan specifying the proper warm-up and cool-down activities and the principles of exercise for each of the five components of health-related physical fitness.

4.2   Identify appropriate physical activities that can be performed if one's physical fitness program is disrupted by inclement weather, travel from home or school, or a minor injury.

4.3   Identify ways of increasing physical activity in routine daily activities.

4.4   Identify and apply basic principles in weight/resistance training and safety practices.

4.5   Explain the effects of nutrition and participation in physical activity on weight control, self-concept, and physical performance.

4.6   Explain the different types of conditioning for different physical activities.

STANDARD 5

Students demonstrate and utilize knowledge of psychological and sociological concepts, principles, and strategies that apply to the learning and performance of physical activity.

Self-Responsibility

5.1   Abide by the decisions of the officials, accept the outcome of the game, and show appreciation toward participants.

5.2   Organize and work cooperatively with a group to achieve the goals of the group.

Grade Eight

5.3   Identify and evaluate three preferences for lifelong physical activity and determine one's responsibility for developing skills, acquiring knowledge of concepts, and achieving fitness.

Social Interaction

5.4   Identify the contributions of members of a group or team and reward members for accomplishing a task or goal.

Group Dynamics

5.5   Accept the roles of group members within the structure of a game or activity.

5.6   Describe leadership roles and responsibilities in the context of team games and activities.

5.7   Model support toward individuals of all ability levels and encourage others to be supportive and inclusive of all individuals.

4

Standards-Based Physical Education: Grades Nine Through Twelve

The high school experience represents the culmination of physical education instruction for California's kindergarten through grade twelve students. Throughout their school years, students have experienced a planned sequence of formal physical education instructional experiences. From kindergarten through fifth grade, the content is delivered incrementally to best enable student learning at the appropriate developmental level. In sixth through eighth grade, the content is consolidated and students' skills are refined, representing a natural progression of skill sophistication. When students reach ninth grade, they are ready to integrate all that they know with all that they can do. They become capable of higher-order thinking and of more skilled performance. The high school courses provide a blueprint for delivering content in a manner that equips students to make a successful transition from the physical education instructional program to participation in physical activity during adulthood.

Beginning with High School Course 1, the five overarching standards for kindergarten through grade eight are consolidated into overarching three standards for grades nine through twelve. Essentially High School Standard 1 incorporates Overarching Standards 1 and 2 from kindergarten through eighth grade; High School Standard 2 incorporates Overarching Standards 3 and 4; and High School Standard 3 incorporates Overarching Standard 5. These standards are extremely rigorous, as is appropriate for a high school experience that represents the culmination of physical education. In the high school courses, the foundation for a physically active lifestyle is firmly laid so that students become independent learners who initiate and monitor their own participation in physical activity.

To fulfill the requirement for high school graduation, students must take at least two years of physical education in high school, pursuant to *Education Code* Section 51225.3(a)(1)(F). High School Courses 1 and 2 are designed to meet this requirement and to provide the foundation for high school instruction. In those courses, students develop proficiency in their movement skills, expand their capabilities for independent learning, and examine practices that allow sound decision making to enhance successful participation in movement activities. *Education Code* Section 33352(b)(7) lists eight content areas for high school physical education which, when included in a course of study, provide a wide variety of physical activities necessary to develop the skills and knowledge essential to an individual for the selection of lifetime pursuits. The California Department of Education has the responsibility of monitoring the extent to which high schools provide a course of study having these eight areas. These content areas are:

- Effects of physical activity upon dynamic health
- Mechanics of body movement
- Aquatics
- Gymnastics and tumbling
- Individual and dual sports

115

Chapter 4
Standards-Based
Physical Education:
Grades Nine
Through Twelve

- Rhythms and dance
- Team sports
- Combatives

Course 1 addresses three content areas (aquatics, rhythms and dance, and individual and dual activities) as well as the effects of physical activity upon dynamic health and mechanics of body movement. The content area of aquatics is a unique activity in that it does not easily cross over into other physical activities. Whereas the skill of striking is utilized in various sport activities (e.g., softball, golf, tennis) and is addressed throughout the students' physical education experiences, this crossover does not occur with aquatics. Knowledge of aquatic skills and safety is essential for California's students, many of whom live near or travel to pools, lakes, rivers, and the ocean. Although aquatic facilities may be limited or nonexistent for some schools, aquatics can still be taught by stressing water safety, rescue techniques, dry-land stroke and kick practice, and buoyancy principles. At a minimum, students should learn drowning-prevention strategies. It is important to note that dry-land instruction will not ensure that students are able to swim in water or under real-life circumstances.

Course 2 addresses three other content areas (combatives, gymnastics and tumbling, and team activities) as well as the effects of physical activity upon dynamic health and mechanics of body movement. Self-defense is one option for addressing the content area of combatives. Because it is directly related to student safety, it is an important area for physical educators to teach and students to learn. The emphasis of this unit is on how to *defend,* not how to fight. The unit begins with students learning about potentially unsafe situations and how to avoid them. Safety skills are the initial focus of instruction. Only after learning safety skills do students begin to learn how to protect themselves should they be attacked.

As noted above, Courses 1 and 2 continue to emphasize the importance of physical activity and personal fitness. Students are provided with opportunities to improve their health-related physical fitness as well as to understand advanced concepts related to physical fitness and physical activity. Students learn how to achieve physical fitness and the importance of maintaining an active lifestyle throughout their lifetime.

Participation in physical activity also can be an important venue for the social, psychological, and emotional development of young adults. Social skills and personal responsibility skills need to be taught and practiced with feedback.[1] Physical education courses provide an ideal setting for adolescents to learn appropriate social interaction skills, suitable ways to express and control emotions, and opportunities to solve complex problems.

High School Courses 3A through 3F and 4A through 4D provide students with the opportunity to explore a variety of physical activities in search of those that they can enjoy and participate in for a lifetime. Course 3 classes are designed for students who have completed High School Courses 1 and 2. Course 3 classes

---

[1]Feedback is most effective when it is specific and positive or specific and corrective.

provide students with their first opportunity to learn advanced knowledge and skills in a self-selected activity (e.g., outdoor activities, aerobics) that meets their particular needs and interests. Course 4 classes are designed as a continuation of the Course 3 classes. They are intended for students who have completed Course 3 and want an intensive experience in the same activity. The purpose of Course 4 classes is to deepen student understanding of the content, building a foundation for future fitness and career needs (see Appendix K). Course 4 classes are designed for students who have completed High School Courses 1 and 2 as well as Course 3 in the same content area.

This chapter incorporates the physical education model content standards for High School Courses 1 through 4, providing an explanation of the physical education content areas underlying the model content standards and outlining activities that are consistent with the intent of the standards. The activities in this chapter are examples of one way in which the standards may be approached. The examples are not to be interpreted as requirements for the physical education classroom or as the only way to approach a particular standard. The physical education model content standards set forth what students are to know and be able to do; they do not prescribe how to provide instruction.

Content mastery does not occur simply because students have received a particular explanation or participated in a particular activity; students must have many opportunities to practice and apply physical education concepts, principles, and skills. Mastery of an individual standard is achieved when students have learned the concept, principle, or skill.

High School Course 1

The developmental range of high school students is diverse. Students experience numerous physical and physiological changes during their high school years. Ninth-grade boys typically experience a period of rapid growth until about fourteen or fifteen years of age. Then, a slower rate of growth follows until around twenty-one years of age. By ninth grade, girls are already experiencing their slower rate of growth. As adolescents attain maturity, their body proportions become more congruent, increasing their potential for higher skill performance. Some students may not have mastered the standards of earlier grade levels, so differentiated instruction becomes increasingly important in high school.

Ninth-grade students operate using higher-order thinking skills. They evaluate performance, analyze data, reflect on personal goals, and adjust behavior as necessary. Students are now at the cognitive stage when they can synthesize much of what they have learned in the earlier grade levels and apply it to new learning situations.

Ninth-grade students are still very concerned about body image and what other people think of them. They are caught somewhere between adolescence and young adulthood as they continue to mature emotionally. Their personal experiences help to formulate their attitudes and beliefs about the world.

Course 1 addresses aquatics, rhythms/dance, and individual and dual activities. Instruction on the effects of physical activity on dynamic health and the mechanics of body movement is integrated throughout the school year. Course 1 is designed to be taken before Course 2, and, therefore, is most appropriate for ninth-grade students or other students taking their first high school physical education course.

At a Glance

STANDARD 1
Students demonstrate knowledge of and competency in motor skills, movement patterns, and strategies needed to perform a variety of physical activities.

Standard 1 builds on the motor skill proficiency developed in kindergarten through eighth grade. Proficiency gives the student the capacity for success leading to advanced levels of performance, thereby increasing the likelihood of continued participation well into adulthood. By the end of Course 1, students demonstrate proficiency in aquatics, rhythms/dance, and individual and dual activities skills. If a swimming pool is unavailable, students still learn water-safety skills (e.g., swim parallel to the coast when caught in a riptide) and dry-land strokes. However, dry-land instruction does not ensure that a student knows how to swim in the water.

Students combine movement patterns to perform advanced offensive, defensive, and transition strategies in aquatics and individual and dual activities. Once students perform, they evaluate the effectiveness of the strategy. Students also combine movement patterns to create more complex rhythmic activities and dances.

Ninth-grade students learn to use biomechanics (see the Glossary) to analyze and improve performance, such as leverage, force, inertia, rotary motion, opposition, and buoyancy. Students work on the skill-related fitness components to enhance their performance. The skill-related fitness components are speed, power, agility, coordination, reaction time, and balance. Students use their understanding of training and conditioning practices to improve skill acquisition and performance. Understanding the three areas (biomechanics, skill-related fitness, and training and conditioning), along with the role of emotions, provides learners with the comprehensive knowledge for improving performance in aquatics, rhythms/dance, and individual and dual activities.

On their path to becoming independent learners of movement skills, students improve their understanding of motor learning concepts. By the end of ninth grade, students can create practice plans for improving their own performance in aquatics, rhythms/dance, and individual and dual activities. These practice plans are based on each student's strengths and weaknesses as identified through feedback from proprioception, from others, and from the performance of complex movement activities.[2]

STANDARD 2
Students achieve a level of physical fitness for health and performance while demonstrating knowledge of fitness concepts, principles, and strategies.

Understanding the role of physical activity in the prevention of disease enables students to see the connections between current physical lifestyle habits and future health care costs. Students continue to participate in enjoyable and challenging activities at a moderate to vigorous level for a minimum of four days each week. The activities address the five components of health-related fitness. To expand on the variety of activities in which they participate, students identify available fitness resources in the community.

Throughout the year students are assessed through scientifically based health-related physical fitness assessments to determine whether they meet health-related fitness performance standards. Students set goals based on the outcome of those assessments and develop and implement monthly

---

[2]Feedback is most effective when it is specific and positive or specific and corrective.

Chapter 4
Standards-Based
Physical Education:
Grades Nine
Through Twelve

High School
Course 1

personal physical fitness plans. By the end of Course 1, students meet the minimum health standards on a scientifically based health-related physical fitness assessment.

Looking toward the future, students learn to transfer their knowledge of fitness to real-world situations. They identify the physical fitness requirements of future occupation choices (see Appendix K). They also analyze consumer physical fitness products and programs for use in their future fitness plans. Finally, now that students are older and more mature, they learn the inherent risks associated with physical activity in extreme environments.

STANDARD 3

Students demonstrate knowledge of psychological and sociological concepts, principles, and strategies that apply to the learning and performance of physical activity.

This standard addresses self-responsibility, social interaction, and group dynamics. Students in Course 1 evaluate their psychological responses to physical activity. They set goals and then describe the positive feelings they experience from successful participation in physical activity. They share the responsibility for creating and maintaining a physically and emotionally safe and nonthreatening environment for all. And finally, they act independently and ignore negative peer pressure during physical activity.

By the end of Course 1, students discuss the changing psychological and sociological needs of a diverse society in relation to physical activity. They understand that physical activity is universal, and all cultures around the world perform physical activities. Through participation in activities from different parts of the world, students gain greater insights into the history and traditions of different cultures. Students extend this learning to social interaction and cooperation at home as well as in their future workplace.

Students learn that each group member brings different strengths and abilities and that it is important for the group to identify and utilize the strengths of each member to be successful in physical activities. They understand that success can be achieved only when students cooperate and interact positively with others.

Chapter 4
Standards-Based
Physical Education:
Grades Nine
Through Twelve

High School
Course 1

Learning Snapshots

STANDARD 1

1.1 Combine and apply movement patterns, simple to complex, in aquatic, rhythms/dance, and individual and dual activities.

Aquatics is one of the content areas listed in the *California Code of Regulations, Title 5,* Section 10060. (See Appendix A.) Providing aquatics instruction is a challenge for schools without a pool. Schools in this situation should investigate opportunities in the community for pool access or consider purchasing a porta-pool. Even without a pool, swimming strokes can be taught. Students are grouped in pairs and assigned to a bench. The teacher hands out task cards on the flutter kick, crawl arm stroke, crawl breathing, and complete crawl stroke. Lying prone on the bench, one student performs each part of the crawl stroke while the second student provides feedback. Once the student has mastered each part, the entire stroke can be attempted. It cannot be assumed that students who have mastered a stroke on dry land are able to swim safely in water.

1.2 Demonstrate proficient movement skills in aquatic, dance/rhythms, and individual and dual activities.

This standard asks students to demonstrate proficiency in movement skills in the content areas of aquatics, rhythms/dance, and individual and dual activities. At this level of skill development, the students are refining their skills. They are becoming more successful and consistent in their performance. Students at this level of skill require variable practice as well as less frequent feedback. In terms of variable practice, the teacher plans instruction so that a different variable of a skill or a different skill is practiced on each trial. The variable may be speed, distance, direction, or trajectory. For example, students should not practice the same badminton stroke twice in a row. Instead, they should perform the badminton overhead smash, forehand clear, drop shot, and serve in turn. As the student's level of learning advances, less feedback is needed for effective learning.

1.7 Analyze and evaluate feedback from proprioception, from others, and from the performance of complex motor (movement) activities to improve performance in aquatic, rhythms/dance, individual activities, and dual activities.

Proprioception refers to the ability to sense the position, location, orientation, and movement of one's body and its parts. This lesson focuses on individual and dual activities. The students are assigned to groups of two. One student performs the golf swing, while the second student provides feedback. During closure, the performers analyze the feedback they received from proprioception and their partner to determine what they need to do to improve their performance. The performers write their analysis.

121

Chapter 4
Standards-Based
Physical Education:
Grades Nine
Through Twelve

1.12 Demonstrate independent learning of movement skills.

This standard prepares students as lifelong learners of movement skills. Each student selects one movement skill from the content areas of aquatics, rhythms/dance, or individual and dual activities. The students are instructed to research the correct technique for their chosen skill and develop learning cues for practicing the correct technique. Then they determine the best type of practice to use to learn the particular skill. Finally, students create and implement their own practice plan.

STANDARD 2

2.9 Explain the inherent risks associated with physical activity in extreme environments.

This lesson begins with the teacher explaining the inherent risks of physical activities in some environments. For example, the desert environment has high temperatures, the mountain environment has low temperatures and high altitude (less oxygen), and the ocean environment has riptides. Students conduct research on an extreme environment in California (e.g., ocean, mountains) in which they would like to participate in physical activity. Students create a written report based on their research on the inherent risks associated with the selected environment.

2.10 Identify and list available fitness resources in the community.

This standard provides students with an opportunity to use the Internet for physical education instruction. The Web site http://www.bam.gov provides information on physical activities students might enjoy. Students conduct an Internet search to find appropriate resources in their community for the physical activities that interest them. For those without Internet access, the activity can be completed using community directories. Students compile a list of resources for review and feedback by the teacher.

2.11 Explain the role of physical activity in the prevention of disease and the reduction of health care costs.

This standard provides students with an opportunity to research a topic related to physical education. The school's teacher librarian can assist the students with finding materials in the school library/media center and on the Internet. Students create a written report based on their research. The physical educator connects this activity to the English-language arts content standards for grade nine by assigning a report that incorporates the grades nine and ten writing strategies and writing applications standards.

STANDARD 3

3.8 Recognize the value of physical activity in understanding multiculturalism.

Students are assigned to groups of four based on their interest in a particular culture. The groups research the significant physical activities, dances, and

**High School
Course 1**

recreational activities of that culture. Each group selects a game or a dance from the culture. They learn the game or dance well enough to teach it to the rest of the class. While teaching the game or dance to others, the group also explains how the dance or game connects to the culture of origin. During closure, the teacher asks students to select two games or dances from different cultures for comparison. The students write a comparison of the relationship between each physical activity and its culture of origin.

High School Course 1
Physical Education Model Content Standards

STANDARD 1
Students demonstrate knowledge of and competency in motor skills, movement patterns, and strategies needed to perform a variety of physical activities.

1.1 Combine and apply movement patterns, simple to complex, in aquatic, rhythms/dance, and individual and dual activities.

1.2 Demonstrate proficient movement skills in aquatic, rhythms/dance, and individual and dual activities.

1.3 Identify, explain, and apply the skill-related components of balance, reaction time, agility, coordination, explosive power, and speed that enhance performance levels in aquatic, rhythms/dance, and individual and dual activities.

1.4 Explain and demonstrate advanced offensive, defensive, and transition strategies in aquatic and individual and dual activities.

1.5 Explain the use of the principles of biomechanics (leverage, force, inertia, rotary motion, opposition, and buoyancy); apply the principles to achieve advanced performance in aquatic, rhythms/dance, and individual and dual activities; and evaluate the performance based on the use of the principles.

1.6 Examine the physical, emotional, cognitive, and scientific factors that affect performance and explain the relationship between those factors.

1.7 Analyze and evaluate feedback from proprioception, from others, and from the performance of complex motor (movement) activities to improve performance in aquatic, rhythms/dance, and individual activities, and dual activities.

1.8 Analyze and explain which training and conditioning practices have the greatest impact on skill acquisition and performance in aquatic, rhythms/dance, and individual and dual activities.

1.9 Create or modify practice/training plans based on evaluative feedback of skill acquisition and performance in aquatic, rhythms/dance, and individual and dual activities.

1.10 Analyze situations and determine appropriate strategies for improved performance in aquatic, rhythms/dance, and individual and dual activities.

1.11 Assess the effect/outcome of a particular performance strategy in aquatic, rhythms/dance, and individual and dual activities.

1.12 Demonstrate independent learning of movement skills.

Chapter 4
Standards-Based
Physical Education:
Grades Nine
Through Twelve

High School
Course I

STANDARD 2

Students achieve a level of physical fitness for health and performance while demonstrating knowledge of fitness concepts, principles, and strategies.

2.1   Participate in moderate to vigorous physical activity at least four days each week.

2.2   Participate in enjoyable and challenging physical activities that develop and maintain the five components of physical fitness.

2.3   Meet health-related physical fitness standards established by a scientifically based health-related fitness assessment.

2.4   Use physical fitness test results to set and adjust goals to improve fitness.

2.5   Improve and maintain physical fitness by adjusting physical activity levels according to the principles of exercise.

2.6   Identify the physical fitness requirements of an occupation.

2.7   Develop and implement a one-month personal physical fitness plan.

2.8   Analyze consumer physical fitness products and programs.

2.9   Explain the inherent risks associated with physical activity in extreme environments.

2.10   Identify and list available fitness resources in the community.

2.11   Explain the role of physical activity in the prevention of disease and the reduction of health care costs.

STANDARD 3

Students demonstrate knowledge of psychological and sociological concepts, principles, and strategies that apply to the learning and performance of physical activity.

Self-Responsibility

3.1   Accept personal responsibility to create and maintain a physically and emotionally safe and nonthreatening environment for physical activity.

3.2   Act independently of negative peer pressure during physical activity.

3.3   Identify and evaluate personal psychological response to physical activity.

3.4   Describe the enjoyment, self-expression, challenge, and social benefits experienced by achieving one's best in physical activities.

3.5   Develop personal goals to improve one's performance in physical activities.

Social Interaction

3.6   Discuss the changing psychological and sociological needs of a diverse society in relation to physical activity.

3.7   Analyze the role that physical activity plays in social interaction and cooperative opportunities in the family and the workplace.

3.8   Recognize the value of physical activity in understanding multiculturalism.

Group Dynamics

3.9   Recognize and evaluate the role of cooperation and positive interactions with others when participating in physical activity.

3.10   Identify and utilize the potential strengths of each individual in physical activity.

125

Chapter 4
Standards-Based
Physical Education:
Grades Nine
Through Twelve

High School
Course 2

High School Course 2

As noted in Course 1, the developmental range of high school students is very diverse. However, by tenth grade, most students are experiencing a slower rate of growth. This slowdown in growth rate, along with increases in the length and breadth of muscles, produces a higher level of motor ability and fitness. Students are becoming more interested in their personal development and recognize the value of high-level physical performance for their future lives and careers.

Tenth-graders continue to improve their cognitive functioning. They are experiencing an expansion of their knowledge base; an increase in their ability to absorb, process, and retrieve information; a refinement of their language and communication skills; an increase in their attention capacity; and an increase in their ability to conceptualize, reason, and analyze information. They are moving toward their full intellectual potential, which is usually achieved between sixteen and twenty-five years of age.

As tenth-graders mature, their egocentrism decreases. Through social inter-action they learn they are not the sole focus of attention. They are learning to express their emotions in more appropriate ways, and their moral reasoning is becoming increasingly sophisticated. Peer groups and dating activities dominate their social lives. They are ready to assume more formal leadership roles during physical activities.

For some high school students, Course 2 is their last opportunity for formal instruction in physical education. Course 2 addresses combatives, gymnastics/tumbling, and team activities. Instruction on the effects of physical activity on dynamic health and the mechanics of body movement is integrated throughout the school year. Course 2 is designed to be taken after Course 1 is completed. Typically, tenth-graders enroll in Course 2, though some students will take Course 2 as eleventh- or twelfth-graders.

At a Glance

STANDARD 1
Students demonstrate knowledge of and competency in motor skills, movement patterns, and strategies needed to perform a variety of physical activities.

The standards in Course 2 are similar to those in Course 1. The difference is in the content areas addressed in each grade level. By the end of Course 2, students demonstrate proficiency in combatives, gymnastics/tumbling, and team activities. A personal defense class in which students learn how to avoid dangerous situations as well as how to defend themselves meets the combatives requirement. Proficiency gives the student the capacity for success leading to advanced levels of performance that increase the

Chapter 4
Standards-Based
Physical Education:
Grades Nine
Through Twelve

High School
Course 2

likelihood of continued participation well into adulthood. Students can combine movement patterns to perform advanced offensive, defensive, and transition strategies in team sport situations. Once performed, students can evaluate the effectiveness of the strategy. Students can also combine movement patterns to create more complex gymnastics/tumbling routines and combative combinations.

Tenth-grade students learn to use biomechanics (see the Glossary) to analyze and improve performance, such as leverage, force, inertia, rotary motion, and opposition. Students also explain and use the skill-related fitness components to enhance their performance. The skill-related fitness components are speed, power, agility, coordination, reaction time, and balance. Students can also use their understanding of training and conditioning practices to improve skill acquisition and performance. Understanding these four areas (biomechanics, motor learning, skill-related fitness, and training and conditioning), along with the role of emotions, provides learners with the comprehensive knowledge for improving performance in combatives, gymnastics/tumbling, and team sport activities.

On their path to becoming independent learners of movement skills, students increase their understanding of motor learning concepts. By the end of tenth grade, students create practice plans for improving their own performance in combatives, gymnastics/tumbling, and team sport activities. These practice plans are based on their personal strengths and weaknesses as identified by the students through feedback from proprioception, from others, and from the performance of complex movement activities.[3]

STANDARD 2

Students achieve a level of physical fitness for health and performance while demonstrating knowledge of fitness concepts, principles, and strategies.

For some students, Course 2 may be the last opportunity to learn about physical fitness and achieve levels of excellence in physical fitness beyond the performance standards established by scientifically based health-related fitness assessments. Students should be assessed on each of the health-related fitness components throughout the school year, so that physical activity can be adjusted to accommodate changes in age, growth and development, and goals. Students continue to develop an exercise habit by participating in challenging activities at a moderate to vigorous level for a minimum of four days each week based on individual needs and interests.

During Course 2, students learn to be wise consumers by evaluating fitness products and programs, as well as fitness resources in the community.

---

[3]Feedback is most effective when it is specific and positive or specific and corrective.

They also learn the facts about ergogenic aids that claim to enhance body composition, appearance, physical fitness, and performance. By the end of Course 2, students can develop and describe a physical fitness plan that enhances personal health and performance. Their plans also take into consideration future leisure and workplace activities. Besides planning their own fitness programs, students can also develop and implement appropriate personal physical fitness programs for family or community members.

STANDARD 3

Students demonstrate knowledge of psychological and sociological concepts, principles, and strategies that apply to the learning and performance of physical activity.

In Course 2, students learn to identify and participate in those activities that they enjoy. They learn that their choice of physical activities may change throughout their lives. They understand that physical activities may need to be modified to allow participation by individuals of various ages and those with special needs. Students realize they will need to evaluate and refine their personal goals continually to improve performance in physical activities. Through their participation in regular physical activity, students learn the psychological benefits of physical activity. They can explain the role of attitude, motivation, and determination in achieving personal satisfaction from challenging physical activities.

As their social skills mature, tenth-grade students identify the effects of individual differences on preference for and participation in physical activity. These differences may include age, gender, ethnicity, socioeconomic status, and culture. As to age and special needs, students learn how to select and modify physical activities so that everyone can participate.

In terms of group dynamics, students learn to identify leadership skills. They learn to perform planned leadership assignments and also assume spontaneous leadership roles. By the end of Course 2, students know how to encourage others to be supportive and inclusive of individuals at all ability levels.

Chapter 4
Standards-Based
Physical Education:
Grades Nine
Through Twelve

High School
Course 2

Learning Snapshots

STANDARD 1

1.4 Explain and demonstrate advanced offensive, defensive, and transition strategies and tactics in combative, gymnastic/tumbling, and team activities.

This complex standard is designed to be addressed over many lessons in different content areas. All offensive strategies are based on opening up space. One example involves teaching students the offensive strategy known as the "vertical stack" in the game called Ultimate. In this strategy the offense forms a straight line—a stack—along the length of the field. The stack usually lines up in the middle of the field, thereby opening up two lanes along the sidelines. The individual with the flying disc throws the disc into a lane without a defender as a receiver quickly cuts into the lane to catch the disc. Students explain and demonstrate this advanced offensive strategy.

1.7 Analyze and evaluate feedback from proprioception, from others, and from the performance of complex motor (movement) activities to improve performance in combative, gymnastic/tumbling, and team activities.

Proprioception refers to the ability to sense the position, location, orientation, and movement of one's body and its parts. The students are assigned to groups of four to work on the roundoff, a common gymnastics/tumbling skill. One person performs the roundoff, one person is the spotter, one person provides feedback, and one person is the recorder. Students rotate roles after each trial. During closure, the performers analyze the feedback they received through proprioception and from others to determine what they need to do to improve their performance.

STANDARD 2

2.3 Identify and achieve levels of excellence in physical fitness that enhance physical and mental performance beyond the standards established by scientifically based health-related fitness assessments.

This standard challenges students to exceed minimum health-related physical fitness performance standards. The first step in this process is for students to determine their current levels of fitness. This step links to Standard 2.11 that calls for students to assess themselves on the five components of health-related physical fitness. The second step is for students to analyze the results of the assessment and to set realistic goals for improvement. The third step is for students to participate in challenging physical fitness activities using the principles of exercise to meet their individual needs and interests. (This step links to Standard 2.2.) Throughout the year, students reassess their levels of fitness to monitor their

129

Chapter 4
Standards-Based
Physical Education:
Grades Nine
Through Twelve

progress. They also meet with the teacher to refine and adjust their goals. If necessary, they revise their personal fitness plans. Most students will need to implement fitness programs both in and out of school to raise their fitness levels above minimum performance standards.

2.8   Explain how to evaluate consumer physical fitness products and programs.

The teacher provides students with a list of some important points to consider when they select physical fitness products and programs. For example:

- Take time to compare prices, features, and quality.
- Try out any piece of equipment or program before making a purchase.
- Gather evidence about the program or product.
- Evaluate the credibility of claims about the product or program.
- Buy only quality equipment.
- Make sure you have a convenient place to use the equipment or that the program is available close to where you live.
- Decide on the features you really need.
- Decide whether there are less expensive ways to achieve the same goals without the product or program.
- Make sure there is a warranty.

As a learning activity, students select a product or program in the community that they think will help them with their fitness. Students can use the list noted above as a starting point to evaluate the product or program. Students investigate the product or program. Each student must also write a summary statement explaining whether the product or program is worth the price. This activity provides extension activities for use with other subject areas. For example, students could apply the analysis skills in the history–social science standards by analyzing the costs and benefits of a fitness product or program. Or, they could apply English–language arts standards by writing a persuasive essay to support their conclusion about whether the product or program is worth the price.

STANDARD 3

3.8   Identify leadership skills, perform planned leadership assignments, and assume spontaneous leadership roles.

Leadership skills include being an active group member, facilitating group interactions, teaching peers, encouraging group members, and sharing leadership responsibilities with others. The specific leadership style that one assumes depends on the people involved, the task, and the environmental factors. The teacher discusses those skills with the students so that they understand the role of a leader. As students participate in leadership situations, the teacher provides the students with feedback so they can improve. To address this standard, all students must be given

**High School
Course 2**

the opportunity to assume planned leadership assignments and must be positioned to assume spontaneous leadership roles. Those opportunities do not happen simply by chance. Situations must be carefully planned and simulated by the teacher, and students must have learned the skills, concepts, and confidence to be successful in leadership roles. Every student is to be provided with opportunities to be group leader for a cooperative activity or group project.

High School Course 2
Physical Education Model Content Standards

STANDARD 1

Students demonstrate knowledge of and competency in motor skills, movement patterns, and strategies needed to perform a variety of physical activities.

1.1 Combine and apply movement patterns, from simple to complex, in combative, gymnastic/tumbling, and team activities.

1.2 Demonstrate proficient movement skills in combative, gymnastic/tumbling, and team activities.

1.3 Explain the skill-related components of balance, reaction time, agility, coordination, explosive power, and speed that enhance performance levels in combative, gymnastic/tumbling, and team activities and apply those components in performance.

1.4 Explain and demonstrate advanced offensive, defensive, and transition strategies and tactics in combative, gymnastic/tumbling, and team activities.

1.5 Explain the use of the principles of biomechanics (leverage, force, inertia, rotary motion, and opposition); apply the principles to achieve advanced performance in combative, gymnastic/tumbling, and team activities; and evaluate the performance based on use of the principles.

1.6 Evaluate the relationships of physical, emotional, and cognitive factors affecting individual and team performance.

1.7 Analyze and evaluate feedback from proprioception, from others, and from the performance of complex motor (movement) activities to improve performance in combative, gymnastic/tumbling, and team activities.

1.8 Analyze and explain which training and conditioning practices have the greatest impact on skill acquisition and performance in combative, gymnastic/tumbling, and team activities.

1.9 Create or modify practice/training plans based on evaluative feedback from skill acquisition and performance in combative, gymnastic/tumbling, and team activities.

1.10 Analyze situations to determine appropriate strategies to use in combative, gymnastic/tumbling, and team activities.

1.11 Assess the effect/outcome of a particular performance strategy used in combative, gymnastic/tumbling, and team activities.

1.12 Evaluate independent learning of movement skills.

Chapter 4
Standards-Based
Physical Education:
Grades Nine
Through Twelve

High School
Course 2

STANDARD 2

Students achieve a level of physical fitness for health and performance while demonstrating knowledge of fitness concepts, principles, and strategies.

2.1   Participate in moderate to vigorous physical activity at least four days each week.

2.2   Participate in challenging physical fitness activities using the principles of exercise to meet individual needs and interests.

2.3   Identify and achieve levels of excellence in physical fitness that enhance physical and mental performance beyond the standards established by scientifically based health-related fitness assessments.

2.4   Assess levels of physical fitness and adjust physical activity to accommodate changes in age, growth, and development.

2.5   Justify the use of particular physical activities to achieve desired fitness goals.

2.6   Develop and describe a physical fitness plan that enhances personal health and performance in future leisure and workplace activities.

2.7   Develop and implement an appropriate personal physical fitness program for a family or community member.

2.8   Explain how to evaluate consumer physical fitness products and programs.

2.9   Identify and evaluate ergogenic aids that claim to enhance body composition, appearance, physical fitness, and performance.

2.10   Evaluate the availability and quality of fitness resources in the community.

2.11   Use and analyze scientifically based data and protocols to assess oneself on the five components of health-related physical fitness.

STANDARD 3

Students demonstrate knowledge of psychological and sociological concepts, principles, and strategies that apply to the learning and performance of physical activity.

Self-Responsibility

3.1   Participate in physical activities for personal enjoyment.

3.2   Examine and explain the ways in which personal characteristics, performance styles, and preferences for activities may change over a lifetime.

3.3   Evaluate the psychological benefits derived from regular participation in physical activity.

3.4   Explain and analyze the role of individual attitude, motivation, and determination in achieving personal satisfaction from challenging physical activities.

3.5   Evaluate and refine personal goals to improve performance in physical activities.

Chapter 4
Standards-Based
Physical Education:
Grades Nine
Through Twelve

High School
Course 2

Social Interaction

3.6   Identify the effects of individual differences, such as age, gender, ethnicity, socioeconomic status, and culture, on preferences for and participation in physical activity.

3.7   Explain how to select and modify physical activities to allow for participation by younger children, the elderly, and individuals with special needs.

Group Dynamics

3.8   Identify leadership skills, perform planned leadership assignments, and assume spontaneous leadership roles.

3.9   Encourage others to be supportive and inclusive of individuals of all ability levels.

Chapter 4
Standards-Based
Physical Education:
Grades Nine
Through Twelve

High School
Course 3

High School Course 3

Eleventh- and twelfth-graders are experiencing various systemic changes on their journey to adulthood. When males and females have reached the ages of eighteen and sixteen, respectively, they have grown to approximately 98 percent of their adult height. Final growth often occurs by the age of eighteen for young women and by age twenty-one for young men. As their bodies change and they grow taller, adolescents also put on weight. Girls often gain 35 pounds during adolescent years, while boys gain 45 pounds (Payne and Issacs 1995). Eleventh- and twelfth-grade students are often interested in achieving and maintaining optimal levels of fitness if only for the sake of personal appearance.

Eleventh- and twelfth-grade students are also moving toward their full intellectual potential. Their increased knowledge and experience provide them with the ability to select those activities in which they would like to improve. These students like structure and want to know what is expected of them. The teacher should therefore make it a point to share lesson objectives and standards with the students.

Eleventh- and twelfth-grade students are continuing their social development in preparation for adulthood. Their personal system of values is becoming more integrated. They are beginning to adjust their self-concept because of developmental changes and experiences. Their self-esteem is improving as they become more competent.

By the eleventh and twelfth grades, students are prepared to focus on the activities they plan to pursue independently after graduation from high school. They can explain why an individual's pursuit of excellence in any arena is an evolving process requiring commitment, courage, confidence, initiative, and perseverance. These students design their own learning schedules and are often able to attain high levels of specialized skills if they apply the motor learning principles. They have learned that self-expression through physical activity is of great value in developing and maintaining the healthy mind and body needed to excel in their personal as well as professional life.

As part of a sequential curriculum, Course 1 and 2 classes are designed as prerequisites for Course 3 classes. Course 3 classes are designed as prerequisites for Course 4 classes. Students who have not completed a Course 3 class covering the same content area may not be prepared to take the Course 4 class. Each course has its own unique content and specific standards for students to learn, although there may be some similarities.

The six content areas identified for Course 3 are:

Course 3A, Adventure/Outdoor Activities
Course 3B, Aerobic Activities
Course 3C, Individual and Dual Activities
Course 3D, Dance
Course 3E, Aquatics
Course 3F, Weight Training and Fitness

135

Chapter 4
Standards-Based
Physical Education:
Grades Nine
Through Twelve

At a Glance

STANDARD 1

Students demonstrate knowledge of and competency in motor skills, movement patterns, and strategies needed to perform a variety of physical activities.

The focus of Standard 1 is to help students apply previously learned movement concepts and principles to the attainment of advanced knowledge and skills in physical activities that they wish to pursue after graduation from high school. Students learn about the safety issues related to their selected activity so that they can enjoy it without injury. They also learn the characteristics and critical elements of the specialized skills required for participation in their chosen activity along with the biomechanics in the performance of these skills. Finally, they learn to be independent learners capable of creating their own learning plans.

STANDARD 2

Students achieve a level of physical fitness for health and performance while demonstrating knowledge of fitness concepts, principles, and strategies.

Students are expected to improve or maintain their physical fitness level by adjusting their levels of physical activity according to the principles of exercise. Students learn to incorporate their selected activity into their personal fitness program. They learn to analyze the effects of their selected activities on their overall health, personal physical fitness program, and personal levels of health-related physical fitness. Course 3F provides additional opportunities for students to engage in the examination of the discipline of exercise physiology and the body's physiological response to different conditioning programs.

STANDARD 3

Students demonstrate knowledge of psychological and sociological concepts, principles, and strategies that apply to the learning and performance of physical activity.

Students taking Course 3 are prepared to focus on the activities they plan to pursue for recreation or as a career after graduation from high school. Students are given the opportunity to select the activities in which they would like to participate. During the course they learn how to explain why this activity is personally enjoyable. Students assume responsibility for developing personal goals to improve performance in their selected activities and for engaging in their selected activities both in and outside school. They also learn to evaluate the potential risks associated with

Chapter 4
Standards-Based
Physical Education:
Grades Nine
Through Twelve

High School
Course 3

participation in their activity of choice. Students use that knowledge to avoid foreseeable injuries.

Students learn to analyze the role of social interaction in the successful participation in and enjoyment of their selected activity. They extend their inclusion skills by learning how to select and modify activities to allow participation by younger children, the elderly, and individuals with special needs.

Leadership is a major skill for eleventh- and twelfth-grade students. Students learn to compare and contrast effective leadership strategies used in their selected activity. Students willingly accept leadership assignments and analyze and respond appropriately when their leadership is necessary. They are also able to cooperate with others who assume leadership roles.

Learning Snapshots

STANDARD 1

High School Course 3E, Aquatic Activities, Standard 1.3:

> Apply previously learned movement concepts to the learning and development of motor skills required for successful participation in aquatic activities.

To meet this standard, students use their motor learning knowledge to help them improve their aquatic skills. The first step is for students to analyze their current aquatic performance. Students seek feedback from the teacher or a peer.[4] Students can also have their performances recorded on video, so that they can analyze their own performance. On the basis of feedback for a particular skill (e.g., butterfly stroke), students classify themselves as beginners, intermediate, or advanced learners. The students then review the various practice protocols (e.g., closed skill practice, part practice, random practice), selecting those protocols that are appropriate for their level of performance. The last step in the process is for students to implement the practice protocol when practicing aquatic skills.

High School Course 3B, Aerobic Activities, Standard 1.4:

> Identify and apply the principles of biomechanics necessary for the safe and successful performance of aerobic activities.

At the beginning of the school year, the teacher reviews previously learned biomechanics principles, including the following:

- Force must be applied to change an object's state of motion (application of Newton's First Law).

---

[4] Feedback is most effective when it is specific and positive or specific and corrective.

- For every action, there is an equal and opposite reaction (Newton's Third Law).
- If one object is to change the motion of another by exerting pressure (for example, when the palm of the hand exerts pressure on the surface of a ball as the ball is caught or struck), the maximum pressure needed can be reduced by increasing the duration of the pressure or by increasing the area that applies the pressure.

As the teacher reviews each concept, he or she leads a discussion with the students regarding its application to aerobic activities. For example, at the beginning of an aerobic activity the performers are stationary and must push on the ground so that the ground will push on them so they can start to move. Throughout the year, the teacher orally quizzes the students regarding the application of biomechanics (see the Glossary) to performance in aerobic activities.

STANDARD 2

High School Course 3F, Weight Training and Fitness, Standard 2.7:

Develop and use a personal physical fitness log to record all workout data on a daily basis.

This course requires students to assume responsibility for their own workouts. Accordingly, students develop and maintain a personal physical fitness log as evidence that they have performed daily workouts. Important information in their log should include date, weight training exercise, number of repetitions, number of sets, and amount of weight lifted. Teachers check the logs that students develop at the beginning of the school year and monitor them throughout the year. Periodically throughout the school year or course, students and teachers discuss the student's progress using the data in the log.

STANDARD 3

High School Course 3A, Adventure/Outdoor Activities, Standard 3.9:

Engage in adventure/outdoor activities both in school and outside school.

Students enrolled in High School Course 3A will participate in adventure/outdoor activities in school. Finding opportunities outside school, however, may be more difficult. It is the student's responsibility to develop a list of community resources for adventure and outdoor activities. It is also the student's responsibility to plan time to participate in these activities and to arrange for transportation to and from the activity center. The teacher provides students with a log, so that they can record the date, time, location, and type of activity in which they engage. Throughout the school year, the teacher meets periodically with each student to review his or her log.

Chapter 4
Standards-Based
Physical Education:
Grades Nine
Through Twelve

High School
Course 3

High School Courses 3A Through 3F
Physical Education Model Content Standards

High School Course 3A: Adventure/Outdoor Activities

High School Courses 1 and 2 are designed to be completed before a student enrolls in High School Course 3A.

STANDARD 1

Students demonstrate knowledge of and competency in motor skills, movement patterns, and strategies needed to perform a variety of physical activities.

1.1   Demonstrate advanced knowledge and skills in two or more adventure/outdoor activities.

1.2   Identify the characteristics and critical elements of a highly skilled performance in adventure/outdoor activities and demonstrate them.

1.3   Apply previously learned movement concepts and principles to the learning and development of the motor skills required for successful participation in adventure/outdoor pursuits and activities.

1.4   Identify and apply the principles of biomechanics necessary for the safe and successful performance of adventure/outdoor activities.

1.5   List the safety equipment required for participation in outdoor pursuits and adventures; describe and demonstrate the use of such equipment.

1.6   Demonstrate independent learning of movement skills in adventure/outdoor activities.

STANDARD 2

Students achieve a level of physical fitness for health and performance while demonstrating knowledge of fitness concepts, principles, and strategies.

2.1   Participate in adventure/outdoor activities that improve health-related physical fitness.

2.2   Analyze the effects of adventure/outdoor activities on a personal physical fitness program and personal levels of health-related physical fitness.

2.3   Improve or maintain physical fitness by adjusting physical activity levels according to the principles of exercise.

2.4   Explain the relationship between participation in adventure/outdoor activities and health.

STANDARD 3

Students demonstrate knowledge of psychological and sociological concepts, principles, and strategies that apply to the learning and performance of physical activity.

Self-Responsibility

3.1   Compare and contrast the effective leadership skills used in adventure/outdoor activities and those used in other physical activities.

139

Chapter 4
Standards-Based
Physical Education:
Grades Nine
Through Twelve

High School
Course 3

3.2   Develop personal goals to improve performance in adventure/outdoor activities.

3.3   Identify and analyze adventure/outdoor physical activities that enhance personal enjoyment.

3.4   Evaluate the risks and safety factors that may affect participation in adventure/outdoor activities throughout a lifetime.

Social Interaction

3.5   Explain how to select and modify adventure/outdoor activities to allow for participation by younger children, the elderly, and individuals with special needs.

3.6   Analyze the role of social interaction in the successful participation in and enjoyment of adventure/outdoor activities.

Group Dynamics

3.7   Accept and perform planned and spontaneous leadership assignments and roles in adventure/outdoor activities.

3.8   Analyze the role that cooperation and leadership play in adventure/outdoor activities.

3.9   Engage in adventure/outdoor activities both in school and outside school.

High School Course 3B: Aerobic Activities

High School Courses 1 and 2 are designed to be completed before a student enrolls in High School Course 3B.

STANDARD 1
Students demonstrate knowledge of and competency in motor skills, movement patterns, and strategies needed to perform a variety of physical activities.

1.1   Demonstrate advanced knowledge and skills in two or more aerobic activities, selecting one or more from each of the following categories:

Category 1	*Category 2*
Aerobic dance	Cross-country skiing
Running	Cycling
Skating	Rowing
Swimming	Triathlon
	Walking

1.2   Identify the characteristics and critical elements of a highly skilled performance in aerobic activities and demonstrate them.

1.3   Apply previously learned movement concepts to the learning and development of the motor skills required for successful participation in aerobic activities.

1.4   Identify and apply the principles of biomechanics necessary for the safe and successful performance of aerobic activities.

Chapter 4
Standards-Based
Physical Education:
Grades Nine
Through Twelve

High School
Course 3

1.5   List the safety equipment required for participation in aerobic activities; describe and demonstrate the use of such equipment.

1.6   Demonstrate independent learning of movement skills in aerobic activities.

STANDARD 2

Students achieve a level of physical fitness for health and performance while demonstrating knowledge of fitness concepts, principles, and strategies.

2.1   Identify and achieve a personal level of excellence in physical fitness.

2.2   Engage independently in physical activity that increases aerobic capacity.

2.3   Evaluate goal-setting and other strategies as effective tools for maintaining and increasing adherence to a personal physical activity program.

2.4   Measure health-related physical fitness periodically and adjust physical activity to achieve fitness goals.

2.5   Identify and explain the positive effects of participation in aerobic activity on personal health.

STANDARD 3

Students demonstrate knowledge of psychological and sociological concepts, principles, and strategies that apply to the learning and performance of physical activity.

Self-Responsibility

3.1   Engage independently in aerobic activities.

3.2   Develop personal goals to improve performance in aerobic activities.

3.3   Compare and contrast the effective leadership skills used in aerobic activities and those used in other physical activities.

3.4   Identify and analyze aerobic activities that enhance both personal enjoyment and the challenge.

3.5   Evaluate the risks and safety factors that may affect participation in aerobic activities throughout a lifetime.

Social Interaction

3.6   Invite others to join in aerobic activity.

3.7   Explain how to select and modify aerobic activities to allow for participation by younger children, the elderly, and individuals with special needs.

3.8   Analyze the role of social interaction in the successful participation in and enjoyment of aerobic activities.

Group Dynamics

3.9   Accept and perform planned and spontaneous leadership assignments and roles in aerobic activities.

3.10   Analyze the role that cooperation and leadership play in aerobic activities.

3.11   Engage in aerobic activities both in school and outside school.

141

Chapter 4
Standards-Based
Physical Education:
Grades Nine
Through Twelve

High School
Course 3

High School Course 3C: Individual and Dual Activities

High School Courses 1 and 2 are designed to be completed before a student enrolls in High School Course 3C.

STANDARD 1
Students demonstrate knowledge of and competency in motor skills, movement patterns, and strategies needed to perform a variety of physical activities.

1.1 Demonstrate advanced knowledge and skills in two or more individual and dual activities, selecting one or more from each of the following categories:

Individual	*Dual*
Archery	Badminton
Cycling	Handball
Golf	Racquetball
Gymnastics/Tumbling	Squash
Skating	Tennis
Skiing	Two-player volleyball
Surfing	
Yoga	

1.2 Identify the characteristics and critical elements of a highly skilled performance in individual and dual activities and demonstrate them.

1.3 Apply previously learned movement concepts to the learning and development of the motor skills required for successful participation in individual and dual activities.

1.4 Identify and apply the principles of biomechanics necessary for the safe and successful performance of individual and dual activities.

1.5 List the safety equipment required for participation in individual and dual activities; describe and demonstrate the use of such equipment.

1.6 Demonstrate independent learning of movement skills in individual and dual activities.

STANDARD 2
Students achieve a level of physical fitness for health and performance while demonstrating knowledge of fitness concepts, principles, and strategies.

2.1 Meet physical fitness standards that exceed those of a scientifically based health-related fitness assessment.

2.2 Participate in individual and dual activities that improve or maintain health-related physical fitness.

2.3 Analyze the effects of individual and dual activities on a personal physical fitness program and personal levels of health-related physical fitness.

2.4 Improve or maintain physical fitness by adjusting physical activity levels according to the principles of exercise.

2.5 Explain the relationship between participation in individual and in dual activities and health.

Chapter 4
Standards-Based
Physical Education:
Grades Nine
Through Twelve

High School
Course 3

2.6   Demonstrate the ability to develop criteria and analyze factors to consider in the purchase of fitness products and programs related to individual and dual activities.

2.7   Develop and implement a month-long personal physical fitness plan that includes individual and dual activities.

STANDARD 3

Students demonstrate knowledge of psychological and sociological concepts, principles, and strategies that apply to the learning and performance of physical activity.

Self-Responsibility

3.1   Compare and contrast the effective leadership skills used in individual and dual activities and those used in other physical activities.

3.2   Develop personal goals to improve performance in individual and dual activities.

3.3   Identify and analyze individual and dual physical activities that enhance personal enjoyment.

3.4   Evaluate the risks and safety factors that may affect participation in individual and dual activities throughout a lifetime.

Social Interaction

3.5   Explain how to select and modify individual and dual activities to allow for participation by younger children, the elderly, and individuals with special needs.

3.6   Analyze the role of social interaction in the successful participation in and enjoyment of individual and dual activities.

Group Dynamics

3.7   Accept and perform planned and spontaneous leadership assignments and roles in individual and dual activities.

3.8   Analyze the role that cooperation and leadership play in individual and dual activities.

3.9   Engage in individual and dual activities both in school and outside school.

High School Course 3D: Dance

High School Courses 1 and 2 are designed to be completed before a student enrolls in High School Course 3D.

STANDARD 1

Students demonstrate knowledge of and competency in motor skills, movement patterns, and strategies needed to perform a variety of physical activities.

1.1   Demonstrate advanced knowledge and skills in two or more dance activities, selecting one or more from each of the following categories:

143

Chapter 4
Standards-Based
Physical Education:
Grades Nine
Through Twelve

High School
Course 3

Category 1	Category 2
Ballet	Modern
Folk	Social
Jazz	Square

1.2 Identify the characteristics and critical elements of a highly skilled performance in dance activities and demonstrate them.

1.3 Apply previously learned movement concepts to the learning and development of the motor skills required for successful participation in dance activities.

1.4 Identify and apply the principles of biomechanics necessary for the safe and successful performance of dance activities.

1.5 List the safety equipment and facilities required for participation in dance activities; describe and demonstrate the use of such equipment and facilities.

1.6 Demonstrate independent learning of movement skills in dance activities.

STANDARD 2
Students achieve a level of physical fitness for health and performance while demonstrating knowledge of fitness concepts, principles, and strategies.

2.1 Meet physical fitness standards that exceed those of a scientifically based health-related fitness assessment.

2.2 Participate in dance activities that improve or maintain personal levels of health-related physical fitness.

2.3 Analyze the effects of dance activities on a personal physical fitness program and personal levels of health-related physical fitness.

2.4 Improve or maintain one's physical fitness by adjusting physical activity levels according to the principles of exercise.

2.5 Explain the relationship between participation in dance activities and health.

2.6 Demonstrate the ability to develop criteria and analyze factors to consider in the purchase of products and programs related to dance activities.

2.7 Develop and implement a month-long personal physical fitness plan that includes dance activities.

STANDARD 3
Students demonstrate knowledge of psychological and sociological concepts, principles, and strategies that apply to the learning and performance of physical activity.

Self-Responsibility

3.1 Compare and contrast the effective leadership skills used in dance activities and those used in other physical activities.

3.2 Develop personal goals to improve performance in dance activities.

3.3 Identify and analyze dance activities that enhance personal enjoyment.

144

Chapter 4
Standards-Based
Physical Education:
Grades Nine
Through Twelve

High School
Course 3

3.4   Evaluate the risks and safety factors that may affect participation in dance activities throughout a lifetime.

Social Interaction

3.5   Explain how to select and modify dance activities to allow for participation by younger children, the elderly, and individuals with special needs.

3.6   Analyze the role of social interaction in the successful participation in and enjoyment of dance activities.

Group Dynamics

3.7   Accept and perform planned and spontaneous leadership assignments and roles in dance activities.

3.8   Analyze the role that cooperation and leadership play in dance activities.

3.9   Engage in dance activities both in school and outside school.

High School Course 3E: Aquatic Activities

High School Courses 1 and 2 are designed to be completed before a student enrolls in High School Course 3E.

STANDARD 1

Students demonstrate knowledge of and competency in motor skills, movement patterns, and strategies needed to perform a variety of physical activities.

1.1   Demonstrate advanced knowledge and skills in two or more aquatic activities, selecting one or more from each of the following categories:

Category 1	*Category 2*
Diving	Life guarding
Kayaking/Canoeing/Rowing	Scuba diving
Snorkeling	Synchronized swimming
Swimming	Water polo

1.2   Identify the characteristics and critical elements of a highly skilled performance in aquatic activities and demonstrate them.

1.3   Apply previously learned movement concepts to the learning and development of motor skills required for successful participation in aquatic activities.

1.4   Identify and apply the principles of biomechanics necessary for the safe and successful performance of aquatic activities.

1.5   List the safety equipment required for participation in aquatic activities; describe and demonstrate the use of such equipment.

1.6   Demonstrate independent learning of movement skills in aquatic activities.

1.7   Identify and practice the safety skills necessary for entering swimming pools, lakes, rivers, and oceans (e.g., walking, jumping, falling, and diving).

145

Chapter 4
Standards-Based
Physical Education:
Grades Nine
Through Twelve

High School
Course 3

1.8   Demonstrate and explain basic water rescue with and without equipment.

1.9   Demonstrate and explain basic cardiopulmonary resuscitation.

STANDARD 2

Students achieve a level of physical fitness for health and performance while demonstrating knowledge of fitness concepts, principles, and strategies.

2.1   Meet physical fitness standards that exceed those of a scientifically based health-related fitness assessment.

2.2   Participate in aquatic activities that improve or maintain health-related physical fitness.

2.3   Analyze the effects of participation in aquatic activities on levels of health-related physical fitness activities and a personal fitness program.

2.4   Improve or maintain one's physical fitness by adjusting physical activity levels according to the principles of exercise.

2.5   Explain the relationship between participation in aquatic activities and indicators of good health.

2.6   Demonstrate the ability to develop criteria and analyze factors to consider in the purchase of products and programs related to aquatic activities.

2.7   Develop and implement a month-long personal physical fitness plan that includes aquatic activities.

2.8   Explain how aquatic activities contribute to the development and maintenance of health-related physical fitness.

2.9   Create and implement aquatic programs that improve health-related physical fitness.

STANDARD 3

Students demonstrate knowledge of psychological and sociological concepts, principles, and strategies that apply to the learning and performance of physical activity.

Self-Responsibility

3.1   Compare and contrast the effective leadership skills used in aquatic activities and those used in other physical activities.

3.2   Develop personal goals to improve performance in aquatic activities.

3.3   Identify and analyze aquatic activities that enhance personal enjoyment.

3.4   Evaluate the risks and safety factors that may affect participation in aquatic activities throughout a lifetime.

3.5   Identify and demonstrate personal responsibilities for safety and hygiene in the aquatics setting.

Social Interaction

3.6   Explain how to select and modify aquatic activities to allow for participation by younger children, the elderly, and individuals with special needs.

3.7   Analyze the role of social interaction in the successful participation in and enjoyment of aquatic activities.

Group Dynamics

3.8   Accept and perform planned and spontaneous leadership assignments and roles in aquatic activities.

3.9   Analyze the role that cooperation and leadership play in aquatic activities.

3.10   Engage in aquatic activities both in school and outside school.

High School Course 3F: Weight Training and Fitness

High School Courses 1 and 2 are designed to be completed before a student enrolls in High School Course 3F.

STANDARD 1
Students demonstrate knowledge of and competency in motor skills, movement patterns, and strategies needed to perform a variety of physical activities.

1.1   Explain the principles of biomechanics of first-, second-, and third-class levers and apply those principles to a variety of lifting techniques.

1.2   Observe and analyze the lifting techniques of another person (or oneself through video) and write an analysis of the performance.

1.3   Demonstrate proper spotting techniques for all lifts and exercises that require spotting.

1.4   Observe and analyze the techniques of another person (or oneself through video) performing a plyometric exercise and write an analysis of the performance.

1.5   Measure and assess multiple performances of another person in the following areas: balance, reaction time, agility, coordination, power, and speed.

1.6   Identify and apply the principles of biomechanics necessary for the safe and successful performance of weight training.

1.7   List the safety equipment required for participation in weight training; describe and demonstrate the use of such equipment.

1.8   Demonstrate independent learning of movement skills in weight training.

STANDARD 2
Students achieve a level of physical fitness for health and performance while demonstrating knowledge of fitness concepts, principles, and strategies.

2.1   Establish a set of personal physical fitness goals, using the principles of training, and create a strength-training and conditioning program.

2.2   Identify the prime mover muscles, antagonistic muscles, and stabilizer muscles for each of the major weight-training exercises.

2.3   Assess multiple performances of another person in the following areas: muscular strength, muscular endurance, cardiorespiratory endurance, and flexibility.

2.4   Explain how the principles of biomechanics, muscle development, gender, age, training experience, training technique, and specificity affect performance related to strength training.

2.5   Demonstrate and explain the techniques and concepts of three types of weight-training programs.

2.6   Demonstrate and explain the concepts of two different conditioning programs.

2.7   Develop and use a personal physical fitness log to record all workout data on a daily basis.

2.8   Meet increasingly higher levels of speed, strength, power, and endurance.

2.9   Meet physical fitness standards that exceed those of scientifically based health-related fitness assessments.

STANDARD 3
Students demonstrate knowledge of psychological and sociological concepts, principles, and strategies that apply to the learning and performance of physical activity.

Self-Responsibility

3.1   Display safe and responsible behavior while training.

3.2   Describe the role of motivation in physical activity.

3.3   Describe how the perception of effort and quality is a personal assessment and describe the role that perception plays in achieving fitness goals.

3.4   Develop personal goals to improve performance in weight training and fitness.

3.5   Identify and analyze weight-training and fitness activities that enhance personal enjoyment.

3.6   Evaluate the risks and safety factors that may affect participation in weight training and fitness throughout a lifetime.

Social Interaction

3.7   Explain how to select and modify weight-training and fitness activities to allow for participation by younger children, the elderly, and individuals with special needs.

3.8   Analyze the role of social interaction in the successful participation in and enjoyment of weight-training and fitness activities.

Group Dynamics

3.9   Assist others in the achievement of their fitness goals.

Chapter 4
Standards-Based
Physical Education:
Grades Nine
Through Twelve

High School
Course 4

High School Course 4

Twelfth-graders are experiencing systemic changes on their journey to adulthood. By twelfth grade, most students have attained approximately 98 percent of their adult height. As their bodies change and they grow taller, adolescents also put on weight. Girls typically gain 35 pounds during adolescent years, while boys typically gain 45 pounds (Payne and Issacs 1995). Twelfth-grade students are physically able to attain high levels of skills as they continue to specialize in activities of their own choosing.

Adolescents' development brings them to the upper limits of their cognitive potential sometime between sixteen and twenty-five years of age. Twelfth-graders can operate in higher-order thinking. They evaluate their performances, analyze data, reflect on personal goals, and adjust physical activities and goals as necessary. Twelfth-graders want to know why as well as how things work. Teachers explain to students why skills are performed a certain way, practiced in a particular manner, and used in a particular way during physical activity.

Twelfth-graders are becoming more interested in the problems experienced by society. They are narrowing their own career options and lifetime choices. They like to make their own decisions to show their independence. They also are ready to assume a wide variety of leadership roles.

By the twelfth grade, students are prepared to focus on the activities they plan to pursue for recreation or as a career after graduation from high school. Students who complete Course 4 classes are well prepared to continue the activity on their own. They apply social skills acquired in physical education activities to enhance their own experience and the experience of others with whom they are involved in physical and social activities. They are encouraged to support and participate in community organizations that promote health and fitness by providing recreational opportunities for people of all ages.

The Course 4 classes are designed as a continuation of the Course 3 classes. Students who have not completed Course 3 in the same content areas may not be prepared to take Course 4. Because Courses 1, 2, and 3 are designed are prerequisites for Course 4, generally only grade twelve students are enrolled in Course 4. The purpose of Course 4 classes is to deepen student understanding of the content, so that they can meet their health-related physical fitness needs throughout their adulthood.

There are four content areas identified for Course 4:

Course 4A, Advanced Adventure/Outdoor Activities
Course 4B, Advanced Aerobics
Course 4C, Advanced Individual and Dual Activities
Course 4D, Advanced Dance

At a Glance

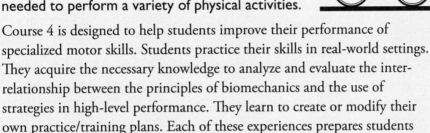

STANDARD 1

Students demonstrate knowledge of and competency in motor skills, movement patterns, and strategies needed to perform a variety of physical activities.

Course 4 is designed to help students improve their performance of specialized motor skills. Students practice their skills in real-world settings. They acquire the necessary knowledge to analyze and evaluate the inter-relationship between the principles of biomechanics and the use of strategies in high-level performance. They learn to create or modify their own practice/training plans. Each of these experiences prepares students for lifelong participation in the activity.

STANDARD 2

Students achieve a level of physical fitness for health and performance while demonstrating knowledge of fitness concepts, principles, and strategies.

In Course 4, students learn to design a personal physical fitness program that can be completed at home or in a gym. They learn to modify their personal program based on the demands of their selected physical activity. Students continue their exercise program to achieve a level of fitness that improves health and performance and prepares them for participation in and enjoyment of their selected activity.

STANDARD 3

Students demonstrate knowledge of psychological and sociological concepts, principles, and strategies that apply to the learning and performance of physical activity.

In Course 4, students learn to evaluate changes in self-responsibility as their skill level in the selected activity improves. They continue to set personal goals for improved performance and enjoyment of the activity. They also learn to perform planned and spontaneous leadership assignments during participation in their activity and to continuously evaluate and improve their leadership skills.

Chapter 4
Standards-Based
Physical Education:
Grades Nine
Through Twelve

High School
Course 4

Learning Snapshots

STANDARD 1

High School Course 4C, Advanced Dual and Individual Activities, Standard 1.3

Create or modify practice/training plans based on evaluative feedback from skill acquisition and performance.

This standard asks students to create a practice plan for improving their performance in their activity of choice. If students are enrolled in a golf class, they create personal golf practice plans. The first step is for the students to analyze their current golf performances. They ask for feedback from the teacher or a peer, or they can have their performances recorded and perform their own analysis.[5] On the basis of feedback for a particular skill (e.g., difficult lie in golf), students classify themselves as beginning, intermediate, or advanced learners. The students then review the various practice protocols (e.g., open skill practice, whole practice, variable practice), selecting those protocols that are appropriate for their level of performance. The last step in the process is for students to create or modify their practice plans.

STANDARD 2

High School Course 4A, Advanced Adventure/Outdoor Activities, Standard 2.2

Design a personal physical fitness program to be completed in a home or gym and that will be consistent with the demands of an adventure/ outdoor activity.

To meet this standard, students design their own physical fitness program. Students first assess themselves using a health-related physical fitness test. They analyze their scores, looking for areas of fitness to maintain and areas for improvement. For each area of health-related physical fitness, they write a personal fitness goal. As they begin to design a fitness program, students list the activities and exercises in which they will engage as a part of their adventure/outdoor education activity course. Finally, they design a personal physical fitness program to maintain their level of fitness and address any areas of improvement that will not be addressed in their physical education course. For example, if a student's upper body strength and cardiorespiratory endurance systems are not at the desired level, she or he may determine that the adventure/outdoor activity course addresses her or his upper body strength needs, but not her or his cardiorespiratory endurance needs. To improve cardiorespiratory endurance, the student develops and implements a cardiorespiratory endurance program outside school.

---

[5] Feedback is most effective when it is specific and positive or specific and corrective.

151

Chapter 4
Standards-Based
Physical Education:
Grades Nine
Through Twelve

STANDARD 3

High School Course 4A, Advanced Adventure/Outdoor Activities, Standard 3.2

Set personal goals for improved performance and enjoyment of adventure/outdoor activities.

Students are asked to develop goals related to improving their performance and enjoyment of adventure/outdoor activities. Students determine their current level of performance and enjoyment. Based on those findings, they write clear, measurable, and achievable goals. The goals are presented to the teacher for feedback and rewritten as necessary.

High School Course 4D, Advanced Dance, Standard 3.3

Perform planned and spontaneous leadership assignments and roles in high-level dance activities.

The content area of dance provides many opportunities for both formal (e.g., choreographer) and informal (e.g., assisting a small group of performers with a particular movement) leadership exercises. The specific leadership style that one assumes depends on the people involved, the task, and the environmental factors. The teacher discusses leadership skills with the students so that they understand the role of a leader. Students are provided with instructional materials, so that they can learn about dance leaders. As students participate in leadership situations, the teacher provides the students with feedback so they can improve.

Chapter 4
Standards-Based
Physical Education:
Grades Nine
Through Twelve

High School
Course 4

High School Courses 4A Through 4D
Physical Education Model Content Standards

High School Course 4A: Advanced Adventure/Outdoor Activities

High School Courses 1, 2, and 3A are designed to be completed before a student enrolls in High School Course 4A.

STANDARD 1

Students demonstrate knowledge of and competency in motor skills, movement patterns, and strategies needed to perform a variety of physical activities.

1.1 Demonstrate expertise in one adventure/outdoor activity.

1.2 Analyze and evaluate the interrelationship of the principles of biomechanics and the use of strategies in high-level performance.

1.3 Create or modify practice/training plans based on evaluative feedback from skill acquisition and performance of adventure/outdoor activities.

1.4 Practice adventure/outdoor activities in real-world settings.

STANDARD 2

Students achieve a level of physical fitness for health and performance while demonstrating knowledge of fitness concepts, principles, and strategies.

2.1 Achieve a level of fitness that improves health and performance and provides opportunities for enjoyment and challenge in an adventure/outdoor activity.

2.2 Design a personal physical fitness program to be completed in a home or gym and that will be consistent with the demands of an adventure/outdoor activity.

STANDARD 3

Students demonstrate knowledge of psychological and sociological concepts, principles, and strategies that apply to the learning and performance of physical activity.

Self-Responsibility

3.1 Evaluate changes in self-responsibility as skill levels in adventure/outdoor activities improve.

3.2 Set personal goals for improved performance and enjoyment of adventure/outdoor activities.

Group Dynamics

3.3 Perform and evaluate planned and spontaneous leadership assignments and roles in high-level adventure/outdoor activities.

153

Chapter 4
Standards-Based
Physical Education:
Grades Nine
Through Twelve

High School Course 4B: Advanced Aerobic Activities

High School Courses 1, 2, and 3B are designed to be completed before a student enrolls in High School Course 4B.

STANDARD 1

Students demonstrate knowledge of and competency in motor skills, movement patterns, and strategies needed to perform a variety of physical activities.

1.1   Demonstrate expertise in two or more of the following aerobic activities, preferably one from each category:

Category 1	*Category 2*
Aerobic dance	Cross-country skiing
Running	Cycling
Skating	Rowing
Swimming	Triathlon
	Walking

1.2   Analyze and evaluate the interrelationship of the principles of biomechanics and the use of strategies in high-level performance.

1.3   Create or modify practice/training plans based on evaluative feedback from skill acquisition and performance.

1.4   Practice aerobic activities in real-world settings.

STANDARD 2

Students achieve a level of physical fitness for health and performance while demonstrating knowledge of fitness concepts, principles, and strategies.

2.1   Identify and achieve levels of personal excellence in health-related physical fitness.

2.2   Adjust personal fitness goals on the basis of fitness assessment measures to improve performance in aerobic activities.

2.3   Design a personal physical fitness program in preparation for the demands of a competitive aerobic activity.

STANDARD 3

Students demonstrate knowledge of psychological and sociological concepts, principles, and strategies that apply to the learning and performance of physical activity.

Self-Responsibility

3.1   Demonstrate a physically active lifestyle that provides for enjoyment and challenge through aerobic activity.

3.2   Identify the qualities of aerobic activity that enhance personal enjoyment.

3.3   Evaluate changes in self-responsibility as skill levels in aerobic activities improve.

3.4   Set personal goals for improved performance and enjoyment of aerobic activities.

Chapter 4
Standards-Based
Physical Education:
Grades Nine
Through Twelve

High School
Course 4

Group Dynamics

3.5   Perform and evaluate planned and spontaneous leadership assignments and roles in high-level aerobic activities.

High School Course 4C: Advanced Individual and Dual Activities

High School Courses 1, 2, and 3C are designed to be completed before a student enrolls in High School Course 4C.

STANDARD 1

Students demonstrate knowledge of and competency in motor skills, movement patterns, and strategies needed to perform a variety of physical activities.

1.1   Demonstrate expertise in two or more of the following individual and dual activities, preferably one from each category:

Individual	*Dual*
Archery	Badminton
Cycling	Handball
Golf	Racquetball
Gymnastics/Tumbling	Squash
Skating	Tennis
Skiing	Two-player volleyball
Surfing	
Yoga	

1.2   Analyze and evaluate the interrelationship of the principles of bio-mechanics and the use of strategies in high-level performance in individual and dual activities.

1.3   Create or modify practice/training plans based on evaluative feedback from skill acquisition and performance.

1.4   Practice individual and dual activities in real-world settings.

STANDARD 2

Students achieve a level of physical fitness for health and performance while demonstrating knowledge of fitness concepts, principles, and strategies.

2.1   Develop personal physical fitness standards that exceed those of a scientifically based health-related physical fitness assessment.

2.2   Demonstrate the ability to develop criteria and analyze factors to consider in the purchase of products and programs related to individual and dual activities.

2.3   Achieve a level of fitness that improves health and performance and provides opportunities for enjoyment and challenge in individual and dual activities.

2.4   Design a personal physical fitness program to be completed in a home or gym and that will be consistent with the demands of a selected individual or dual activity.

155

Chapter 4
Standards-Based
Physical Education:
Grades Nine
Through Twelve

High School
Course 4

STANDARD 3
Students demonstrate knowledge of psychological and sociological concepts, principles, and strategies that apply to the learning and performance of physical activity.

Self-Responsibility

3.1   Evaluate changes in self-responsibility as skill levels in individual and dual activities improve.

3.2   Set personal goals for improved performance and enjoyment of individual and dual activities.

Group Dynamics

3.3   Perform and evaluate planned and spontaneous leadership assignments and roles in high-level individual and dual activities.

High School Course 4D: Advanced Dance

High School Courses 1, 2, and 3D are designed to be completed before a student enrolls in High School Course 4D.

STANDARD 1
Students demonstrate knowledge of and competency in motor skills, movement patterns, and strategies needed to perform a variety of physical activities.

1.1   Demonstrate expertise in two or more of the following dance activities, preferably one from each category:

Category 1	*Category 2*
Ballet	Modern
Folk	Social
Jazz	Square

1.2   Analyze and evaluate the interrelationship of the principles of bio-mechanics and the use of strategies in high-level performance in dance activities.

1.3   Create or modify practice/training plans based on evaluative feedback from skill acquisition and performance.

1.4   Practice dance in real-world settings.

1.5   Demonstrate skills in choreography.

STANDARD 2
Students achieve a level of physical fitness for health and performance while demonstrating knowledge of fitness concepts, principles, and strategies.

2.1   Achieve a level of fitness that improves health and performance and provides opportunities for enjoyment and challenge in a dance activity.

2.2   Design a personal physical fitness program to be completed in a home or gym and that will be consistent with the demands of a dance activity.

2.3   Adjust personal fitness goals on the basis of fitness assessment measures to improve performance in dance activities.

STANDARD 3

Students demonstrate knowledge of psychological and sociological concepts, principles, and strategies that apply to the learning and performance of physical activity.

Self-Responsibility

3.1   Evaluate changes in self-responsibility as skill levels in dance activities improve.

3.2   Set personal goals for improved performance and enjoyment of dance activities.

Group Dynamics

3.3   Perform planned and spontaneous leadership assignments and roles in high-level dance activities.

5

Assessment

Assessment of student learning is a critical component of a standards-based physical education program. It focuses instruction on student learning. Because assessment and instruction are inextricably linked in standards-based instruction, and decisions regarding assessment are made before those on instruction, the assessment chapter has been purposely placed before the chapters related to instruction. This sequence serves as a reminder that if it is important enough for students to learn, then it is important enough to assess. The question teachers ask is no longer "Did I teach the material?" The questions that must be answered are "Did my students learn?" and "What evidence of that learning do I have?" When assessment is used appropriately, it is a powerful instructional tool. It provides evidence of what students have learned and reveals the concepts and skills on which students need additional instruction and practice. Effective teachers use assessment to develop and to alter their instructional plans based on the instructional needs of their students.[1]

Standards-based assessment is an ongoing process of collecting evidence generated by the student's performance measured against the grade- or course-level standards. High-quality assessment is valid, reliable, and objective and answers the critical question "Have the students mastered the standards?" It challenges students to proficiently apply the skills, knowledge, and attitudes called for in the model content standards. Therefore, assessment results are reported to each student in a timely manner, with a focus on the student's strengths and areas in need of improvement.

Types of Assessment

Assessment informs instruction at the beginning (entry level), during (progress monitoring), and at the end (summative) of the learning experience. Those three types of assessment are essential for student learning because they provide direction for instruction. Taken together, they designate the starting place, route to take, point at which to change routes, and the destination.

Entry-Level Assessment

Entry-level assessment measures student mastery of preceding grade- or course-level standards that serve as prerequisite building blocks for the content forthcoming. It also helps the teacher determine which of the current grade- or course-level standards the students have already mastered. For example, the teacher may design a lesson during which students demonstrate their basketball skills at a number of stations at the beginning of the eighth-grade basketball unit to determine students' current levels of performance. The results provide the teacher with information regarding instructional starting points.

---

[1]Many examples and suggestions are provided in this chapter. As with all examples and suggestions in this framework, they are not to be interpreted as requirements or as the only way to assess student learning.

Progress-Monitoring Assessment

Assessment can also reveal the effectiveness of the teacher's instructional decisions and provide insight into how physical education teachers can make learning more meaningful. Quality assessment informs students, teachers, and parents of students' progress toward mastery of the standards throughout the school year.

The most critical guideline for the monitoring of progress is that it should occur at frequent intervals and the assessment data reviewed immediately to adjust instruction. Collecting and acting on information frequently during instruction is a sign of a highly effective program. To ensure the progress of every student, data are examined at the classroom level as well as the individual student level. Because the monitoring of progress is a collaborative professional activity, the data are shared among teachers at the same grade or course level and analyzed to identify student needs and determine which strategies work most effectively.

In standards-based learning, progress monitoring becomes a crucial component of instruction for every student. It is only through such monitoring that teachers can continually adjust instruction so that all students are constantly progressing. No student should languish and be left behind because of a teacher's failure to recognize the student's need for extra help or for a different approach. Similarly, students should not spend time practicing standards already mastered because of a teacher's failure to recognize that they are ready to move on. Assessment that monitors student progress helps steer instruction in the right direction. It signals when alternative routes need to be taken or when the student needs to backtrack to gain more forward momentum.

In one sense, everything students do during instruction is an opportunity for progress monitoring. Teachers continually look for indicators among student responses and performances and in student work. Monitoring can be as simple as demonstrating a skill and asking students to indicate, using thumbs up or thumbs down, whether the skill was performed correctly. It can include checking homework or observing students' performances. Or, it may be a more formal type of assessment, such as short, objective assessments (written quiz, structured observation, skills checklist, etc.) to ensure that student learning of the standard is consistent for the entire class.

The value of using performance data as the basis for making well-informed adjustments to instruction cannot be overstated. Teachers need a solid basis for answering such questions as these:

- Should I move ahead or spend more time on the current phase of instruction?
- Are students able to practice what they have learned through independent activities, or do I need to provide additional instruction?
- Can I accelerate the planned instruction for some or all students and, if so, what is the best way to do that?

Summative Assessment

Summative assessment, which has characteristics similar to those of entry-level assessment, is done to determine whether the student has attained a standard or group of standards. Summative assessment answers questions such as these: Does the student know and understand the concepts? Can he or she perform the skills? Can he or she apply the knowledge? Has he or she reached a sufficiently high level of mastery to move on?

Summative assessment measures in a more formal way the progress students have made toward meeting the standards. Typically, it comes at the end of an instructional unit, course, or school year. The most critical aspect of summative assessment is that it measures the ability of students to transfer what they have learned to related applications. For example, sixth-grade Standard 4.2 states, "Develop a one-day personal physical fitness plan specifying the intensity, time, and types of physical activities for each component of health-related physical fitness." Throughout the school year, teachers may conduct progress-monitoring assessment that asks students to identify the intensity, time, and type of physical activity for each component of health-related physical fitness. However, the summative assessment for this standard requires that students create a one-day personal fitness plan. This plan may take the form of a written schedule, a videotape of the program, or a computer-generated plan. Regardless of the form, the assessment is based on the application of three of the four fitness principles: intensity, time, and type.

Principles of Assessment

The following principles of effective assessment are integrated into the assessment design:

- Select the best evidence of student performance related to the standard.
- Examine the extent to which all students are achieving the grade- or course-level standards.
- Ensure that the assessment measures what it intends to measure as directly as possible (validity).
- Ensure that the assessment produces the same results when repeated (reliability).
- Ensure that the results can be measured the same way by any qualified professional and are not based on that professional's opinion (objectivity).
- Provide assessments that are ongoing and integrated with instruction (embedded assessment).
- Communicate expectations for student achievement at the beginning of the task.
- Create a process of continuous feedback for the student.[2]
- Include student self-reflection and self-assessment as part of the assessment system.
- Ensure that assessments are not biased as to gender, language, or ethnicity.
- Ensure that assessments do not place students with disabilities at a disadvantage.

---

[2]Feedback is most effective when it is specific and positive or specific and corrective.

Standardized assessments meet the principles noted above and the ones below:

- Standardized assessments should be administered under the same conditions to all students.
- Standardized assessments should be administered using the same directions to all students.
- Standardized assessments should be scored in scaled increments small enough to detect varying degrees of skills and knowledge.

Assessment Tools

A variety of assessment tools are used to assess student learning in physical education: structured observations, selected-response/forced-choice items, essay questions, logs, journals, performance tasks, reports, projects, and student portfolios. For some assessment tools (essays, performance tasks, and reports), rubrics are developed to evaluate student learning. Teachers typically use these tools, especially for formal assessments. However, self-assessment and peer assessment are also effective methods.

Students can assess themselves when given lists of performance objectives and directed to judge their own achievement. This procedure is facilitated by the videotaping of the student's performance for follow-up viewing by the student. The results of these assessments demonstrate how students use skills, solve movement problems, and progress over time. Self-assessment also helps motivate students to assume responsibility for their own learning.

In peer assessment, one student compares and contrasts another student's performance according to the criteria established by the teacher, which are based on clear expectations for student achievement. Peer assessment is conducted live or videotaped. As students develop their peer assessment skills, they learn the importance of giving and receiving support and constructive feedback. The results can be communicated verbally or visually using a task card, rating scale, or checklist. However, the teacher is always ultimately responsible for the evaluation of student learning.

Structured Observations

Observation refers to looking at a performance and assessing that performance. This type of assessment has often been criticized for being too subjective. The term "structured observation" refers to observing a performance and assessing the performance using criteria known by both the teacher and students. The use of specific criteria moves the assessment from the subjective side of the assessment continuum to the objective side of the continuum. This tool is especially effective for assessing student performance related to movement, motor, and social skills.

For example, Standard 1.1 for grade seven states, "Demonstrate mature techniques for the following patterns: overhand, sidearm, and underhand throwing; catching; kicking/punting; striking; trapping; dribbling (hand and foot); and volleying." One assessment tool for this standard is the structured observation.

For it to be an objective measure, there must be criteria against which student performance is measured. (See the sample six-point rubric for this standard under the "Rubrics" section later in this chapter.)

Structured observations are conducted through a variety of methods, including station approach and embedded assessment. In the station-approach scenario, students are assigned to one of several stations in a circuit. Some stations involve exercising, while others involve motor skill practice and mini-games. One station is designated as the testing station where students meet with the teacher for motor skills assessment. Embedded assessment refers to the assessment of learning as students are practicing skills—it occurs simultaneously with instruction. The assessment can take place periodically throughout the learning sequence (progress monitoring) or at the conclusion of the unit (summative assessment).

Selected-Response/Forced-Choice Items

Selected-response and forced-choice items are written test questions to assess students' cognitive learning. In selected-response and forced-choice questions, students select a single correct response. This type of assessment has a valid role in assessing pure knowledge and facts, but it is possible for students to guess the correct response to these questions instead of actually demonstrating their learning. Examples of selected-response/forced-choice items include traditional multiple-choice items, matching tests, true/false tests, and fill-in-the blanks from a list of choices.

For example, Standard 2.12 for grade two states, "Identify the different points of contact when striking a balloon upward and striking a balloon forward." This standard can be assessed using a multiple-choice question. The correct answer and distracters (incorrect answers) are illustrations appropriate for each point of contact and the questions are written at the second-grade reading level.

1. How do you make the balloon go up?
   a. Hit the right side.
   b. Hit the left side.
   c. Hit the bottom.
   d. Hit the top.

Standard 2.6 for fourth grade states, "Distinguish between punting and kicking and describe the similarities and differences." Using a Venn diagram, students are asked to fill in (from a list) the similarities and differences between punting and kicking.

Essay Questions

Essay questions are useful for exploring in greater depth students' ability to apply the facts, concepts, principles, and theories learned in physical education. The questions typically take more time than multiple-choice or short-answer tests, and they are also more complex to grade. They are usually graded with a rubric that is created by the teacher and shared with the students in advance. In evaluating essay responses in physical education, teachers need to be careful to differenti-

ate between students' actual lack of knowledge (or misunderstanding) of physical education content and limited reading or writing ability. Examples follow.

Standard 4.7 for grade three states, "Describe the relationship between the heart, lungs, muscles, blood, and oxygen during physical activity." One example of an essay question for this standard is:

How do your heart, lungs, muscles, blood, and oxygen work together when you are physically active?

Standard 2.6 for grade four states, "Distinguish between punting and kicking and describe the similarities and differences." One example of an essay question for this standard reads:

How are punting and kicking the same and how are they different?

Standard 4.12 for grade five states, "Explain how technology can assist in the pursuit of physical fitness." One example of an essay question for this standard reads:

Describe one type of technology that can help improve your personal physical fitness. Tell how this technology can help you meet your personal fitness goals.

Standard 4.3 for grade seven states, "Match personal preferences in physical activities with each of the five components of health-related physical fitness." One example of an essay question for this standard reads:

List the types of physical activities you enjoy doing and describe how that activity matches one or more of the components of health-related physical fitness.

High School Course 1, Standard 2.11 states, "Explain the role of physical activity in the prevention of disease and the reduction of health care costs." One example of an essay question is:

You have learned that physical activity will help you live a longer and healthier life. Explain the role physical activity plays in the prevention of disease and the reduction of health care costs.

High School Course 1, Standard 3.4 states, "Describe the enjoyment, self-expression, challenge, and social benefits experienced by achieving one's best in physical activities." One example of an essay question for this standard reads:

Today you participated in a timed long-distance run, and you achieved your personal best time. Describe the enjoyment, self-expression, challenge, and social benefits you experienced by achieving this personal best.

High School Course 2, Standard 2.8 states, "Explain how to evaluate consumer physical fitness products and programs." One example of an essay question for this standard reads:

What are the factors that you would consider when evaluating physical fitness products? How would you use these factors to evaluate fitness products?

Logs

Logs provide students with the opportunity to record data. Teachers periodically review the data with the students and provide feedback on the student's progress. These data can include:

- Physical activity performed outside the school day
- The frequency, intensity, time, and type of exercise performed daily
- Scores on motor skill assessments to demonstrate improvement over time

It is important to match the log to a specific standard. For example, Standard 3.3 for grade three states, "Participate three to four days each week, for increasing periods of time, in continuous moderate to vigorous physical activities that require sustained movement of the large-muscle groups to increase breathing and heart rate."

Students use logs to monitor their participation. Each student's log includes space to record the date, activity, and amount of time engaged in activities that meet the criteria (sustained movement of large-muscle groups, increased breathing and heart rate).

Standard 4.11 for grade five states, "Measure and record the heart rate before, during, and after vigorous physical activity."

Students record their heart rates in a log. The log includes columns for the date and heart rate before activity, during activity, and after activity.

Standard 3.6 for grade seven states, "Assess periodically the attainment of, or progress toward, personal physical fitness goals and make necessary adjustments to a personal physical fitness program."

Students monitor their physical fitness progress in a log. The log can be used on a monthly or bimonthly basis and includes the fitness goals and columns for the name of the fitness test, date the test was administered, and the student's score.

Journals

Journals provide students with the opportunity to record their insights, reactions, and reflections. They are especially effective for assessing student learning related to Overarching Standard 5 (kindergarten through grade eight) and Overarching Standard 3 (high school). Through the journal-writing process, students document their own growth over time. Journal writing may take place during lesson closure or as a homework assignment. At the elementary school level, journal writing can also be done after the physical education lesson when students are back in the classroom. The journal may be specific to physical education or a history-social studies journal or a language arts journal or another subject related to the prompt. Examples of writing prompts for student journals used as an assessment tool in physical education are as follows:

Standard 5.8 for grade five states, "Appreciate physical games and activities reflecting diverse heritages." An appropriate journal prompt for this standard is:

What did you appreciate most about the heritage of the game you played today? Why did you appreciate that aspect of the game?

Standard 5.4 for grade seven states, "Evaluate the effect of expressing encouragement to others while participating in a group physical activity." An appropriate journal prompt for this standard is:

At the beginning of the lesson we identified ways to express encouragement both verbally and nonverbally. During the lesson you had the opportunity to use these ideas. How did someone's encouragement affect your participation in the activity? When you encouraged others, what was the result of that encouragement?

High School Course 1, Standard 3.10 states, "Identify and utilize the potential strengths of each individual in physical activities." An appropriate journal prompt for this standard is:

Today you were involved in a team building activity. Identify the strengths of your team members and tell how you utilized their strengths for your team to be successful.

Performance Tasks

Performance tasks require students to accomplish complex tasks by using prior knowledge and recent learning and skills. These tasks demonstrate a deeper understanding of the content and skills and increase student engagement. Performance assessment involves students in situations where they must construct responses that clearly illustrate higher-level thinking skills. These tasks often have more than one acceptable response; therefore, when assessing student responses, teachers allow for novel responses. Creating a list of possible solutions ahead of time provides the teacher with an objective method for assessing the performance task.

For example, Standard 1.4 for second grade states, "Create a routine that includes two types of body rolls (e.g., log roll, egg roll, shoulder roll, forward roll) and a stationary balance position after each roll."

For this performance task, students demonstrate their ability in a routine of their own creation to perform smoothly two types of body rolls and their ability to balance, in a moment of stillness, after each roll.

Standard 1.1 for fifth grade states, "Perform simple small-group balance stunts by distributing weight and base of support."

For this performance task, students in groups of four perform a minimum of five balance stunts. Each stunt includes all members of the group. All five stunts must use a wide base of support, and the weight of the group must be evenly distributed among group members.

Standard 1.2 for eighth grade states, "Create and perform a square dance."

For this performance task, small groups of students create a novel square dance that uses eight of the calls previously taught. Students set their square dance routine to music and perform it for the class.

Standard 2.6 for eighth grade states, "Develop and teach a team game that uses elements of spin or rebound, designated offensive and defensive space, a penalty system, and a scoring system."

For this performance task, students develop a game that uses elements of spin or rebound, and they teach their game to other students. The new game must include a method of scoring, an organizational pattern, player movement, limitations (rules), and penalties for rule violation. The students write down the game rules and required components and then teach the game to other students. The writing and the teaching are both performance tasks.

High School Course 2, Standard 1.10 states, "Analyze situations to determine appropriate strategies to use in combative, gymnastic/tumbling, and team activities."

For this performance task, students are provided with an attack situation in combatives that they must analyze to determine the best defensive response. In gymnastics/tumbling a performance task may include analyzing a routine carefully to select where best in the routine to add a balance sequence. Once students have determined the appropriate strategies, they defend their choice. This defense can be either oral or written.

Reports

Reports require students to search through a variety of resources in the classroom or library/media center (e.g., video clips, books, magazines, online databases, or other Internet resources); find the most relevant, accurate, and up-to-date information on a specific topic; and write a summary. Writing reports is an option for every standard that has a cognitive component. For example, High School Course 1, Standard 2.11 states, "Explain the role of physical activity in the prevention of disease and the reduction of health care costs." Assigning a written report would be an appropriate way to assess students' mastery of the standard. Students are given time during class or receive a homework assignment to research the topic and write the report following carefully selected criteria. The teacher explains the criteria when assigning the report. Reports may also be delivered as oral presentations using visual aids such as computer-based presentations.

Other standards for which reports are an appropriate way to assess achievement include:

- Standard 4.5 for fourth grade: "Explain why the body needs water before, during, and after physical activity."

- Standard 2.1 for fifth grade: "Explain the importance of open space in playing sport-related games."

- Standard 2.1 for sixth grade: "Explain how to increase force based on the principles of biomechanics."

- Standard 4.4 for seventh grade: "Explain the effects of physical activity on heart rate during exercise, during the recovery phase, and while the body is at rest."

- Standard 2.2 for eighth grade: "Explain the rotation principles used in performing various manipulative skills."

Projects

Projects are activities that may require as much as several weeks to complete. Numerous products may be created for a project, including graphs, posters, calendars, presentations, electronic presentations (using a computer and projection system), and multimedia products that combine text, still images, digitized sound, and digitized video clips. Multimedia projects are ideal for interdisciplinary work because students can integrate content from physical education, computer skills from their computer class, and writing and speaking skills from their English-language arts class in the development of the project.

Whether the project is for a single subject or interdisciplinary, students need to focus both on the individual components of the project and on putting those components into a complete project. Examples of projects are as follows:

Standard 2.5 for grade seven states, "Compare and contrast the effectiveness of practicing skills as a whole and practicing skills in smaller parts."

In motor learning language, this is known as whole and part practice. Students are asked to research the two different types of practice and then to present their findings in the format of a graphic organizer (e.g., table or chart, Venn diagram) to the entire class.

Standard 4.5 for grade seven states, "Describe the role of physical activity and nutrition in achieving physical fitness."

Students research one aspect of physical activity or nutrition that has a possible effect on physical fitness. Students create a visual aid (such as a poster or graph) and prepare a commercial (or public service announcement) to present live or on videotape emphasizing the positive effect of the activity or aspect of nutrition.

Other standards for which projects could be assigned for assessment purposes include:

- Standard 4.6 for second grade: "Compare and contrast the function of the heart during rest and during physical activity."

- Standard 2.10 for fourth grade: "Design a routine to music that includes even and uneven locomotor patterns."

- Standard 1.11 for sixth grade: "Design and perform smooth, flowing sequences of stunts, tumbling, and rhythmic patterns that combine traveling, rolling, balancing, and transferring weight."

- Standard 4.1 for eighth grade: "Develop a two-week personal physical fitness plan specifying the proper warm-up and cool-down activities and the principles of exercise for each of the five components of health-related physical fitness."

- High School Course 2, Standard 1.12: "Evaluate independent learning of movement skills."

Student Portfolios

Portfolios are collections of students' work related to the grade- or course-level standards and may be either paper or digital. Portfolios help students observe improvement in their work and assist teachers with assessing student progress and the effectiveness of their teaching strategies. When the portfolios are reviewed according to predetermined criteria, the teacher and students can determine the levels of content mastery already achieved. Portfolios can also be used to demonstrate to parents how far students have advanced toward the goal of content mastery.

There are several types of portfolios:

Process portfolios. Process portfolios demonstrate the student's mastery over time. During the school year or length of the course, teachers and students periodically discuss the work in the portfolio to determine progress and areas needing improvement. An ideal use of the process portfolio in physical education is monitoring student performance of motor skills throughout the school year. Students are videotaped on a periodic basis, and their performances are inserted into a digital portfolio. Students and their parents can view the development of their skill performance throughout the school year.

Portfolios of assessment tasks. Portfolios of assessment tasks include a series of specific tasks or assignments usually related to the mastery of a set of specific content. An example of an assessment portfolio for physical education is a fitness portfolio. A fitness portfolio includes assessments related to each of the standards under the overarching fitness standards.

Best-work portfolios. The portfolios showcase students' best work related to each grade-level or course-level standard throughout the school year. Usually the teacher and the student jointly select the items. The portfolios are typically used in formal and informal reviews of student progress. An example of a best-work portfolio in physical education is a comprehensive portfolio with at least one assessment related to each grade-level or course-level standard.

Digital portfolios. Digital portfolios are an electronic extension of the paper portfolio. Using a computer, students can store text, graphics, video clips, and audio clips along with complete multimedia projects in a digital format. The digital version provides both students and teacher with a means of tracking and accessing large amounts of data from a variety of formats in a short period of time.

Rubrics

Whenever a performance assessment tool is used, a rubric of explicit criteria for evaluating students' work is determined by the teacher and shared with the students before the assessment is conducted. A rubric is a fixed scale showing the characteristics of performance for each point on the scale. If the student's performance is between two levels, his or her score is the lower number. Rubrics are most often used to rate performance tasks and essays, but they can be modified for many types of assessment tools. A teacher developing rubrics should consider the following points:

- The scale includes three or more levels.
- The points of the scale (levels of student performance) are equidistant on a continuum.
- Descriptors are meaningful.
- Descriptors clearly define each level of performance.
- The highest point indicates exemplary performance.

Six-point rubrics and four-point rubrics are the most common formats. On a six-point rubric, levels 5 and 6 describe competency beyond "meeting the standard" in order to motivate highly skilled students. Level 4 describes "meeting the standard." Levels 2 and 3 describe moving toward the standard, and level 1 represents a lack of any knowledge or skill related to the standard.

On a four-point rubric, level 3 denotes "meeting the standard" of minimum competency. Level 4 describes competency beyond "meeting the standard," level 2 describes a beginner, and level 1 represents a lack of any knowledge or skill related to the standard.

Here is an example of a six-point rubric for assessing a portion of Standard 1.1 for grade seven: "Demonstrate the mature technique for the following patterns: overhand, sidearm, and underhand throwing; catching; kicking/punting; striking; trapping; dribbling (hand and foot); and volleying." Remember, level 4 is the minimum competency level for a six-point rubric; so there is a direct match between the standard and the student's performance at this level. Level 2 describes the beginning stage of learning, and level 3 describes the intermediate stage of learning. These two levels are derived from research on motor development that delineates the stages of development for fundamental movement and motor skills (Gallahue and Ozmun 2006). Levels 5 and 6 are beyond the mastery level called for in the standard. Level 5 requires the student to demonstrate the correct technique while generating additional force (distance) and accuracy, and level 6 requires the student to demonstrate the correct technique in an open environment.

Sample Rubric

Level 6	*Demonstrates the mature stage for the overhand pattern in a game setting.*

Level 5	*Demonstrates the mature stage for the overhand pattern along with accuracy from a variety of distances.*

Level 4 *Demonstrates the mature stage for the overhand pattern:*
1. Player stands with side to target.
2. Arm is swung upward, sideways, and backward to position of elbow flexion.
3. Trunk rotates to the throwing side.
4. Player steps forward with nondominant foot transferring weight.
5. Body rotation forward occurs through lower body, then upper body, and then shoulders.
6. Elbow leads arm movement, followed by forearm extension and wrist snap.
7. There is arm follow-through in the direction of the target.

Level 3 *Demonstrates the elementary stage for the overhand pattern:*
- Player faces target with feet parallel.
- Arm is swung upward, sideways, and backward to position of elbow flexion.
- Player steps forward incorrectly with foot on same side of body as throwing arm.
- Body rotates and body weight shifts forward with the step.
- Elbow leads the way in the arm movement.

Level 2 *Demonstrates the initial stage for the overhand pattern:*
- Player stands facing the target.
- Action is mainly from the elbow.
- Action resembles a push.
- There is little or no rotation.
- Feet remain stationary.
- Follow-through is forward and downward.

Level 1 *Demonstrates random attempts to throw the ball:*
- Player stands erect facing the target.
- Force originates from flexing the hip.
- The ball is thrown with very little arm action.

Assessing the Skills and Concepts Learned

Students are assessed on the model content standards to determine the degree of student learning. The following five-step process for assessing student learning related to each standard is one approach to ensuring that the assessment aligns with the standard:

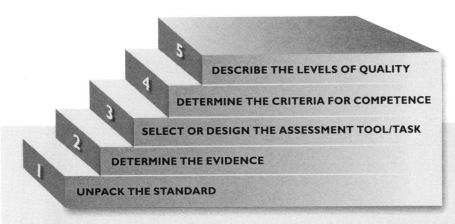

Step 1: Reveal all the content in the standard by "unpacking" a standard. Unpacking reveals the depth and breadth of the content in each standard and provides the foundation for knowing what learning should be assessed.

Step 2: Determine the evidence students must generate to demonstrate that they have learned the content.

Step 3: Select or design the assessment tool/task that allows students to demonstrate their learning.

Step 4: Determine the criteria for competence.

Step 5: Describe levels of quality.

An example of the five-step process for assessment in action follows. As with all examples in this framework, the example is not to be interpreted as a requirement or as the only way to assess this standard.

GRADE 7, STANDARD 1.1

Demonstrate mature techniques for the following patterns: overhand, sidearm, and underhand throwing; catching; kicking/punting; striking; trapping; dribbling (hand and foot); and volleying.

1 UNPACK THE STANDARD

Demonstrate mature technique for the hand dribble.

What is the verb: *Demonstrate*

What is the level of proficiency (if available): *Mature technique*

What is the skill or content: *Hand dribble*

2 DETERMINE THE EVIDENCE

Hand dribble a ball with mature technique.

3 SELECT OR DESIGN THE ASSESSMENT TOOL/TASK

Structured observation: *Students demonstrate with mature technique the hand dribble.*

4 DETERMINE THE CRITERIA FOR COMPETENCE

1. Bend slightly at waist and knees.
2. Keep head up with eyes looking forward.
3. Push the ball down and slightly forward with spread fingers of dominant hand.
4. Flex wrist and extend elbow to impart force.
5. Keep the ball below waist.

5 DESCRIBE THE LEVELS OF QUALITY

Level 6	*Demonstrates the mature stage for dribbling in a game setting*
Level 5	*Demonstrates the mature stage for dribbling when moving around stationary objects*
Level 4	*Demonstrates the mature stage for dribbling* 1. Bend slightly at waist and knees. 2. Keep the head up with eyes looking forward. 3. Push the ball down and slightly forward with spread fingers of dominant hand. 4. Flex wrist and extend elbow to impart force. 5. Keep the ball below waist.
Level 3	*Demonstrates the elementary stage of development for dribbling* • Hold the ball with both hands. • Position one hand on top and the other near the bottom of the ball. • Slap the ball with the hand for subsequent bounces. • Use inconsistent force for downward thrust. • Lean slightly forward with the ball at chest level.
Level 2	*Demonstrates the initial stage of development for dribbling* • Hold the ball with both hands. • Place hands on the sides of the ball with palms facing each other. • Use both arms for downward thrust. • Bounce the ball so it contacts the ground and is close to the body. • Repeat bounce-and-catch pattern.
Level 1	*Demonstrates random attempts to dribble the ball* Slap at the ball.

Assessment of Motor Skills

The most common tool for assessing motor skill performance is structured observation. It is the assessment tool used for each of the examples in this section. Structured observation is typically used together with a rubric, although a checklist or criterion-referenced scale may also be used. The three standards in this section all relate to catching to illustrate assessment at different grade levels.

GRADE 1, STANDARD 1.13
Catch, showing proper form, a gently thrown ball.

1 UNPACK THE STANDARD

What is the verb: *Catch*
What is the level of proficiency (if available): *Proper form*
What is the skill or content: *Catch (gently thrown ball)*

2 DETERMINE THE EVIDENCE

Catch a ball that is gently thrown to them, demonstrating proper form for catching.

3 SELECT OR DESIGN THE ASSESSMENT TOOL/TASK

Structured observation: *Students demonstrate the skill of catching when receiving a gently thrown ball by another student or the teacher.*

4 DETERMINE THE CRITERIA FOR COMPETENCE

1. Watch the ball.
2. Extend arms.
3. Grasp the ball with both hands.
4. "Give" with the ball on contact to reduce impact force.

5 DESCRIBE THE LEVELS OF QUALITY

Level 6	*Demonstrates the mature stage for catching in an open environment*
Level 5	*Demonstrates the mature stage for catching a ball tossed off center*
Level 4	*Demonstrates the mature stage (all four critical elements) for catching* 1. Watch the ball. 2. Extend arms. 3. Grasp the ball with both hands. 4. "Give" with the ball on contact to reduce impact force.
Level 3	*Demonstrates the elementary stage of development for catching* Prepares for the catch by lifting arms, bending arms slightly, attempting to make contact with hands first, and using the chest as a backstop.
Level 2	*Demonstrates the initial stage of development for catching* Makes an anticipatory movement, holds arms in front of body, with elbows extended and palms up; bends arms at elbows; cradles ball.
Level 1	*Demonstrates random attempts to catch the object* Attempts to trap the ball.

GRADE 2, STANDARD 1.10

Catch a gently thrown ball below the waist, reducing the impact force.

1 UNPACK THE STANDARD

What is the verb: *Catch*
What is the skill or content: *catch (gently thrown ball below the waist)*

2 DETERMINE THE EVIDENCE

Catch a gently thrown ball below the waist while clearly displaying the body positions and movements needed to reduce impact force.

3 SELECT OR DESIGN THE ASSESSMENT TOOL/TASK

Structured observation: *Students demonstrate the skill of catching below the waist when receiving a gently thrown ball by another student or the teacher.*

4 DETERMINE THE CRITERIA FOR COMPETENCE

1. Watch the ball.
2. Point fingers down.
3. Extend both arms.
4. Grasp the ball with both hands.
5. "Give" with the ball on contact.

5 DESCRIBE THE LEVELS OF QUALITY

Level 6	*Demonstrates the mature stage for catching in an open environment*
Level 5	*Demonstrates the mature stage for catching a ball tossed off center*
Level 4	*Demonstrates the mature stage (all five critical elements) for catching* 1. Watch the ball. 2. Point fingers down. 3. Extend both arms. 4. Grasp the ball with both hands. 5. "Give" with the ball on contact.
Level 3	*Demonstrates the elementary stage of development for catching* Prepares for the catch by lifting arms, bending arms slightly, attempting to make contact with the hands first, and using the chest as a backstop.
Level 2	*Demonstrates the initial stage of development for catching* Makes an anticipatory movement, holds arms in front of body, with elbows extended and palms up; bends arms at elbows; cradles ball.
Level 1	*Demonstrates random attempts to catch the object* Attempts to trap the ball.

GRADE 7, STANDARD 1.1

Demonstrate the mature technique for catching.

1 UNPACK THE STANDARD.

What is the verb: *Demonstrate*
What is the level of proficiency: *Mature technique*
What is the skill or content: *Catching*

2 DETERMINE THE EVIDENCE

Catch a ball while displaying mature technique.

3 SELECT OR DESIGN THE ASSESSMENT TOOL/TASK

Structured observation: *Students demonstrate the mature technique for catching.*

4 DETERMINE THE CRITERIA FOR COMPETENCE

1. Watch the ball.
2. Move to the ball.
3. Position one foot ahead of the other.
4. Hands are positioned with fingers pointing up if the ball is above the waist, and hands are positioned with fingers pointed down if ball is below the waist.
5. Extend both arms.
6. Grasp the ball with two hands.
7. "Give" with the ball on contact.

5 DESCRIBE THE LEVELS OF QUALITY

Level 6	*Demonstrates the mature stage for catching in a game setting*
Level 5	*Demonstrates the mature stage for catching a variety of thrown balls*
Level 4	*Demonstrates the mature stage (all seven key elements in place) for catching* 1. Watch the ball. 2. Move to the ball. 3. Position one foot ahead of the other. 4. Hands are positioned with fingers pointing up if the ball is above the waist, and hands are positioned with fingers pointing down if the ball is below the waist. 5. Extend both arms. 6. Grasp the ball with two hands. 7. "Give" with the ball on contact.
Level 3	*Demonstrates the elementary stage of development for catching* Prepares for the catch by lifting arms, bending arms slightly, attempting to make contact with hands first, and using the chest as a backstop.
Level 2	*Demonstrates the initial stage of development for catching* Makes an anticipatory movement, holds arms in front of body, with elbows extended and palms up; bends arms at elbows; cradles ball.
Level 1	*Demonstrates random attempts to catch the object* Attempts to trap the ball.

Assessment of Movement Concepts, Principles, and Strategies

The most common tools for assessing standards related to movement concepts, principles, and strategies are selected-response questions, essay questions, reports, and projects. The first two examples in this section address information related to critical features, and the third example addresses information related to game tactics.

Critical Features

KINDERGARTEN, STANDARD 2.8

Describe the position of the fingers in the follow-through phase of bouncing a ball continuously.

1   UNPACK THE STANDARD.

What is the verb: *Describe*
What is the skill or content: *Follow-through phase of bouncing a ball continuously*

2   DETERMINE THE EVIDENCE

An oral description of the position of the fingers during the follow-through phase of bouncing a ball continuously.

3   SELECT OR DESIGN THE ASSESSMENT TOOL/TASK

Question (oral response): *When you are bouncing a ball, what is the position of the fingers when the ball hits the ground (follow-through phase)?*

4   DETERMINE THE CRITERIA FOR COMPETENCE

1. Student responds that fingers point down when the ball hits the ground.

5   DESCRIBE THE LEVELS OF QUALITY

Level 4	*Student describes that the fingers point down in the follow-through phase and adds that the fingers point up in the initial contact phase.*
Level 3	*Student describes that the fingers point down.*
Level 2	*Student describes that the fingers point anywhere but down.*
Level 1	*Student does not respond.*

GRADE 7, STANDARD 2.1

Identify and describe key elements in the mature performance of dribbling (hand).

UNPACK THE STANDARD

What is the verb: *Identify and describe*
What is the level of performance: *Mature performance*
What is the skill or content: *Hand dribbling*

2 **DETERMINE THE EVIDENCE**

Must be able to identify the key elements for dribbling when presented with those and other choices that may not be considered key elements for dribbling. A description (written or oral) of the key elements in mature performance of hand dribbling constitutes evidence of student learning.

3 **SELECT OR DESIGN THE ASSESSMENT TOOL/TASK**

Both actions (verbs) must be assessed. The selected-response question addresses identification, and the essay question addresses description of the key elements.

Selected Response/Forced Choice

Which of the following techniques are key elements in the mature performance of the hand dribble?

[List a variety of correct and incorrect responses for the student to choose.]

Essay Question

What are the key elements in the mature performance of a hand dribble?

4 **DETERMINE THE CRITERIA FOR COMPETENCE**

Student identifies (selected response) and describes (essay question) the following:

1. Ball dribbled with fingers
2. Ball rebounds to waist height
3. One hand dribbles the ball at a time
4. Look up

5 **DESCRIBE THE LEVELS OF QUALITY**

Selected Response/Forced Choice	
Level 4	*Correctly identifies the four key elements of a hand dribble plus an additional correct answer from the list*
Level 3	*Correctly identifies the four key elements of a hand dribble*
Level 2	*Correctly identifies two of the key elements of a hand dribble*
Level 1	*Does not correctly identify any key elements of a hand dribble*
Essay Question	
Level 4	*Correctly describes the four key elements of a hand dribble plus an additional correct answer from the list*
Level 3	*Correctly describes the four key elements of a hand dribble*
Level 2	*Correctly describes two key elements of a hand dribble a ball*
Level 1	*Does not respond*

Game Tactics

HIGH SCHOOL COURSE 2, STANDARD 1.4

Explain and demonstrate advanced offensive, defensive, and transition strategies and tactics in combative, gymnastic/tumbling, and team activities.

1 UNPACK THE STANDARD

What is the verb: *Explain and demonstrate*
What is the level of proficiency: *Advanced*
What is the skill or content: *Offensive, defensive, and transition strategies for volleyball*

2 DETERMINE THE EVIDENCE

An explanation (written or oral) of advanced offensive, defensive, and transition strategies and tactics in combative, gymnastic/tumbling, and team activities. A demonstration of advanced offensive, defensive, and transition strategies and tactics in combative, gymnastic/tumbling, and team activities.

3 SELECT OR DESIGN THE ASSESSMENT TOOL/TASK

Because there are two verbs, this item requires that students provide evidence of learning both skills. Two assessments are used in this example, each assessing one of the verbs.

Project
Explain three advanced offensive strategic concepts, three transition strategic concepts, and three defensive strategic concepts used in volleyball.

Structured observation
Demonstrate three advanced offensive strategic concepts, three transition strategic concepts, and three defensive strategic concepts used in volleyball.

4 DETERMINE THE CRITERIA FOR COMPETENCE

Advanced offensive strategic concepts for volleyball

1. Create space.
   - Send the ball to an open space.
   - Send the ball to a weak player.
   - Fake a hit in one direction and then send the ball in a different direction.
2. Send the ball low over the net to opponents to reduce the time that they have to return the ball.
3. Change positions so players are placed according to their strengths (e.g., move the setter to the center front position).

Advanced defensive strategic concepts for volleyball

1. Maintain an unobstructed view of the net and the opposing team.
2. Close space.
   - Cover all court space (e.g., w formation on serve receive).
   - Cover the areas where the ball is most likely to land (e.g., block formation when defending against a spike).
3. Prepare for all possible attacks.
   - Be prepared to cover the space of the court against a spike or less forceful hit over the net.

Advanced transition strategies for volleyball

1. Transition from defense to offense by immediately moving from block coverage to a w formation.
2. Transition from offense to defense by immediately moving from a spike coverage setup to a block coverage setup.
3. Support the spiker by covering all possible space where a spike could be returned.

5 DESCRIBE THE LEVELS OF QUALITY

Project	
Level 4	*Players are able to explain correctly all nine strategic concepts and give a specific example of each one.*
Level 3	*Players are able to explain correctly all nine strategic concepts.*
Level 2	*Players are able to explain correctly two strategic concepts each for offense, defense, and transitions.*
Level 1	*Players are unable to explain any strategies.*

Structured Observation	
Level 4	*Players are able to demonstrate correctly all nine strategic concepts during a game situation.*
Level 3	*Players are able to demonstrate correctly all nine strategic concepts.*
Level 2	*Players are able to demonstrate correctly two strategic concepts each for offense, defense, and transitions.*
Level 1	*Players are unable to demonstrate any strategic concepts.*

Assessment of Physical Fitness Performance

Fitness assessment is an ongoing process that helps students to improve their personal fitness. Therefore, many standards in this section build from one grade or course level to the next. Verbs commonly used for standards related to physical fitness performance are *perform*, *participate*, and *demonstrate*. Assessment tools for those standards include structured observation and log.

GRADE 5, STANDARD 3.4

Perform an increasing number of oblique curl-ups on each side.

1 UNPACK THE STANDARD

What is the verb: *Perform*
What is the skill or content: *Oblique curl-ups on each side*

2 DETERMINE THE EVIDENCE

Data collected from a sequence of performances that spans time and shows an increasing number of oblique curl-ups.

3 SELECT OR DESIGN THE ASSESSMENT TOOL/TASK

Structured observation: *Count the number of oblique curl-ups performed on each side during a pretest and post-test.*

DETERMINE THE CRITERIA FOR COMPETENCE

1. Increases the number of oblique curl-ups performed on each side

 DESCRIBE THE LEVELS OF QUALITY

Level 4	*Increases the number of oblique curl-ups performed on each side by at least five*
Level 3	*Increases the number of oblique curl-ups performed on each side by at least one*
Level 2	*Increases the number of oblique curl-ups performed on one side by at least one*
Level 1	*There is no increase in the number of oblique curl-ups performed*

GRADE 6, STANDARD 3.4

Participate in moderate to vigorous physical activity a minimum of four days each week.

 UNPACK THE STANDARD

What is the verb: *Participate*

What is the skill or content: *Physical activity*

 DETERMINE THE EVIDENCE

Data to demonstrate participation at least four days a week in moderate to vigorous physical activity.

 SELECT OR DESIGN THE ASSESSMENT TOOL/TASK

Log noting the type of activity, level of activity (moderate, vigorous), and date performed

 DETERMINE THE CRITERIA FOR COMPETENCE

1. Four days each week
2. Moderate to vigorous level

DESCRIBE THE LEVELS OF QUALITY

Level 4	*Logs moderate to vigorous activity five times or more per week*
Level 3	*Logs moderate to vigorous activity four times a week*
Level 2	*Logs moderate to vigorous activity two times a week*
Level 1	*Logs no moderate to vigorous activity*

Assessment of Physical Fitness Concepts and Principles

The physical fitness concepts and principles are cognitive standards. Common assessment tools for cognitive standards are selected response-questions and essay questions. However, reports and projects may also be used.

GRADE 3, STANDARD 4.14

Identify flexibility exercises that are not safe for the joints and should be avoided.

1 **UNPACK THE STANDARD**

What is the verb: *Identify*
What is the skill or content: *Unsafe flexibility exercises*

2 **DETERMINE THE EVIDENCE**

From a list of several flexibility exercises, students identify those that are not safe for joints.

3 **SELECT OR DESIGN THE ASSESSMENT TOOL/TASK**

Selected response:

Circle the exercises below that are not safe for joints.

The teacher provides a work sheet illustrated with pictures of the lower back stretch, hurdler stretch, reverse hurdler stretch, ballistic windmills, back saver sit-and-reach, neck circles, straight-leg standing toe touches, forward lunges, arm circles, and across-chest stretch.

4 **DETERMINE THE CRITERIA FOR COMPETENCE**

The student identifies any four of the following exercises as unsafe:
hurdler stretch, neck circles, straight leg standing toe touches, arm circles, and ballistic windmill.

5 **DESCRIBE THE LEVELS OF QUALITY**

Level 4	Correctly identifies five (hurdler stretch, neck circles, straight-leg standing toe touches, arm circles, and ballistic windmills) as unsafe exercises
Level 3	Correctly identifies four unsafe exercises
Level 2	Correctly identifies two unsafe exercises
Level 1	Does not identify any unsafe exercises

HIGH SCHOOL COURSE 2, STANDARD 2.8

Explain how to evaluate consumer physical fitness products and programs.

1 **UNPACK THE STANDARD.**

What is the verb: *Explain*
What is the skill or content: *Consumer physical fitness products and programs*

2 **DETERMINE THE EVIDENCE**

An explanation (written or oral) of how to evaluate fitness products and programs.

SELECT OR DESIGN THE ASSESSMENT TOOL/TASK

Essay question: *You are setting up a home gym. How would you evaluate the physical fitness products you would use in your home gym? Provide an example of one piece of equipment.*

4 DETERMINE THE CRITERIA FOR COMPETENCE

- Take time to compare costs, features, and quality.
- Try out any piece of equipment or program before you spend your money.
- Document the evidence that supports the program or product.
- Evaluate the credibility of claims about the product or program.
- Buy only quality equipment.
- Make sure you have a convenient place for the equipment or that the program is available close to where you live.
- Decide on the features you really need.
- Decide whether there are less expensive ways to achieve the same goals without the product or program.
- Make sure there is a warranty.

5 DESCRIBE THE LEVELS OF QUALITY

Level 4	All nine points are included in the response, and an example is provided.
Level 3	All nine points are included in the response.
Level 2	Five points are included in the response.
Level 1	Four or fewer of the points are included in the response.

Assessment of Psychological and Sociological Concepts, Principles, and Behaviors

The standards that focus on psychological and sociological concepts, principles, and behaviors encompass cognitive, psychomotor, and affective learning. Common tools for assessing cognitive learning are written responses and reports. The most common tool for assessing psychomotor learning is the structured observation. For assessing affective learning, the most common tool is the journal. Examples of an appropriate assessment tool for each type of learning are shown below.

Cognitive Learning

GRADE 8, STANDARD 5.6

Describe leadership roles and responsibilities in the context of team games and activities.

 UNPACK THE STANDARD

What is the verb: *Describe*
What is the skill or content: *Leadership roles and responsibilities*

2 DETERMINE THE EVIDENCE

Description of leadership roles and responsibilities in the context of team games and activities.

3 SELECT OR DESIGN THE ASSESSMENT TOOL/TASK

Essay question: *What are the leadership roles and responsibilities for team games and activities?*

4 DETERMINE THE CRITERIA FOR COMPETENCE

1. Student describes the following leadership roles:
   Communicator
   Organizer
   Motivator

2. Student describes the following leadership responsibilities:
   Resolves conflicts
   Develops offensive and defensive strategies
   Empowers teammates

5 DESCRIBE THE LEVELS OF QUALITY

Level 4	*Meets level 3 and describes one additional leadership role and one additional leadership responsibility*
Level 3	*Describes the three leadership roles and three leadership responsibilities identified under criteria for competence*
Level 2	*Describes two leadership roles and two leadership responsibilities identified under criteria for competence*
Level 1	*Fails to describe any leadership roles or leadership responsibilities*

Psychomotor Learning

GRADE 5, STANDARD 5.6

Acknowledge orally the contributions and strengths of others.

1 UNPACK THE STANDARD

What is the verb: *Acknowledge*
What is the skill or content: *Contributions and strengths of others*

2 DETERMINE THE EVIDENCE

Orally acknowledge contributions and strengths of others.

3 SELECT OR DESIGN THE ASSESSMENT TOOL/TASK

Structured observation: *track on a chart the number of acknowledgments during an activity*

4 DETERMINE THE CRITERIA FOR COMPETENCE

1. Orally acknowledges two other students

5 DESCRIBE THE LEVELS OF QUALITY

Level 4	*Orally acknowledges the contributions and strengths of three or more students*
Level 3	*Orally acknowledges the contributions and strengths of two other students*
Level 2	*Orally acknowledges the contributions and strengths of one other student*
Level 1	*Does not orally acknowledge the contributions and strengths of others*

Affective Learning

GRADE 5, STANDARD 5.7

Accommodate individual differences in others' physical abilities in small-group activities.

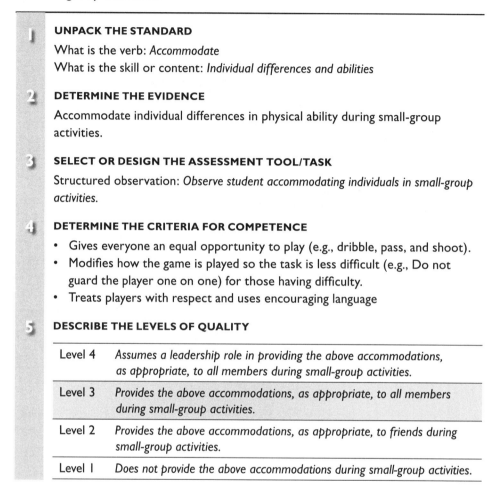

1 UNPACK THE STANDARD

What is the verb: *Accommodate*

What is the skill or content: *Individual differences and abilities*

2 DETERMINE THE EVIDENCE

Accommodate individual differences in physical ability during small-group activities.

3 SELECT OR DESIGN THE ASSESSMENT TOOL/TASK

Structured observation: *Observe student accommodating individuals in small-group activities.*

4 DETERMINE THE CRITERIA FOR COMPETENCE

- Gives everyone an equal opportunity to play (e.g., dribble, pass, and shoot).
- Modifies how the game is played so the task is less difficult (e.g., Do not guard the player one on one) for those having difficulty.
- Treats players with respect and uses encouraging language

5 DESCRIBE THE LEVELS OF QUALITY

Level 4	*Assumes a leadership role in providing the above accommodations, as appropriate, to all members during small-group activities.*
Level 3	*Provides the above accommodations, as appropriate, to all members during small-group activities.*
Level 2	*Provides the above accommodations, as appropriate, to friends during small-group activities.*
Level 1	*Does not provide the above accommodations during small-group activities.*

State-Required Physical Performance Test

Education Code Section 60800 requires every school district and charter school in California with pupils in grades five, seven, and nine to administer the physical performance test (designated by the State Board of Education) to each pupil in those grades during the months of February, March, April, or May. All students in those three grade levels must be tested; there are no provisions for parents requesting that their children not be tested. Students in grades five, seven, and nine having an IEP (individualized education program) or 504 Plan should also have a provision for taking the state physical performance test included in their IEP or 504 Plan. Results of the physical performance test administrations are to be submitted to the California Department of Education (CDE), upon request, at least once every two years. The CDE is required to compile the results in a report to the state Legislature and the Governor every two years. Districts must also report the aggregate results of the physical performance test in their annual school accountability report card.

Currently, the designated physical performance test is the FITNESSGRAM® (Third Edition), which is designed to assess six key fitness areas that represent three broad components of fitness: (1) aerobic capacity, (2) body composition, and (3) muscle strength, endurance, and flexibility.[3] Performance on each of the fitness-area tests is divided into two general areas: a Healthy Fitness Zone (HFZ) or needs improvement (i.e., not in the Healthy Fitness Zone). The desired performance standard for each fitness-area test is the HFZ, established by the test developers, that reflects reasonable levels of physical fitness attainable by most students. HFZs vary by student age and gender. For students in grade nine, *Education Code* Section 51241(b)(1) defines passing of the physical performance test as meeting satisfactorily (performing within the HFZ) at least five of the six standards of the test.

As with the administration of other statewide standardized tests, regulations and protocols for the FITNESSGRAM® (Third Edition) test battery must be carefully followed to ensure the validity of the test. District administrators are responsible for being aware of current statutes and regulations and ensuring compliance. In addition, the administrators are responsible for ensuring that staff members responsible for testing are properly trained and provided with any resources and assistance they may require. The administration of the FITNESS-GRAM® (Third Edition) test battery requires specialized training because the teacher's judgment comes into play (e.g., evaluating the performance of push-ups). In addition, careful planning is necessary to create a safe environment for all students, one that preserves the dignity of each student. District administrators are encouraged to create a fitness-testing plan that conforms to the test administration manual and complies with current statutory and regulatory requirements for administering the assessment and reporting results.

Resources

Information about the FITNESSGRAM® (Third Edition) is available on the CDE Web site at http://www.cde.ca.gov/ta/tg/pf/. The CDE manual for test administration and data reporting, *Physical Fitness Test (PFT): Preparation Manual for Testing and Reporting,* may be downloaded from that site.

Assessment and the Use of Technology

New media and electronic technologies for assessment can be valuable to physical educators and students. Educators who do not have access to the technology devices and software noted here may want to apply for competitive grants or seek categorical funds. Chapter 9 covers the instructional uses of technology, while this section is focused on using technology to enhance the assessment process.

---

[3]As of January 2009, the state-designated physical performance test is the FITNESSGRAM® (Third Edition).

Electronic Testing

Test-generation software assists teachers with the development of written tests. The teacher enters the test questions into the software along with the answers. The software stores the information and allows the teacher to sort and select stored questions for inclusion on a test. The software also formats and prints the test, or the students can take the test online and the software scores it. Some test-generation programs come with test questions. When selecting questions for inclusion in a test, teachers consider the content taught and what is to be measured to ensure alignment between standards-based instruction and assessment.

A student-response system provides the added feature of capturing all students' responses simultaneously and displaying a summary of the results immediately. Each student is provided with a remote keypad for use in answering the teacher's questions. The systems can be used for formal and informal assessments.

Fitness-Reporting Software

Fitness-reporting software analyzes raw fitness scores, prints summaries, and stores data for pre- and post-test comparisons. Some fitness-reporting programs have the capacity to follow a student from kindergarten through grade twelve, providing year-to-year comparisons. However, data entry can be a time-consuming task unless the software interfaces with a handheld computer. Trial versions of fitness-reporting software are sometimes posted on the Internet. It is recommended that teachers experiment with several programs before selecting one.

Fitness-reporting software supports the assessment of several standards, including:

Grade 4, Standard 3.8: Measure and record changes in aerobic capacity and muscular strength, using scientifically based health-related physical fitness assessments.

Grade 7, Standard 3.1: Assess one's own muscle strength, muscle endurance, aerobic capacity, flexibility, and body composition by using a scientifically based health-related fitness assessment.

High School Course 1, Standard 2.4: Use physical fitness test results to set and adjust goals to improve fitness.

Nutritional Analysis Software

Nutritional analysis software uses a student's age, weight, height, gender, and amount of physical activity to calculate the student's nutritional needs. The student records the types and amounts of foods he or she has eaten. Then the program creates a report of calories ingested, the nutrient values for each food, and the total of all nutrients ingested. Students use these reports to analyze their food consumption. Some programs also analyze the type and quantity of physical activity. These programs calculate calories expended for a specified amount of time and the relationship between caloric intake and caloric output.

Nutritional analysis software supports the assessment of several standards, including:

Grade 5, Standard 4.1: Record and analyze food consumption for one day and make a plan to replace foods with healthier choices and adjust quantities to enhance performance in physical activity.

Grade 6, Standard 4.7: Compile and analyze a log noting the food intake/ calories consumed and energy expended through physical activity.

Digital Cameras/Camcorders

Digital cameras and camcorders are used to record what the teacher is observing. This is especially beneficial when the teacher is using structured observation as the assessment tool. Teachers can view recordings to assess performance later, or they can view the recording with the student to enhance student learning.

Digital recordings can also be used with video-analysis software to analyze movement performances. The student's performance is recorded and then transferred to the computer. The recording speed (frames per second) and the length (in inches) of a physical object in the field of view are entered in the software. Those two variables allow the software to analyze the movement for factors such as displacement, velocity, and acceleration. The students use this information for deeper analysis of their performance.

Video analysis supports the assessment of a few standards, including:

Grade 6, Standard 2.3: Analyze and correct errors in movement patterns.

Grade 7, Standard 2.2: Analyze movement patterns and correct errors.

Pedometers/Accelerometers

Pedometers accurately measure the number of steps that an individual takes. Accelerometers accurately measure the quantity and intensity of movement in one or more dimensions. Both devices provide a valid indicator of overall physical activity when students are instructed in the correct protocol.

Pedometers and accelerometers support the assessment of several standards, including the following ones:

Grade 5, Standard 3.3: Participate three to four days each week, for increasing periods of time, in continuous moderate to vigorous physical activities at the appropriate intensity for increasing aerobic capacity.

Grade 6, Standard 3.4: Participate in moderate to vigorous physical activity a minimum of four days each week.

High School Course 2, Standard 2.1: Participate in moderate to vigorous physical activity at least four days each week.

Heart Rate Monitors

Heart rate monitors measure heart rate before, during, and after physical activity. Some monitors can be programmed to record data, so that students can review the numbers after the workout. Other heart rate monitors interface with a computer and print out a hard copy that students can analyze at their leisure.

Heart rate monitors support the assessment of several standards, including:

Grade 5, Standard 4.10: Compare target heart rate and perceived exertion during physical activity.

Grade 5, Standard 4.11: Measure and record the heart rate before, during, and after vigorous physical activity.

Grade 6, Standard 3.6: Monitor the intensity of one's heart rate during physical activity.

Body Composition Analyzers

Body composition analyzers measure the ratio of fat-free mass to fat mass. There are a variety of body composition analyzers, including bioelectrical impedance, skinfold measurements, and hydrostatic weighing. Body composition analyzers support the assessment of several standards, including the following ones:

Grade 6, Standard 3.1: Assess the components of health-related fitness (muscle strength, muscle endurance, flexibility, aerobic capacity, and body composition) by using a scientifically based health-related fitness assessment.

Grade 7, Standard 3.1: Assess one's own muscle strength, muscle endurance, aerobic capacity, flexibility, and body composition by using a scientifically based health-related fitness assessment.

Grade 8, Standard 3.1: Assess the components of health-related physical fitness (muscle strength, muscle endurance, aerobic capacity, flexibility, and body composition) by using a scientifically based health-related physical fitness assessment.

Grading Practices in Standards-Based Physical Education

Grading policies and practices are generally developed at the school district level. Implementation of standards-based physical education may require changes in grading policies and practices. District-level involvement and approval are necessary steps in developing or modifying grading policies and practices. Grades symbolize the progress and cumulative achievements of individual students in a form that can be communicated to them and to their parents. Periodic assessments on standards taught during the grading period are the basis of the grade for that period. By the end of the year, all standards have been assessed because students will have had the opportunity to learn them all. Grading based on the achievement of clearly stated criteria emphasizes what students know and can do. The physical education grade is based on the individual's progress toward all the grade- or course-level standards. Throughout the grading period students are required to generate evidence of having met or exceeded the grade- or course-level standards. As with other subject areas, grading in physical education is based on the achievement of standards instead of being based on dressing, effort, and participation. (See *EC* Section 49066[c] in Appendix A.) The grade for citizenship, behavior, or work habits is appropriate for reporting attendance, participation, dressing, and effort.

For grading to be valid and fair, the student and teacher must share a common understanding of what is to be accomplished. Grading practices are explained to students at the beginning of the year or course. Throughout the school year or course, students are kept informed of their grades. The criteria for an assignment are clearly explained to the students prior to its implementation, and students are provided with enough time for instruction and practice.

The depth and breadth of knowledge and skills in each standard vary. When basing grades on grade- or course-level standards, teachers must decide how much weight to give each standard. Standards-based grading is most beneficial for students and parents when a standards-based report card is used. (See Appendixes G and H for examples of standards-based report cards.) This type of report card shows the student's grades for each overarching standard or specific standards in a grade level or course level so that parents and students can clearly understand the student's areas of strength and areas that need improvement.

Technology is also available to assist with the creation of grade reports. There are numerous generic software grading programs on the market and several software programs specific to grading physical education. Many of the programs allow data collection using a handheld computer. Portability is convenient for physical educators who primarily work away from their offices. Many grading programs are similar, prompting the user for the names of students, tests and assignments, and grading practices. The teacher enters data throughout the school year or grading period, and the software calculates the final grade. Some programs produce standards-based report cards. Some publishers of grading programs post trial versions of their software on the Internet. It is highly recommended that teachers experiment with several programs to determine whether a software grading program is an appropriate use of funds and which program best meets their needs.

6

Instruction

S tandards-based physical education instruction focuses on student learning so that each student has the opportunity to master all the grade-level or course-level physical education model content standards. This framework provides a road map for the design of standards-based physical education lessons. Teachers start by selecting the grade- or course-level standard(s) for instruction, determine and design assessment strategies, and then create instructional opportunities for students to engage in the content. (See information on standards-based instructional design and unpacking standards in Chapter 1.) All learning opportunities (e.g., drills, games, cognitive activities) are directly aligned with the grade- or course-level standards.

Lessons are planned logically and sequentially for maximum instructional time and learning. Effective instructional units are of sufficient length to allow students to develop skills and competence in the areas being taught. These instructional units build upon skills and knowledge that have been learned previously and prepare students to reach future grade- or course-level standards.

Skilled teachers design instruction based on the content or skill to be taught, the strategies available to teach it, and the needs of their students. No single method of instruction is the best or most appropriate in all situations. Teachers must thoughtfully consider the impact of their decisions on the instructional process and evaluate those decisions as to their effect on the learning process. Instructionally sound lessons are carefully developed and are designed to engage all members of the class in learning activities focused on student mastery.

Prior to instruction students are assessed to determine whether they are ready for the new content. If they are not, then instruction is provided to bring them up to grade or course level. Once students are at grade or course level, then the current grade- or course-level standards are addressed. Lessons need to be designed so that students are constantly exposed to new information while practicing skills and reinforcing their understanding of information introduced previously. The teaching of standards-based physical education is holistic: several standards may be taught simultaneously in the same lesson or sequence of lessons.

To guide educators in designing instructional strategies, this chapter is organized into eight main sections:

Instructional Models
Establishing a Safe Environment
Class Management
Effective Teaching Behaviors
Principles of Motor Learning
A Sample Physical Education Lesson
Instructional Strategies
Multidisciplinary Opportunities

Instructional Models

Physical education instruction takes place in many settings; therefore, a variety of instructional models need to be developed for physical education. Those models that are ultimately selected and implemented provide each student with the opportunity to learn in the most effective manner. Student learning of physical education content, rather than mere participation in physical activity programs, is the foundation for decisions related to instructional models.

The traditional setting refers to physical education instruction in a regular school environment. Other environments include juvenile court and alternative education settings (e.g., continuation schools, court and community schools, independent study schools, etc.). Regardless of the setting, all students are expected to receive instruction in physical education that provides them with the skills and knowledge specified in the content standards and enables them to demonstrate learning related to all grade- and course-level physical education model content standards. In addition, students must be provided with the minimum minutes of physical education required for their grade level. (See Appendix A for statutory requirements.) Development of standards-based instructional programs in all settings requires careful planning to ensure that the instructional program provides a comprehensive curriculum.

In some situations, the use of an independent study course to obtain credit for physical education may be an opportunity to meet students' educational needs. Independent study is an instructional strategy, not an alternative curriculum. Independent study shall not be provided as an alternative curriculum (*Education Code* Section 51745[a][3]). Independent study physical education courses incorporate the depth and breadth of the physical education curriculum.

Appropriate Use of Independent Study

- Outside learning may address an individual student's needs in a particular learning sequence more appropriately than the physical education course.

Inappropriate Use of Independent Study

- It should not be a replacement for the physical education course.
- Content of the outside activity is not of equivalent depth and breadth as the standards-based curriculum.
- It is inappropriate to use the amount of time spent in an outside activity or sport as a rationale for choosing independent study as an instructional strategy.

Distance learning, virtual schools, interactive video, and online courses are other instructional models. For some students, technology-based instructional models may prove to be an adequate setting for physical education instruction. Online physical education courses must be carefully evaluated to determine whether they address the model content standards, appropriately assess student learning and provide evidence of such, and have authentic measures as an integral part of the program. Chapter 9 provides specific information on evaluating online courses.

Establishing a Safe Environment

A safe environment in physical education has two components: the physical and the psychological. The first refers to the physical environment and the need to ensure that the facilities and equipment are safe, staff is prepared to handle emergencies, class size is conducive to providing a safe environment, communication systems are in place so that physical education teachers can connect quickly to the main office or health office, students use equipment and facilities in a safe manner, and there is proper supervision of all physical activities. (See the "Facilities" section of Chapter 9 for additional information on facility safety.) The second component refers to the psychological environment and the need to ensure that students feel physically, emotionally, and socially safe during the instructional process.

Teachers establish, teach, and enforce safety rules. Provisions are made to ensure that every student understands rules and expectations regarding safety. The safety rules are specific to the school site; they include rules stating that students must use materials only for their intended purpose and that students must always use safety materials (e.g., catcher's protective equipment, shin guards for soccer, mats for climbing wall). If an activity has an inherent risk (e.g., the risk of drowning during swimming), students are made aware of this inherent risk ahead of time along with ways to ensure their personal safety. All safety rules are documented in the teacher's lesson plans, as well as school and district policy and procedures documents.

Students should wear proper attire in physical education. Proper attire is non-restrictive, with adequate ventilation to prevent heat- and cold-related illnesses. Appropriate shoes offer support and prevent slippage. School districts may want to evaluate and adopt dressing policies and procedures that are appropriate to their individual programs. All policies are communicated to students and parents and guardians. Elementary teachers clearly communicate the physical education schedule to parents and guardians, so that parents and guardians know the days and times of physical education instruction and can help their children plan appropriate attire for those days.

Adequate supervision, based on the nature of the activity as well as the ages, maturity levels, and skill levels of the students, is always provided during physical activity. In addition, closer supervision is provided for high-risk activities or stations. Schools and teachers help create a safe learning environment by implementing the following supervision principles:

- Always be in the immediate vicinity (within sight and sound) of the students.
- Constantly scan the area for clues that may indicate a potentially dangerous situation.
- Secure an adequate replacement (not a paraprofessional, student teacher, or custodian) when it is necessary to leave the area.
- Be aware of the health status of every student.
- Provide a buffer zone around all play areas (do not use common boundary lines).

- Carefully match students by size and ability for any activity involving potential contact.
- Create written supervision procedures that designate the responsible staff member and/or certificated personnel (e.g., for the locker room, before class, after class).
- Have access to a telephone or other communication device and post emergency telephone numbers in a handy location.
- Do not use equipment for purposes other than those for which it was intended.
- Do not alter equipment in any manner.
- Do not allow students to use any equipment before they receive instruction on the safe use of the equipment (Mohnsen 2008, 48).
- Plan for weather conditions and air quality.

The psychological side of a safe and healthy environment is less tangible but is equally important. High-quality programs are nonthreatening and encourage every student to succeed in physical education. There is a culture of concern and mutual support among staff members and students. The importance of social values—caring for others, treating others with respect, affirming diversity, and being a responsible member of a group—are clearly stated, recognized, and modeled by all adults. Appropriate social interaction skills are taught and practiced with feedback from the teacher.[1] Demeaning statements or actions directed to staff members or students are not tolerated.

All instructional practices preserve the dignity and self-respect of every student. Physical educators learn and use students' names, help students to feel valued and recognized for who they are and what they are capable of doing, and take students' needs into consideration when planning instructional activities. Practices that do not preserve the dignity of students, such as forming groups or teams through a public selection process, using students as targets in games such as Dodge Ball, and weighing students in front of others, are both harmful and inappropriate.

Teachers are aware of and alert to the different forms of harassment and bullying that may take place during physical education: during class, in the locker room, or on the school grounds before and after class. Physical education takes place in a public venue; therefore, vigilance by physical education teachers and administrators ensures that no individual student or group of students is targeted for humiliation or bullying. In fact, teachers have the legal responsibility to create a school environment free from discriminatory attitudes and practices and acts of violence. In 1982, California voters amended the state Constitution by adding the "Right to Safe Schools" provision, which states: "All students and staff of primary, elementary, junior high, and senior high schools have the inalienable right to attend campuses which are safe, secure, and peaceful." (Cal. Const. art. 1, § 28, subd. [c].)

---

[1] Feedback is most effective when it is specific and positive or specific and corrective.

It is important for teachers to monitor students for inappropriate behavior and to intervene immediately when there is a problem. Early intervention is especially important for sexist, heterosexist, or homophobic behaviors displayed by students. Signs of those behaviors (e.g., inappropriate language, demeaning comments) are frequently ignored by physical educators (Morrow and Gill 2003) and can quickly escalate.

A key factor in the prevention of bullying and harassment is the establishment of an effective and consistent class management system. Additionally, local school boards adopt policies and procedures, as well as administrative regulations, to create school environments that are "free from discriminatory attitudes and practices and acts of hate violence," based on *EC* Section 233(a)(1). Acts of violence include hate crimes as defined below in the California *Penal Code.* The instigator of a hate crime is subject to prosecution.

> A hate crime means a criminal act committed, in whole or in part, because of one or more of the following actual or perceived characteristics of the victim:
>
> 1. Disability.
> 2. Gender.
> 3. Nationality.
> 4. Race or ethnicity.
> 5. Religion.
> 6. Sexual orientation.
> 7. Association with a person or group with one or more of these actual or perceived characteristics (*Penal Code* Section 422.55[a]).

Class Management

An effective class-management system sets the stage for high-quality physical education instruction by providing the time and opportunity for learning to take place. It promotes student engagement and maximizes instructional effectiveness. Effective class management does not just happen; it is carefully and systematically planned.

Preventive class management "refers to the proactive (rather than reactive) strategies teachers use to develop and maintain a positive, predictable, task-oriented class climate in which minimal time is devoted to managerial tasks and optimal time is therefore available for instructional tasks" (Siedentop and Tannehill 2000). Research supports setting high expectations and establishing teaching routines (e.g., handing out equipment), rules, and consequences for students during the first several days of the school year and reinforcing them throughout the year. Class rules are effective when they are few in number, stated in the positive, and posted so that they can be referred to frequently. Examples of effective rules include:

- Dress appropriately.
- Arrive on time.
- Listen to others.

- Respect others.
- Use equipment responsibly.

Potentially, the primary management tool for teachers is the physical education curriculum itself. When students are actively engaged in focused, rigorous, and challenging physical education activities, fewer opportunities for inappropriate behavior arise. When students are successful and their successes are made clear to them, they are more likely to be motivated to work on physical education. This intrinsic motivation is valued over the use of artificial external reward systems (Weiss 2000; Whitehead 1993).

In a physical education program, an effective classroom is characterized by the following management practices:

- Every student is engaged in a learning activity.
- Students are given an opportunity to explore new or unfamiliar equipment before instruction.
- Teachers identify a location for students to place equipment while the teacher is talking (e.g., by their feet).
- Teachers use a signal that can be heard over distance outside to alert students to the next task.
- When providing instructions, teachers position students so that they do not look directly into the sun.
- Teachers constantly move throughout the learning environment to monitor student behavior.
- Disciplinary procedures are appropriate for the infraction, and exercise is never used as punishment or a reward.

Effective class-management practices that teachers use indoors (such as knowing students' names, setting boundaries, using proximity to control behavior, being positive, providing learning activities that promote success for all students, and actively supervising students) also work outdoors.

Effective Teaching Behaviors

Researcher Linda Darling-Hammond (1997, 293) states, "When all is said and done, what matters most for students' learning are the commitments and capabilities of their teachers." Successful teachers have high expectations for every student and use effective teaching behaviors to ensure that every student achieves the grade-level or course-level standards. "Effective teaching behaviors" refer to the decisions that teachers make regarding the use of time and their interaction with students. Physical education teachers use research-based effective teaching behaviors to support student learning. These include:

- Planning for every lesson
- Using time effectively
- Providing effective practice
- Providing specific positive or specific corrective feedback

- Keeping students engaged in moderate-to-vigorous physical activity at least 50 percent of the instructional time (*Healthy People 2010* 2000)
- Keeping students engaged in academic learning time for sufficient time to support student success (Rink 1998; Siedentop 1991).
- Applying motor learning concepts to instructional practices (See Appendix E, "Concepts and Principles of Motor Learning.")

Principles of Motor Learning

Motor learning is the study of change in a person's ability to perform fundamental and specialized movement and manipulative skills. Using research-based principles of motor learning supports student learning most efficiently and effectively. In addition, when teachers point out the principles they are using, it teaches students about the learning process and appropriate ways to practice when working on their own. (See Appendix E.)

Feedback

Feedback is beneficial to learners if it is specific corrective feedback (e.g., "Form a wider triangle with your hands and head to give you a wider base of support—this will make it easier for you to perform the headstand") or specific positive feedback (e.g., "Good job—you bent your elbows as you caught the ball"). Feedback should be delayed about five seconds after the student completes the skill, so that he or she has time to process the proprioception feedback before hearing external feedback. Feedback should be restricted to the features not readily apparent to the learner (e.g., the technique rather than accuracy) and should be limited to one or two specific corrective or specific positive statements at a time. Additionally, the focus of the feedback should match the focus of the lesson. Feedback can be provided by the teacher, a peer, or oneself using mirrors or a video.

Transfer of Learning

The learning of one skill can have a positive or negative effect on the learning of another skill. When the impact is positive, it is called a positive transfer of learning. When the impact is negative, it is called a negative transfer of learning. Providing students with information about the ways in which skills are similar helps them to positively transfer the appropriate learning from the first learned skill to the second. For example, the overhand movement pattern is used in the overhand volleyball serve, tennis serve, and badminton smash. When learning the tennis serve, after having learned the volleyball serve, students should be alerted to the similarities between the two serves. Differences between skills are brought to the attention of the students to minimize the potential interference of the first skill on the learning of the second skill. For example, at the elementary level, students are alerted to the differences between galloping and skipping at the time when the second skill is taught.

Improving Speed and Accuracy

When students are first introduced to new motor skills, it is important to emphasize speed or force instead of accuracy. Otherwise, learners will often choose a poor technique (e.g., dart-throwing technique for the overhand throw) instead of the proper technique (arm back, rotate body, and transfer weight for the overhand throw) to ensure accuracy. As learners progress, they can focus more on accuracy; however, there is always a tradeoff between speed and accuracy.

Practice Schedules

Motor skill practice can be organized in many different configurations. Some configurations lead to efficient learning of motor skills while others do not. This section discusses several different methods of organizing practice and the implications of each one for effective practice in physical education.

Practice can be spaced out over time (distributed practice) or completed in one instructional period (mass practice). Distributed practice generally leads to more effective learning, especially in the early stages. Therefore, students practice several different skills during each class period.

Practice may involve the entire skill (whole practice), or the skill can be broken down into small units (part practice). For example, the triple jump involves a hop, a skip, and a jump. Whole practice would involve performing the hop, skip, and jump together. Part practice would involve practicing the hop, then practicing the skip, and then practicing the jump. Whenever possible, however, whole practice is used—especially when breaking down the skill changes it significantly. For example, a forehand drive in tennis involves a backswing and a forward swing of the racquet. However, practicing just the backswing or just the forward swing changes the skill significantly. In situations where the skill is complex and has relatively independent parts—such as the triple jump—whole practice is used as soon as the learner can demonstrate each part correctly.

Practice can be organized so that the same skill is practiced in the same way (constant practice), or the same skill can be practiced with changing conditions (variable practice). Constant practice for the overhand throw might be throwing and catching with a partner. Variable practice for the overhand throw might include several stations: throwing and catching with a partner, throwing at a stationary target, throwing at a moving target, throwing while being defended, etc.

In physical education, every student practices closed skills using constant practice. Closed skills are those skills that are performed in a static environment. Examples include basketball free throw, volleyball serve, and tennis serve since no one interferes with the player performing these skills. Beginners should practice open skills using constant practice, and intermediate and advanced learners should practice open skills using variable practice. Open skills are those skills performed in a changing environment. Examples of open skills include basketball dribble, volleyball spike, and tennis forehand drive since the execution of the skill depends on the positioning of the defense. Constant practice enhances the learning of closed skills and open skills for beginners only. Variable practice enhances the learning of open skills for intermediate and advanced learners.

	Closed Skills (static environment)	Open Skills (changing environment)
Constant Practice (practice in same way)	All students	Beginners
Variable Practice (practice with changing conditions)	Not applicable	Intermediate and advanced students

Practice that involves several skills during one instructional period may be organized in either a blocked or random manner. In a blocked protocol, each skill is practiced once and for the same amount of time. For example, the volleyball forearm pass is practiced for 10 minutes, then the volleyball set is practiced for 10 minutes, and then the volleyball serve is practiced for 10 minutes. In a random protocol, the skills are practiced in a random order for various lengths of time. For example, the volleyball forearm pass is practiced for 10 minutes, then the volleyball set is practiced for five minutes, then the forearm pass is practiced again for five minutes, then the volleyball serve is practiced for 10 minutes, and then the set is practiced again for five minutes. Blocked practice leads to short-term success; however, random practice leads to long-term success (e.g., performance of the correct technique, improvement in accuracy). Therefore, practice in physical education is either changed frequently or a station approach is used (Schmidt and Wrisberg 2000; Magill 2001).

A Sample Physical Education Lesson

This sample lesson consists of four components: an opening, instruction, practice, and a closing.[2] A visitor to a class in which this lesson plan is followed might observe the following.

Opening

The class opening begins with a preview of the standards to be learned, an overview of the lesson, and an anticipatory set, where the teacher shows the students the value of what they will be learning during the instructional period. The concepts and motor skills being taught and practiced during the lesson are also introduced. Additionally, the organization of skill practice, including grouping, location, and equipment distribution, is explained. To increase student physical activity time, the teacher keeps instruction succinct and provides no more than three directions before having students attempt the skill or activity. Then the teacher provides additional directions as needed.

---

[2] The sample lesson shows one approach to organizing a lesson. As with all suggestions and examples in the framework, the sample lesson is not intended to be a requirement for the physical education classroom.

Instruction

When introducing a new motor skill, the teacher provides a model of the skill by performing it, asking a student who is proficient at the skill to perform it, or providing a video of the skill. When students are used for demonstration purposes, both genders and various ethnicities are proportionally represented over time. Effective models are accurate, highlight the critical features of the skill, provide visual information so that students can form a mental image of the action, and depict the skill in its entirety and at normal speed. The demonstration is accompanied by a brief explanation that is logically sequenced and that focuses on one or two cues. A cue is a short phrase or single word that focuses on the important aspects of the skill to be practiced (e.g., "reach" and "give" for catching).

When introducing a new cognitive concept, the teacher first determines what the students already know. Then the cognitive information is provided through a scaffolding process whereby new information is built upon previous knowledge. The new information is organized and presented in a meaningful way (e.g., graphic organizers) that requires students to actively use the information. During the lesson closure, time is provided for students to discuss the new information.

Prior to the start of practice, the teacher checks the students' understanding of the concept(s) and motor skill(s) presented as well as the directions for practicing the skill(s). Many teachers are unaware that students do not understand their directions until the students try to demonstrate the skill or implement the activity. Checking for understanding, a type of informal progress monitoring, occurs through a variety of techniques: signaled answers, choral responses, or sampling individual students. "Signaled answers" means asking students true or false questions and requesting a thumbs-up or thumbs-down response to indicate their understanding. For a choral response, students call out the answer to a question in unison. The sampling of individual students involves asking a few students to respond to the questions and generalizing the understanding of these students to the entire class.

Providing Effective Practice

Practice time engages students in the maximum amount of practice at the appropriate level of difficulty using the correct technique. The following guidelines support effective practice opportunities for every student:

- Use games with a small number of players (two-on-two basketball instead of five-on-five) for maximum practice opportunities.
- Have sufficient equipment so that no student is waiting for equipment.
- Provide students with specific corrective or specific positive feedback.
- Monitor progress (embedded assessment) to determine when reteaching a skill or concept may be necessary.
- Organize activities so that only a few students are in each group.
- Provide sufficient practice trials to allow every student to achieve success.
- Keep transition times to a minimum.

- Omit any activity that involves students waiting for a turn or being eliminated.
- Provide differentiated instruction at the appropriate level of difficulty for every student through the use of alternative activities at various levels of complexity.
- Actively supervise students during practice to keep them on-task.

Aside from providing students with appropriate motor skill practice, the guidelines help to ensure that students are engaged in moderate to vigorous physical activity during most of the instructional period.

Closing

During closure the content of the lesson is reviewed. If the students have been engaged in physical activity, the students participate in a cool-down. A cool-down involves the gradual slowing down of activity that results in a lowering of body temperature after moderate to vigorous exercise. A cool-down may include walking or stretching.

During the opening of the lesson, students are told what they will learn. During the closure, students review what they have learned, thus bringing the learning experience full circle. The closure is an ideal time to employ a questioning strategy that requires students to use higher-order thinking skills. Asking questions about the why and how of a concept or skill requires students to think deeply about their learning. Students can be asked to journal write or pair share (discuss the question with a partner). An effective use of class time is to check for understanding by having the students discuss the lesson while participating in a cool-down.

Instructional Strategies

Every student is expected to meet or exceed the grade- or course-level standards set forth in the physical education model content standards. The standards define the "what," but it is the instruction that describes the "how." Differentiated instruction refers to the use of a variety of strategies to accommodate differences in students' learning styles, interests, needs, and prior knowledge. No single instructional strategy is the best or most appropriate for all students or in all situations.

Teachers draw from both student-initiated learning strategies and teacher-directed learning strategies to satisfy the learning needs of individual students and to stimulate higher levels of thinking and creativity. Specific strategies can include competency-based learning, contract learning, drill and practice, small games, problem-based learning, lecture, cooperative learning, stations, and role playing. Drawing on their experience and training, teachers determine the instructional strategies most likely to promote high student learning and achievement. Successful teachers constantly reevaluate the effectiveness of the approach they take and modify strategies when students are not moving toward proficiency with the standards.

Examples of Instructional Strategies

The following examples consist of three instructional strategies that could be used to provide instruction on the same standard. There are examples for a grade four, grade seven, and High School Course 2 standard using eight different instructional strategies. The examples represent just some of the ways that a standard could be taught. The examples, like all other examples in this framework, are not to be interpreted as requirements for the physical education classroom or as the only instructional approach to a particular standard. In physical education classes, the teacher determines the most effective strategy or strategies for her or his students.

GRADE 4, STANDARD 1.1

Perform simple balance stunts with a partner while sharing a common base of support.

There are three possible instructional strategies for addressing this standard.

Problem solving

The teacher prompts the students with questions and requests that they respond to physically. For example, "Can you and your partner balance on three body parts?"

Stations with task cards

The teacher sets up three balancing-stunt stations that require students to work with a partner:

1. Bottoms up

   Partners sit facing each other with knees bent, feet held high, and soles touching.

   The objective is to push against a partner's feet until both students' bottoms are off the ground.

2. Partner inchworm

   Partners face each other, sitting on each other's feet.

   Partners grasp one another's elbows or upper arms.

   The objective is for students to move forward or backward while sitting on each other's feet.

3. Back-to-back

   Pairs sit on the ground, back-to-back, knees bent, and elbows linked. The objective is to stand up together.

Lecture and demonstration

The teacher describes and uses a visual aid to demonstrate each partner-balance stunt (see previous strategy) and then has students in pairs replicate the stunt.

GRADE 7, STANDARD 3.4

Plan a weekly personal physical fitness program in collaboration with the teacher.

There are three possible instructional strategies for addressing this standard.

Lecture

The teacher presents a lecture on one aspect of health-related fitness including frequency, intensity, time, and type (F.I.T.T.) concepts each day for a week. The students are asked to take notes on the lecture.

Problem-based learning

The teacher tells the students that they are now fitness trainers and that they have a new client. The client is five feet tall, has 30 percent body fat, and is sixteen years old. The students are provided with a variety of resources and told to create a fitness plan for the client.

Cooperative learning

The teacher organizes students into five groups. Each group is assigned one aspect of health-related fitness to research using library resources. After learning the frequency, intensity, time, and type (F.I.T.T.) concepts for their area of fitness, they teach the information to the rest of the class.

HIGH SCHOOL COURSE 2, STANDARD 3.9

Encourage others to be supportive and inclusive of individuals of all ability levels.

There are three possible instructional strategies for addressing this standard.

Social skill instruction

The teacher starts the class by asking students to brainstorm what encouragement looks like, sounds like, and feels like. The teacher then instructs the students to encourage one another during the physical activity portion of the lesson. At the end of the lesson, the teacher has students report orally on their use of encouragement during the lesson or by writing in their journals.

Lecture and practice

The teacher explains and give students examples of what encouragement looks like, sounds like, and feels like. The teacher then instructs the students to practice encouraging one another during the physical activity portion of the lesson.

Role-play

The teacher tells the students what encouragement looks like and sounds like. The teacher then puts students in trios and has them role-play providing encouragement. One student provides encouragement; one student accepts the encouragement; and the third student gives feedback to the first student on his or her ability to provide encouragement. Students rotate roles so that each student can provide encouragement, accept encouragement, and give feedback.

Multidisciplinary Opportunities

Physical education teachers should continually interact with and support the other subject area teachers, including the teacher librarian. And other subject area teachers should continually interact with and support physical education teachers. The goal of this interaction is to look at the content in different subject areas and find natural connections. Generally, the study of biomechanics aligns well with physical science and physics, the study of fitness (exercise physiology) aligns well with biology and health, sociology (social interaction) and psychology (personal responsibility) align well with health education and history–social science, and the study of movement concepts aligns well with aesthetics (arts). However, when a multidisciplinary approach to instruction is used, it is important to make sure that the content is from the same grade level in each subject area.

The following examples illustrate the alignment of content standards that may benefit from a multidisciplinary approach to instruction:

Table 6.1 Alignment of Physical Education Content with Other Subjects

		Physical Education
Science	**Grade 2** **1c.** Students know the way to change how something is moving is by giving it a push or a pull. The size of the change is related to the strength, or the amount of force, of the push or pull.	**2.8** Compare the changes in force applied to a ball and the ball speed when rolling a ball for various distances.
History–Social Science	**Kindergarten** **K.4.1** Determine the relative locations of objects using the terms near/far, left/right, and behind/in front. **Grade 5** **5.1.2** Describe their varied customs and folklore traditions.	**2.1** Explain the difference between under and over, behind and in front of, next to and through, up and down, forward and backward, and sideways. **5.8** Appreciate physical games and activities reflecting diverse heritages.
Mathematics	**Grade 1** **Measurement and Geometry** **2.3** Give and follow directions about location.	**1.4** Change direction from forward and back and right and left in response to tempos, rhythms, and signals while walking, running, hopping, and jumping (i.e., locomotor skills).

		Physical Education
Mathematics (continued)	**Grade 5** **Number Sense 2.1** Add, subtract, multiply, and divide with decimals; add with negative integers; subtract positive integers from negative integers; and verify the reasonableness of the results.	**4.8** Identify the heart rate intensity (target heart-rate range) that is necessary to increase aerobic capacity. Standard 4.8 requires the following calculation: Maximum heart rate (MHR) = 208 − (.7 × your age) Target heart rate range (THRR) = MHR × .7 to MHR × .8
Visual and Performing Arts	**Grade 4** **3.4** Perform and identify folk/ traditional and social dances from California history. **Grade 4** **3.3** Explain the various ways people have experienced dance in their daily lives (e.g., Roman entertainments, Asian religious ceremonies, baby naming in Ghana, Latin American celebrations).	**1.21** Perform a series of basic square-dance steps. **1.7** Perform folk and line dances.

Effective physical education teachers seek opportunities for interdisciplinary instruction to enrich and deepen student learning. However, these same teachers always keep in mind that their number one goal for physical education instruction is to ensure student learning of the physical education model content standards.

7

Universal Access

The diversity of California students presents unique opportunities and significant challenges for instruction. Students come to California schools with a wide variety of skills, abilities, interests, and levels of proficiency. In any physical education class, there are tall and short students, advanced and remedial learners, and students at different physical, social, and emotional developmental levels. Regardless of the variation of the student population in each physical education class, the teacher's role is to deliver high-quality instruction appropriate to the student's current level of achievement.

The state-adopted model content standards for physical education are for *all* students. The goal of physical education programs in California is to ensure universal access to high-quality curriculum and instruction so that every student can meet or exceed the state's physical education model content standards. To reach that goal, teachers design instruction to meet the instructional needs of every student. Teachers can be well prepared to adapt to the diversity in their classrooms through careful diagnosis and planning and appropriate adaptations of the curriculum, assessment techniques, instruction, environment, and other variables for students with special needs.

There are frequent references to students with special needs throughout this chapter on universal access. The term *students with special needs* is defined as students who are marginalized in physical education, students with cultural and religious practices who need program modifications to participate, English learners, at-risk learners, students with long-term and short-term medical needs, advanced learners, and students with disabilities. Even within these categories there are differences among the students. It could be said that all students have special needs, because each student is unique. Therefore, it is imperative that students receive instruction based on their individual needs and not based on the labels that may be applied to them. Although many special education students receive adapted physical education services and/or modified instruction, not all special education students require them. To ensure that the instructional needs of all students are met, physical education teachers must be provided with information about each student's special needs and medical issues.

The first part of this chapter addresses several strategies that can be used to promote inclusion of every student. These strategies include establishing a safe and inclusive learning environment, using inclusive instructional materials and equipment, and differentiation. A safe and supportive environment for all students is also discussed in Chapter 6. The second part of this chapter addresses appropriate strategies for working with students with specific instructional needs.

Establishing an Inclusive Environment

Physical education is unlike subject areas that focus almost exclusively on cognitive development through written work and oral responses. In most subjects a student's special needs can be kept private between the teacher and student. Learning in physical education, however, takes place in a public environment. Therefore, the need for a safe, supportive, and inclusive environment is heightened. For students to attain standards successfully, there must be a climate of respect and dignity—for oneself, for others, and for physical education generally. Such a climate is especially important when students are being directed in attempts to refine skills or are being disciplined.

Physical education offers unique opportunities to bring students together in nonthreatening ways that emphasize fairness and cooperation. Because physical education involves students working and playing together, students learn the personal and social skills, values, and attitudes needed for effective, positive social interaction. Disparaging remarks about an individual's disabilities, ethnicity, gender, native language, race, religion, or sexual orientation are not tolerated. Sarcasm and "put-downs" are considered inappropriate behavior and addressed with each student according to a student discipline plan, behavior contracts, and the like. Conversely, positive social skills are modeled, taught, reinforced, and assessed regularly.

The following practices promote a safe, supportive, and inclusive environment for students:

- Learn each student's name.
- Listen to every student.
- Be aware of each student's needs (by using resources such as IEPs, counselors, nurses, other educational service providers, parents, and the student).
- Use neutral language (e.g., using "player-to-player defense" instead of "man-to-man defense").
- Use language that recognizes a student as a person who happens to have a disability (e.g., student with autism instead of autistic student).
- Recognize and show appreciation for the abilities of every student (e.g., have a student in a wheelchair with good upper body strength demonstrate an upper body weight-lifting exercise).
- Group students according to the learning objective (e.g., skill practice, cognitive understanding, social skill development).

Instructional Resources That Allow Full Access

Chapter 9 discusses the selection of instructional resources; however, this section focuses on the selection of instructional resources appropriate for students with special needs. A broad range of physical education equipment is selected so that every student can be successful. Both physical-activity and sport equipment may vary in relation to size, weight, pliability, and texture to facilitate student learning regardless of skill level.

Equipment selection should be based on the student's skill level. If a student's force or speed is poor, then more pliable objects should be used until the student can successfully use less pliable objects. If a student's ability to catch or grip an object is poor, then soft-textured objects are selected with the student moving toward using harder-textured objects as skills improve. If a student's timing is poor, then lightweight objects should be used until the student's timing is good enough for a heavier object to be used. If a student's accuracy is poor, larger targets should be selected until the student is ready to kick or throw to smaller targets. Table 7.1 provides examples of ways to adjust instruction to the student.

Table 7.1 Matching Materials and Equipment to Skill Levels

Skill	Individualization method	Progression
Throw and catch	Vary the speed of the object by using objects of different pliability.	First use a fluff ball. Second, use a sponge ball. Next use a beanbag. Then use a playground ball.
Strike objects	Vary the weight of the implement and the object.	First use a balloon and a lightweight short-handle paddle. Second, use a high-density foam tennis ball and a lightweight short-handle paddle. Next use a shuttlecock and a badminton racquet. Then use a tennis ball and tennis racquet.
Kick or throw for accuracy	Vary the size of the target.	First use a large goal formed by cones. Next move the cones closer together. Then use a standard goal.

All instructional materials used in physical education are free of stereotypes and inclusive of all groups (e.g., gender, cultures, ethnicities, students with disabilities). Portraying positive images of diverse individuals participating in a wide variety of physical activities shows students that the activities are for everyone. (More information on adapting instruction is included in Table 7.2 on page 215 and Table 7.3 on page 222.

Differentiation Strategies

Students with special needs can benefit from appropriately challenging curriculum and instruction if systematically planned differentiation strategies are used. The strategies for differentiating instruction for students include pacing, complexity, depth, and novelty.

Pacing is perhaps the most commonly used strategy for differentiation. That is, the teacher speeds up or slows down instruction. This simple, effective, and inexpensive strategy may be used for many students with special needs. The instructional pace for advanced learners can be accelerated (Benbow and Stanley 1996). For example, if assessment indicates a student has mastered the skills for performing a handstand, the student practices a handstand rollout. For students experiencing difficulty, instruction can be slowed down. The key elements in slowing down instruction are to ensure that the content remains rigorous, that the students move ahead as quickly as they can, and that the instruction leads to the mastery of content standards within a reasonable amount of time.

Changing instruction as to depth, novelty, or complexity requires more training and skill on the part of the teacher and instructional materials that lend themselves to such variations. For advanced students, it means enriched instruction that encourages students to address topics at greater depth, learn complex skills in a more challenging environment, or make connections across disciplines not normally expected at that grade level. For example, Standard 4.1 for seventh grade states, "Develop a one-week personal physical fitness plan specifying the proper warm-up and cool-down activities and the principles of exercise for each component of health-related physical fitness." Advanced students may be asked to create multimedia presentations of their plans with video clips of each exercise. For students experiencing difficulty in physical education, the teacher focuses on the F.I.T.T. principles (frequency, intensity, time, and type) for the five components of health-related physical fitness and presents one component to the students at a time. The lessons are tightly organized, sequential, and distilled to ensure that students understand the fundamental concepts or skills needed to master later standards.

Changing the complexity of instruction is also appropriate for the psychomotor domain. For example, Grade 2, Standard 1.14 states, "Hand-dribble, with control, a ball for a sustained period." Advanced students may be asked to dribble while changing direction and switching from the dominant hand to the nondominant hand. For students who learn better when the task is broken into smaller tasks, the teacher begins instruction on Grade 2, Standard 1.14, with bouncing and catching the ball instead of dribbling. The students are then slowly and sequentially introduced to dribbling in place two times, to continuously dribbling, to dribbling with control. Sufficient time is provided for the students to master each stage before they proceed to the next stage. For other students experiencing difficulty in physical education, the physical educator may need to reteach skills that are a prerequisite to those identified in the standard. In some instances, these skills will be found in a lower grade-level standard or may be a fundamental movement pattern.

Experienced teachers develop a repertoire of proven instructional strategies for use in special situations or with certain students. Many of these strategies can be explicitly taught or embedded in instructional materials. To implement successful instructional strategies for all students, the teacher may:

1. Establish a safe, inclusive environment in which the students are encouraged to talk and to ask questions freely when they do not understand.
2. Use a wide variety of ways to explain a concept or an assignment. When appropriate, the concept or assignment is depicted in graphic (e.g., target heart rate calculation) or pictorial form (e.g., correct technique) to accompany oral and written instructions.
3. Introduce in the vocabulary (e.g., hop, jump) to be used for each lesson prior to the lesson and use reinforcement or additional practice afterward. Monitor instructional resources and instruction for ambiguities or language that would be confusing, such as idioms.
4. Set up tutoring for additional assistance. (Tutoring by a qualified teacher is optimal.) Design peer or cross-age tutoring so that it does not detract from the instructional time of either the tutor or student and is supervised by the teacher.

5. Enlist the help of parents at home when possible.

6. Establish special sessions to prepare students for unfamiliar testing situations.

7. Frequently ask each student to communicate his or her understanding of the concept, problem, or assignment.

8. Allow students to demonstrate their understanding and abilities in a variety of ways (e.g., gestures, demonstration, drawing) while reinforcing modes of communication that are standard in the school curricula.

9. Use a variety of ways to check frequently for understanding. Analyze why students do not understand. (This analysis may involve breaking down the skill or concept into parts to determine exactly where the student became confused.)

The strategies for students with special needs include variations in assessment techniques (e.g., drawing a picture, verbalizing the response). Despite the modifications made, however, the focus is always on helping students meet the physical education model content standards to the best of their ability and frequently assessing their progress in attaining the standards.

Students Who Are Marginalized

This section addresses those students who are often marginalized in physical education. It is divided into two parts: gender equity and students with different body types.

Gender Equity

California law and federal law require that students of both sexes be treated equally in integrated physical education classes. California law clearly states, "all students have the right to participate fully in the educational process free from discrimination" (*EC* Section 201[a]). (See also *EC* 200, *EC* 221.5, and *5 CCR* 4940[e] in Appendix A.) Integration by gender is also required by current federal Title IX regulations that, with a few specific exceptions, prohibit single-sex classes or activities. Regarding nondiscrimination on the basis of sex in education programs or activities, *34 CFR* 106.34. states that local educational agencies who are recipients of federal funding:

> . . . shall not provide or otherwise carry out any of its education programs or activities separately on the basis of sex, or require or refuse participation therein by any of its students on the basis of sex.

(See Appendix A.)

When gender equity is practiced, boys and girls are viewed as individuals whose strengths and weaknesses in the physical domain are based on ability and learning opportunities. All students, male and female, are given the teacher's attention and feedback on an equal basis, called on equally to demonstrate new skills, and disciplined equally. Teachers need to ensure gender fairness and support all students equally.

Teachers promote gender equity by using inclusive language (referring to the class as "students" instead of "you guys"), omitting stereotypical phrases (e.g., changing "Perform girl push-ups" to "Perform modified push-ups"), and omitting stereotypical assumptions. Some physical educators, in an effort to include girls in game play, may create a rule: "A girl must touch (e.g., throw, dribble) the ball before a team can score." This type of rule, which is based on a stereotypical assumption, communicates to students that all girls are less competent than all boys and that special rules are necessary to give girls a chance. In practice, this rule results in situations where one girl literally places her hand on the ball to comply with the rule but does not meaningfully contribute to the game. Thus, the assumption that girls are less competent is perpetuated. A better alternative is to use a small number of players in games (e.g., two against two, three against three) so that all students are included in the game by necessity.

Teachers must also refrain from stereotypical assumptions about male students. Statements such as "Boys don't like gymnastics" and "Boys aren't good at rhythmic activities" are inappropriate and limit opportunities for boys to achieve in all areas of physical education. The model content standards for physical education apply equally to all students regardless of gender.[1]

Students with Different Body Types

Physical educators need to be sensitive to students' self-esteem in relation to their body image. Students are aware of differences. Those who are smaller, taller, or larger than the norm are easily identified and singled out, being picked first for a team because they are the tallest for basketball or picked last because they are overweight and run slowly. In either case, some students are sensitive to slights and feel insecure about themselves and their abilities. They may be targeted for bullying. It is imperative that the teacher creates an environment in which every student feels included and has a positive learning experience. Using a variety of methods to create groupings rather than one (peer selection) is the key to creating an environment in which all students have an equal opportunity to achieve success in physical education.

Accommodating Cultural and Religious Practices

Culture represents the customary beliefs and patterns of behavior, both explicit and implicit, that are passed on to future generations by the society in which people live and/or by a social, religious, or ethnic group within it. Culture plays a role in the development of every student. Skilled teachers realize their own cultural experiences shape their perspective and that multiple perspectives, aside from their own, must be considered in planning programs for students.

---

[1]Although the benefit from single-gender education is a topic of public debate, according to a review published by the United States Department of Education (2005), "There is a dearth of quality studies [on single gender education] (i.e., randomized experiments or correlational studies with adequate statistical controls) across all outcomes" of educational achievement.

Appropriate instruction in physical education for culturally diverse populations may require special teaching skills and a focus on students' unique needs. Students from different cultures may respond differently to directions from the teacher, praise and acknowledgment from others, perceived expectations, and physical interaction. Teachers learn to recognize and understand the influence of their students' cultural heritages and learn to accommodate diversity while achieving the goals of the physical education curriculum.

The following key strategies for educators promote consideration of students' beliefs and practices:

- Become aware of cultural differences (e.g., the meaning associated with eye contact and hand gestures).
- Become educated about the religious and ethnic customs of students.
- Have students work in small heterogeneous groups.
- Encourage students to research their cultures and share the dances, sports, and games of their cultures.
- Treat students as individuals, not as members of groups.
- Avoid stereotyping students by groups (i.e., assuming students from a particular culture will prefer certain activities).
- Analyze instructional materials for stereotypical images and language.
- Learn to pronounce students' names correctly.
- Set high expectations for all students.
- Accept students' native language and help students to develop English language skills.
- Teach students about the cultural context of physical activities.
- Recognize that students from different cultures may not possess prior knowledge or experience related to some physical activities.
- Be aware of the fasting that may be the custom during some religious holidays and plan activities that are less demanding.
- Accept and celebrate ethnic and cultural diversity.

There are times when cultural and religious beliefs require special consideration in physical education classes. For example, in some cultures and religions the exposure of any part of the body except the face and hands is not permitted for girls; sharing showers and changing clothes in common rooms is not permitted for boys; and boys and girls must be separated at puberty. These cultural and religious beliefs can raise a variety of issues related to dressing, showering, dancing, and swimming activities. However, there are strategies that can reduce the impact of these issues on the physical education class.

Examples of effective strategies for accommodating students' dressing/showering are as follows:

- Allow students to have lockers near friends.
- Demonstrate changing techniques such as changing a shirt under the cover of another shirt.
- Provide private areas for changing and showering.
- Allow students to wear clothing acceptable to their religious practices.

Examples of effective strategies for reducing physical contact between boys and girls in physical education classes are as follows:

- Assign students to certain roles/positions to prevent physical contact (e.g., quarterback/receiver without defenders).
- Modify the activity to avoid physical contact. (e.g., use a soft object to "tag" students to avoid physical contact).

Examples of effective strategies for accommodating students in dancing are as follows:

- Modify groupings (pair students of the same gender or have the student dance alone).
- Provide the student with an alternate physical activity if the student's religious beliefs forbid dancing.

An example of an effective strategy to accommodate students in swimming is as follows:

- Allow students to wear modified attire instead of traditional swimsuits.

Examples of effective strategies to accommodate student fasting are as follows:

- Modify strenuous activities on the day(s) of the fast.
- Schedule physical education earlier in the school day for students who are fasting.

English Learners

California's diverse student population consists of many different ethnic groups, speaks a variety of languages and dialects, varies in English proficiency, and comes to school with a variety of experiences, both academic and nonacademic. The California Department of Education reported that in the 2007-08 school year, 1.55 million students, 24.7 percent of California public school students, were identified as English learners. More than 50 major languages (other than English) were found to be represented. The top five languages and percentage of English learners using each language were Spanish (85.1 percent), Vietnamese (2.2 percent), Pilipino (1.4 percent), Cantonese (1.4 percent), and Hmong (1.3 percent).

Different instructional approaches are needed for students with limited English. Bilingual interpreters or instructors skilled in sign language may be needed. For teachers who do not speak a second language and for English learners, specially designed academic instruction in English (SDAIE) is another approach that may be used. SDAIE, also known as sheltered instruction (Echevarria, Vogt, and Short 2004; Guarino et al. 2001), provides students with a variety of interactive and multimodal means to access information. With sheltered instruction techniques, teachers modify the language demands of the lesson and:

- Clearly enunciate all words.
- Define advanced words with simpler synonyms (e.g., explain that *cardiorespiratory* means the heart and lungs).

- Use cognates (see the Glossary) when appropriate (e.g., *muscle,* the Spanish word *muscolo; ligament,* the Spanish word *ligamento).*
- Clarify the use of any idiomatic expressions (e.g., "Keep your eye on the ball" means to watch the ball).
- Use contextual cues such as gestures, facial expressions, demonstrations, props, and visual aids (e.g., task cards).
- Use graphic organizers (e.g., Venn diagram).
- Use prior content for introductions (preview/anticipatory set).
- Hold up manipulatives (e.g., beanbags, balls) when describing skill technique.

Cooperative learning has also proved effective in teaching students at various levels of English proficiency because high levels of interaction are associated with enhanced learning of content and English (Echevarria, Vogt, and Short 2000). Feedback for English learners, like that provided to all students, should be specific and positive or specific and corrective, and timely.

Table 7.2 Instructional Modifications for English Learners

Standard	Support for Building Understanding	Tasks/Strategies	Additional Considerations
Grade 2, Standard 4.3: Identify ways to increase time for physical activity outside of school.	Show pictures of students: • Walking to school • Biking to school • Using stairs • Turning off TV and going out to play • Walking an animal	Show chart illustrating sedentary and physically active activities. • Driving to school rather than walking to school • Sitting on a bench rather than playing on playground • Playing a video game indoors rather than playing an outdoor game	Check for understanding using the chart, with students providing thumbs-up and thumbs-down responses. Group or partner English learners who are at Level 1 or Level 2 in English language proficiency.
Grade 3, Standard 1.2: Perform an inverted balance (tripod) by evenly distributing weight on body parts.	Demonstrate the tripod. Provide concrete demonstrations of students successfully performing the tripod. Provide pictures/charts of students correctly performing the tripod technique.	Focus questions on video or student performing tripod. Does making a triangle with hands and elbow assist with performing the tripod? Show video clip of correct technique and incorrect technique.	Partner with like-language student. Orally check for understanding when possible.

In addition to helping English learners gain access to the physical education content, physical education teachers can also provide valuable opportunities for English language development. The following examples show how physical education teachers can foster English language development:

- Letter recognition is reinforced by using beanbags with letters printed on them.
- The names of body parts are taught through their use in physical activities (e.g., the teacher instructs the students to bend the knees as he or she completes movements involving the bending of knees).
- The names of locomotor movements are taught through labeling of demonstrations by other students (e.g., the teacher says, "Skip across the circle," and students demonstrate the movement).
- Writing skills are reinforced by having students write down words used in the lesson that they do not recognize or cannot define.
- Vocabulary is developed through physical activity instruction (e.g., pass the ball through your arms, stand on the blue square, move around the cone, stand behind your partner, throw the ball to the target).

At-Risk Learners

Students are at-risk learners if they are not making reasonable progress toward the standards or are experiencing levels of difficulty for one reason or another. These students may have come from schools or states where different content is taught, or they may simply not have learned the correct or prerequisite technique or information. The achievement deficiency of at-risk learners can often be addressed with minimal assistance by the teacher. When students begin to fall behind in their mastery of physical education model content standards (as evidenced by ongoing assessment), immediate intervention is warranted. Interventions combine practice in material not yet mastered with instruction in new skill areas. Students who are behind will find it a challenge to catch up with their peers and to stay current as new concepts and skills are introduced. Yet the need for remediation cannot be allowed to exclude these students from instruction in new content. In a standards-based environment, students who are struggling to learn or master physical education receive differentiated instruction.

In helping students move from below grade or course level up to their grade or course level, teachers use instructional resources aligned to the standards; however, during a transitional period, students receive instruction aligned with fundamental concepts from previous grade levels or courses that support the standards for their grade level or course level. For example, motor skill standards may be broken down for some students before they can apply them in a game situation, or students may be taught the components of health-related physical fitness before they can create a fitness plan.

Examples of appropriate strategies for working with at-risk students are as follows:

- Increase the wait time after asking a question.
- Call on students so that all students have opportunities to answer questions.

- Probe or delve further when students respond with an incorrect answer by asking questions that help lead students to the correct answers (Los Angeles County Office of Education 1993).
- Understand students' specific learning needs.
- Ask students to share with a partner ("pair share").

Students with Medical Conditions

Students with long-term and short-term medical conditions may include those with scoliosis, asthma, obesity, broken limbs, and those who are pregnant. Students with medical conditions are entitled to an instructional program based on grade-level or course-level standards. The program for those students is designed to address the same standards as that for students without medical conditions. When possible, students with medical conditions engage in the same instructional unit and content area.

A student with an IEP may also have a short-term condition (e.g., a student who receives special education services for a speech disorder and who also has a broken arm). The teacher considers both the IEP requirements and the short-term condition when planning instruction. An instructional plan for a student with a short-term medical condition assigns physical education tasks and physical activities that the student can do in the short term and gradually, as the medical condition allows, moves the student toward full participation.

Physical education teachers work with the student's doctor and other health care providers to design a program for the student. Teachers also communicate with the student's parents or guardians to fully understand what the student can and cannot do. Effective communication between the parents, teachers, and other professionals ensures that a student receives physical education instruction that meets his or her unique needs.

Advanced Learners

Advanced learners are students who demonstrate or are capable of demonstrating performance in physical education at a level significantly above the performance of their age group. Often in physical education, athletes are classified as the advanced learners. However, the physical education model content standards address cognitive and affective learning as well as psychomotor learning. Therefore, the term *advanced learners* in physical education takes on a different meaning. In California, each school district determines its own criteria for identifying gifted and talented students. The percentage of students so identified varies, and each district may choose whether to identify students as gifted based on their ability in physical education.

Standards-based education offers opportunities for students who have the motivation, interest, or ability in physical education to excel. Several research studies (Harrison 2001; Rink 1998) have demonstrated the importance of setting high expectations for all students, including highly skilled students. The physical education model content standards provide students with goals worth reaching and identify the point at which skills and knowledge should be mastered. The natural corollary is that when standards are mastered, students should either move on to standards at higher grade levels or focus on material not covered by the standards.

A common approach is to provide advanced students with enrichment and depth as they study the standards for their grade level. With such an approach, enrichment or extension leads the student to complex, technically sound applications. Care is taken to design instruction that is dynamic and thoughtfully constructed. Lessons can be devised by groups of teachers pooling their expertise in helping advanced students to learn. These teams create innovative methods for assessing student progress to facilitate assignment of students to instructional groups in which teaching is targeted to challenge students and ensure their progress toward mastery of the model content standards.

Some examples of appropriate strategies for advanced learners are as follows:

- Build on basic skills (e.g., reverse layup taught after the layup).
- Provide assistance to peers.
- Plan challenging activities for self.
- Allow for independent study.
- Allow students to expand assignments to meet their interests and needs.
- Adjust instruction to meet student needs.
- Provide a variety of resources.
- Provide complex, in-depth assignments.
- Allow for interdisciplinary projects.
- Provide problem-based assignments.
- Offer assignments geared toward areas of creativity.
- Promote higher levels of thinking.
- Use an inclusive style of teaching,

Students with Disabilities (IEPs and 504 Plans)

Students become eligible for special education services through an assessment process called multidisciplinary team evaluation. The federal regulations (*34 CFR § 300.8*) for the Individuals with Disabilities Education Act (IDEA 2004) identify the following disability categories:

- Mental retardation
- A hearing impairment (including deafness)
- A speech or language impairment
- A visual impairment (including blindness)
- A serious emotional disturbance (referred to as "emotional disturbance")
- An orthopedic impairment
- Autism
- Traumatic brain injury
- Other health impairment

- A specific learning disability
- Deaf-blindness
- Multiple disabilities

Students who have one of these disabilities may require special education. Even if a student with a disability does not require special education classroom instruction, he or she may have special needs for physical education instruction. For example, a student using crutches or one with cerebral palsy may be appropriately placed in a general education classroom. He or she may, however, require specially designed instruction in physical education or adaptations of equipment or facilities to successfully participate in physical education.

Students with disabilities are provided with access to all the model content standards through a rich and supported program that uses instructional materials and strategies that best meet their needs. A student's 504 Plan or individualized education program (IEP) often includes suggestions for techniques to ensure that the student has full access to a program designed to provide him or her with appropriate learning opportunities. Teachers familiarize themselves with each student's 504 Plan or IEP to help the student achieve mastery of the physical education model content standards.

In compliance with the requirements of Section 504 of the federal Rehabilitation Act of 1973, a Section 504 Plan is typically individually designed for a student who, based on an assessment, is determined to have a "physical or mental impairment [that] substantially limits one or more major life activities." The plan specifies agreed-on services and accommodations. In contrast to the federal Individuals with Disabilities Education Improvement Act (IDEA 2004), Section 504 allows a wide range of information to be in a plan: (1) the nature of the disability; (2) the basis for determining the disability; (3) the educational impact of the disability; (4) the necessary accommodations; and (5) the least restrictive environment in which the student may be placed.

An IEP is a written, comprehensive statement of the educational needs of a student with a disability and the specially designed instruction and related services to be employed to meet those needs. An IEP is developed (and annually reviewed and revised) by a team of individuals knowledgeable about the student's disability. The student's parents or guardians are involved in the IEP development as well as the annual review and revision process. The IEP complies with the requirements of the IDEA 2004 and covers such items as the (1) student's present level of performance in relation to the curriculum; (2) measurable annual goals related to the student's involvement and progress in the curriculum; (3) specialized programs (or program modifications) and services to be provided; (4) participation with nondisabled students in regular classes and activities; and (5) accommodation and modification in assessments and instruction.

Some students come to physical education with motor, cognitive, or perceptual deficits; others, with more severe multiple disabilities. Successful participation in physical activities by students with disabilities depends on the teacher's attitude and skill in providing instruction and support to all students. Teachers continually inspire all students to learn and experience maximum enjoyment in physical education by understanding students' specific needs and encouraging students who do not have special needs to accept those students who do.

Students with disabilities, whether they are identified as needing special education and related services or not, have the right to participate in physical education in the least restrictive environment and to have a modification of the regular program if needed. Further, under Section 504 of the Rehabilitation Act of 1973, Amendments of 1991 (Public Law 102–42), and the Americans with Disabilities Act of 1990 (Public Law 101–336), students with disabilities may not be discriminated against by school personnel.

Physical Education Service Delivery Options

Three physical education program options (as defined in *Adapted Physical Education Guidelines in California Schools,* 2003, pages 22–26) are recommended to meet the needs of students with and without disabilities. (See Appendix I.) The IEP team determines which service or combination of services would best meet the student's needs and provide the mandated number of minutes of physical education required for the student's grade level.

General physical education. This option encompasses a full spectrum of game, sport, fitness, and movement activities, including physical and motor fitness, fundamental motor skills and patterns, and skills in aquatics, dance, and individual and group games and sports. The student participates with or without accommodations, adaptations, or modifications that can be made by the general physical education teacher. The IEP should accurately reflect any accommodations, adaptations, or modifications that are necessary for the student to participate successfully in the general physical education program.

Specially designed physical education. Specially designed instruction means the content, methodology, or delivery of instruction is adapted to address the unique needs of the student that result from the student's disability (*34 CFR* § 300.39[b]). If specially designed physical education is prescribed in a child's IEP, the public agency responsible for the education of that child must provide services directly or make arrangements for those services to be provided (*34 CFR* § 300.108). A special education teacher, teaching physical education to the students in her self-contained class, is one example of specially designed physical education. Another example is one class period of middle or high school physical education in which all students need specially designed physical education and are taught by the general physical education teacher.

Adapted physical education. A credentialed adapted physical education specialist provides adapted physical education to students who have instructional needs that cannot be adequately satisfied in other physical education programs as indicated by an assessment and IEP process. Adapted physical education services may be provided through direct instruction, team teaching, the appropriate use of instructional aides, or collaborative consultation as long as appropriate goal(s) and objective(s) are indicated and accurately monitored by the adapted physical education specialist. All such services must be accurately indicated on the student's IEP with appropriate goals and objectives/benchmarks recorded and monitored by the adapted physical education specialist. The frequency and duration of adapted physical education service are based on the needs of the student and are indicated on the IEP. The IEP indicates the frequency with which the adapted physical education specialist provides service for the student. Collaborative consultation is one method of providing instructional service to assist students with participating successfully in the less restrictive settings of general physical education.

Adapted physical education services should be available in all school districts. Every student, including a student with disabilities, must have the minutes of physical education instruction required by statute. The student's time with the adapted physical education specialist is usually only a portion of this time. Instruction for the remaining required physical education time is best provided in consultation with the adapted physical education specialist and should be documented on the IEP.

The physical education teacher seeks out opportunities for informal talks with the adapted physical education specialist or special education teacher to develop methods for working with students with disabilities. The teacher enlists the help of parents, aides, other teachers, community members, administrators, counselors, and diagnosticians, when necessary, and explores the use of technology or other instructional devices as a way to respond to students' individual needs. When students cannot participate safely and successfully in the physical education program and when interventions have been ineffective, the specialist in adapted physical education takes a more active role and an assessment for adapted physical education is conducted, including presentation of results to the IEP team.

Adaptations

Many students with a disability require adaptations that include accommodations or modifications to enhance their learning. An accommodation addresses the instructional needs of the student by removing the effects of the disability but does not alter the performance outcome (e.g., more time, smaller groups, substitutions, and instructional prompts). A modification is also based upon the instructional needs of the student, but it fundamentally alters and usually defines performance that approximates rather than shows mastery of standards (e.g., student plays "one-on-one" hockey instead of team game, steps over stationary rope instead of jumping a self-turned rope, or drops the ball into a container instead of throwing with accuracy). Educators should use caution when deciding whether to modify physical education performance outcomes for standards, as the course content may be changed. All educators should refer to the student's IEP or Section 504 Plan when adapting a standards-based physical education curriculum for a student with a disability (adapted from the State Council on Adapted Physical Education's *Position Paper on Physical Education Content Standards for Students with a Disability*).

Table 7.3 provides examples of possible adaptations for general education programs.

Table 7.3 Adaptations in Physical Education for Students with Disabilities

Category	Examples
Formation (including space, placement within a group, and boundaries of the activity)	• Place hard-of-hearing student near the instructor when instructions are given orally. • Assign a student with asthma, obesity, or reduced stamina to infield positions during a softball unit. • Reduce the court or field size for a student with asthma, obesity, or reduced stamina.
Change of form or language used	• Use gestures and demonstration to augment verbal communication. • Provide written lists of tasks or steps to a student with attention or auditory memory difficulties. • Assign a peer helper to a student with attention, communication, or reading difficulties.
Equipment	• Use lighter or smaller sports equipment for a student with reduced strength or small stature. • Make multiple pieces of the same equipment available to increase practice time for students. • Use equipment that moves at a slower speed when students are learning a new skill.
Task or objective (alter skill level to be taught or practiced during lesson)	• Reduce the number of repetitions of an exercise for a student with reduced strength or mild physical disability. • Set goals for improving individual performance rather than compare performance with other students. • Allow for additional trials for student with lower skills or mild physical disability.
Environment, including social environment	• Assign a peer helper to a student with attention, communication, or reading difficulties. • Teacher selects teams. Do not allow student captains to "choose" teams in front of the group. • Provide specific feedback and positive comments from peers or teacher.
Players (number, groupings of individuals, or organize class into stations)	• Teacher structures groups to ensure equality and opportunity to contribute/participate. • Assign peers to model, assist, or augment participation.
Rules (including game rules and class rules)	• Alter rules for inclusion rather than exclusion. • Alter the dress code during outdoor activities for student who is sensitive to the sun.

Source: Adapted from Seaman et al. (2007), pages 209–10.

Accommodations

The following adaptations are examples of accommodations:[2]

Quantity—Adapt the number of items that the student is expected to learn or complete. For example, if students are expected to learn three dance steps, students with a developmental disability may be able to learn only one.

Time—Adapt the time allotted and allowed for learning, task completion, or testing, such as increasing time allotted to finish an endurance run or swim.

Level of support—Increase the amount of personal assistance for a particular student by utilizing the classroom paraeducator/teacher aide, creating a peer tutor program, or encouraging parent volunteers to assist in class.

Input—Adapt the way instruction is delivered to the student by becoming familiar with each student's style of learning. Some students learn best by watching a demonstration, others through auditory means, and still others by moving their own bodies to replicate the performance.

Difficulty—Adapt the skill level, type of problems, or the rules for how the student may approach the task. Examples include using a ball ramp for bowling or allowing a student to use a crutch to hit or kick a ball.

Output—Adapt how the student responds to instruction. Give a student with a learning disability the option of orally answering test questions on concepts rather than in written form.

Participation—Adapt the extent to which a student is actively involved in the task according to the student's abilities rather than his or her disabilities. If a student is unable to run, another student can do the running part of the activity for the student. If the student has limited understanding of the movement patterns, assign a buddy to help lead him or her through the appropriate pattern or give specific cues or prompts during the movement.

Modifications

Modifications are considered more extreme and are required only when the accommodations are not effective at facilitating the participation of the student in a general education program. The following adaptations are examples of modifications:

Alternate goals—Adapt the goals or outcome expectations while using the same equipment used for students without disabilities. Coordinate the goals and expectations for the class with the IEP of the student with the disability. While the class is working toward acquiring lifetime skills for playing volleyball and expected outcomes include mastery of a variety of volleyball skills, a student with a disability may be focused on playing cooperatively without hitting other students to meet an IEP goal such as "Play cooperatively in a group game at least 15 minutes by the end

---

[2]Examples of accommodations and modifications are adapted from Seaman et al. (2007), pages 281–83.

of the semester." If the class is learning to dribble a ball with one hand while moving, a student with a disability might be expected to master a one-hand dribble while stationary.

Substitute curriculum—A different skill or sport is experienced by the students with disabilities. A unit on track and field instruction may be appropriate for students with disabilities but may require different skills, such as pushing a wheelchair, rather than running. Not all physical education is sport, so if the purpose of an instructional unit is to improve specific health-related parameters, other activities that meet that criterion can be used: swimming or pushing a wheelchair or bicycling can be substituted for running, weight lifting can be substituted for lifting one's body as in tumbling, and a dual sport such as tennis can be substituted for volleyball.

8

Supporting High-Quality Physical Education

The delivery of effective and efficient physical education instruction that meets the needs of every student requires broad support. It is an obligation of everyone, including administrators, teacher leaders, college and university personnel, community members, and parents. Each of these groups is an important contributor. The stakeholders at each school or school district form a support system that assists in the design, implementation, and evaluation of an effective physical education instructional program. These stakeholders also serve an important function as advocates for a sustained focus on the achievement of the physical education model content standards by every student. This chapter addresses the roles and responsibilities of the stakeholders, administrators in particular, in the development, implementation, and maintenance of high-quality, standards-based physical education instructional programs.

Administrative Role and Support

The role of school board members, district administrators, and school administrators is crucial to the success of the physical education program. Setting and clearly articulating high expectations for instruction by all teachers and learning by every student is the foundation of a successful program. It is also essential that administrators express a positive attitude toward physical education and an appreciation for its importance in a comprehensive school setting.

Administrators convey their high expectations by being visible in the physical education setting. Frequent visits to the physical education facility provide administrators with firsthand knowledge of safety and maintenance issues. Frequent class observations allow the school administrator to provide physical education teachers with relevant feedback regarding their instructional practices. In addition, attendance at physical education department meetings increases the administrators' understanding of the unique needs of the physical education staff and program.

District and school administrators, as well as school board members, need to understand the meaning of high-quality physical education to effectively support the program. This understanding includes knowledge of the content addressed in the physical education model content standards, how to establish effective learning environments, how to assess student learning in physical education, and instructional strategies that work in physical education. To this end, district and school administrators are provided with ongoing professional development on the topic of physical education.

Hiring Practices

The first step toward providing a high-quality physical education program is hiring high-quality teachers. Only appropriately credentialed teachers are considered for physical education positions. Appropriate hiring practices also help to ensure that class sizes for physical education are consistent with other subject areas in the school and that students have sufficient opportunities and support to master physical education content.

227

Chapter 8
Supporting
High-Quality
Physical
Education

Supervising Practices

Administrators frequently monitor instruction to ensure teachers are utilizing the best practices for student learning. Administrators prepare for instructional monitoring by becoming knowledgeable about how students learn physical education content, how student learning in physical education is assessed, and the essentials of effective instruction in physical education. Table 8.1 provides quality indicators for administrators making instructional observations. (See Appendix J.)

Table 8.1 Quality Indicators for Instructional Observations

Physical Education Instruction	Quality Indicators
Physical education content	Curriculum is standards-based. Learning sequences are content-rich.
Assessment of student learning	Assessment is embedded. There are multiple data-collection points.
Effective instruction	Lessons maximize learning. Curriculum, assessment, and instruction are aligned. Multiple instructional strategies are utilized.

Administrators observe physical education instruction and provide teachers with feedback to improve their instructional practices. Formal and informal observations take place regularly and focus on physical education content, establishing a positive learning environment, assessment of student learning, teaching strategies, effective teaching behaviors, and legal issues associated with physical education.

High-Quality Professional Development

Successful implementation of the physical education model content standards depends on continuing professional development. Professional development is "a planned, collaborative, educational process of continual improvement for teachers" (*Before It's Too Late* 2000). Professional development is based on the physical education model content standards and guidelines presented in this framework. It is conducted by credentialed and experienced presenters and provided through a variety of professional development opportunities that include workshops, seminars, conferences, and, most importantly, ongoing training programs. Professional development opportunities help to ensure that teachers are provided with the tools to be highly effective.

School and school district administrators support teachers' lifelong learning with release time and funding for ongoing, highly effective, standards-based professional development programs. At the school level, physical education teachers have opportunities to meet regularly with each other and with members of other departments or grade levels to assess the effectiveness of programs and plan revisions. Release time is provided so that teachers can observe one another teaching. Teachers are encouraged to become involved in professional

228

Chapter 8
Supporting
High-Quality
Physical
Education

organizations and to contribute their expertise to professional development projects in physical education at the local, state, and national levels.

The conditions that support powerful learning for adults include attending to what is learned, how it is learned, and where it is learned. High-quality professional development:

- Is a long-term, planned investment in professional development that is strongly supported by the administration and designed to ensure that teachers continue to develop skills and knowledge in physical education content and instructional options
- Provides classroom support for teachers experimenting with new instructional strategies
- Builds in accountability practices and evaluation of professional development programs to provide a foundation for future planning
- Provides time for physical education teachers to work together and to engage in professional dialog regarding new concepts and ideas
- Focuses on student learning, especially tailoring curriculum and instruction to students' needs, all of which is compatible with current research and the physical education model content standards
- Includes ongoing and in-depth activities and a variety of strategies to help educators apply what they have learned and sustain improved instruction
- Provides time for educators to reflect, analyze, and refine their own professional practices and to plan and refine instruction accordingly
- Develops, refines, and expands teachers' pedagogical repertoire, content knowledge, and the skill to integrate both
- Follows the principles of good teaching and learning, including providing comfortable, respectful environments conducive to adult learning

Professional Development Opportunities and Topics

Physical education teachers have numerous opportunities for professional growth. Colleges and universities (including community colleges) offer physical education courses in continuing education or advanced study programs. Many school districts provide in-service training programs for their physical education teachers. In school districts where no in-service training program exists, physical education teachers should request, through appropriate administrative channels, that one be established. Professional organizations offer local, state, and national conferences/conventions, as well as professional journals and opportunities to interact and collaborate with colleagues. Many of these organizations also offer online learning experiences so that busy teachers can learn at their own pace.

All professional development for physical education strives for improved student achievement as the primary objective. To that end, programs are focused on physical education instruction at each teacher's specific grade level or course level and the standards associated with that grade or course level. Ongoing professional development is planned and provided for both generalists who teach physical education and teachers with single-subject credentials in physical education. The generalist who teaches physical education may have little or no

229

Chapter 8
Supporting
High-Quality
Physical
Education

background in physical education or subject matter content knowledge and may want professional development specifically designed to increase his or her subject area knowledge.

Suggested professional development topics appropriate for all teachers of physical education include:

- New research related to teaching physical education
- Content information contained in the state-adopted model content standards
- Assessing student learning
- Understanding child and adolescent development
- Working effectively with a diverse student population: differentiated instruction, inclusion strategies, language acquisition, modifications for special-needs students
- Brain research related to learning
- Effective instructional practices for standards-based instruction
- Using technology in physical education
- Effective use of instructional materials
- Unpacking the standards
- Universal precautions
- Standardized fitness-testing protocols
- Class management techniques

Specific professional development topics for individuals without a background in physical education include:

- Physical education content knowledge
- Motor development
- Lesson development for physical education
- Evaluating, managing, and distributing physical education equipment
- Teaching physical education content (e.g., movement education, tumbling, motor skills)
- How to plan and organize an outdoor learning environment

Program Development

Resources for standards-based physical education curriculum are limited or in early developmental stages; therefore, the responsibility for program development rests upon individual school districts. Local districts create standards-based physical education curricula that are aligned to the model content standards and are adopted by the district board for use throughout the district. The locally adopted curriculum is then implemented throughout the district and evaluated regularly by teachers and administrations. Adjustments are made to the curriculum as determined by periodic evaluations.

Districts hire or designate physical education specialists/consultants to assist with ongoing curricula development and revisions. The role of the physical education specialist/consultant becomes an integral part of implementation of the physical education model content standards. The responsibility of the specialist/consultant is to provide content-specific knowledge, best practices, professional

230

Chapter 8
Supporting
High-Quality
Physical
Education

development, and teacher support. Once districts hire or designate physical education specialists/consultants, the specialists/consultants form a curriculum committee including the specialist/consultant, teacher leaders, district administrators, program consultants, teacher librarians, professional organization representatives, and, when possible, county office curriculum specialists.

The district curriculum committee develops a physical education program and the materials to support implementation of the program. Program materials may include a curriculum guide from which teachers can extract information to assist with lesson design. Other materials, based on the state-adopted model content standards, that support the district curricula include grade- or course-level standards charts, pacing guides or curriculum maps, course descriptions, and model lesson designs. The curriculum committee develops instructional resources and makes them available to teachers. The instructional materials include strategies for individualized instruction, class management, standardized testing procedures and protocols, and equipment organization. The instructional resources also present a sequence of course offerings showing all stakeholders the path of student progress in physical education. District program development highlights the relationship between physical education and academic learning as part of the entire district academic program. The curriculum is viewed as a resource for teachers. Individual unit and lesson plans based on the district-adopted curriculum are then developed by individual teachers at the site level.

Once the program and instructional materials are developed, districts provide physical education teachers with structured planning time and time to receive professional development. Ongoing assistance from the teacher specialist/consultant will ensure that teachers receive the most current information and support in providing high-quality physical education programs.

At the school level, administrators call upon the expertise of physical education teachers to help develop a master schedule for physical education that best meets the needs of every student. Specifically, elementary physical education classes are scheduled throughout the day to make the best use of facilities, equipment, and supplies. In middle school and high school physical education classes, instruction is provided by grade or course level so students learn the grade- and course-level content called for in the physical education model content standards.

In terms of program development, the role of administrators is to take the following measurs:

- Assist the physical education staff with the development of long-term and short-term goals for program improvement.
- Allocate time for the physical education department to discuss the state-adopted physical education model content standards, current research-based instructional practices, and standards-based assessment.
- Facilitate articulation between grade levels and grade spans to ensure that instruction is sequential and supports long-term goals for student achievement.
- Take a leadership role in program evaluation.
- Establish schoolwide systems to ensure that students with special needs are (1) assessed early to determine the need for additional and specialized

231

Chapter 8
Supporting
High-Quality
Physical
Education

instruction; (2) monitored to determine when and what kind of additional support is needed; and (3) included in all state, school district, and schoolwide assessments.

- Support the ongoing use of broad-based school health or wellness councils or advisory committees, as required by federal legislation (Public Law 108-265, Section 204), to develop and implement local wellness policies.
- Showcase physical education instruction and student achievement of the physical education model content standards through newsletters and physical education nights, similar to math nights.

Providing a Safe Learning Environment

Physical education instruction must take place in a safe learning environment. District and site administrators assist by ensuring that school facilities, equipment and supplies, and resources are safe to use and stocked in sufficient quantity. Additionally, they provide an adequately staffed physical education department and ensure that staff members receive health information on every student.

Effective administrators use a variety of funding sources to provide the necessary resources for high-quality physical education programs. Categorical funding, discretionary funding, and general funds are all utilized to provide the optimum learning opportunities for every student. Grant funding may also be used, but it should not become the sole funding source nor should it supplant the regular general education funding of physical education. The selection of instructional resources should be based on the guidelines in Chapter 9.

The administrator's role related to facilities and equipment is to perform the following functions:

- Supervise the installation of equipment.
- Ensure that appropriate space is provided around equipment and that the rules for safe conduct around equipment are clearly stated and posted in a visible location.
- Ensure that equipment and facilities are monitored and maintained.
- Document results of equipment and facilities inspections.
- Arrange for repairs to be made as soon as a defect is found.
- Ensure that insurance protection is adequate and tailored to the school's specific requirements.
- Monitor repairs when a defect is found.
- Work with the risk management department to shut down or condemn unsafe areas until repairs are completed.

Special attention is paid to safety hazards that are common in the physical education environment:

- Holes or cracks in hard, dirt, or turf surfaces
- Water damage and improper irrigation and drainage
- Grass or weeds growing through cracks in hard surfaces
- Debris
- Loose or weakened play structures

- Weathering and dry rot
- Improperly secured or unsupervised swimming pools
- Foundational surfaces that are not properly maintained (excessive wear)

Additionally, the aquatic facility is an area that requires special attention. Safety equipment (e.g. hook, lifeline, ring buoys, spine boards) are conveniently located around pool areas and must be in usable condition. A telephone or other communication device is easily available in the facility for use during emergency situations. Under California *Health and Safety Code* Section 116033, at least one lifeguard must be in attendance during instruction in aquatics.

> Persons providing aquatic instruction, including, but not limited to, swimming instruction, water safety instruction, water contact activities, and competitive aquatic sports, at a public swimming pool shall possess an American Red Cross Emergency Water Safety Course certificate, or have equivalent qualifications, as determined by the state department. In addition, these persons shall be certified in standard first aid and cardiopulmonary resuscitation (CPR). . . The requirements of this section shall be waived under either of the following circumstances: (a) when one or more aquatic instructors possessing the American Red Cross Emergency Water Safety Course Certificate or its equivalent are in attendance continuously during periods of aquatic instruction, or (b) when one or more lifeguards meeting the requirements of Section 116028 are in attendance continuously during periods of aquatic instruction.

An adequately staffed physical education department will also help to ensure a safe and productive learning environment. The National Association for Sport and Physical Education (NASPE) advises the best practices for elementary physical education. The class size ratio is one teacher for every 25 students. For secondary physical education there is to be one teacher for every 30 students (*Teaching Large Class Sizes in Physical Education* 2006; NASPE Recognition Program Criteria for Recognition: STARS Levels 1–3 2006). The *California Code of Regulations, Title 5,* Section 10060, states, "Class size is consistent with the requirements of good instruction and safety." And, *Healthy Children Ready to Learn: Facilities Best Practices* (2007, 17) states, "40 students or fewer is a preferable class size" in middle and high school settings.

A sound practice for physical educators and other staff personnel in contact with students during physical education and physical activity is to be certified in first aid and CPR. They should also receive training in universal blood precautions. Under the "universal precaution" principle, blood and body fluids from all persons should be considered as infected, regardless of the known or supposed health status of the person. At a minimum, plastic gloves are available and used whenever there is the potential of exposure to blood or other body fluids. Schools and districts have written policies for providing emergency first aid, procedures for reporting accidents to parents and school authorities, and plans for handling emergency situations.

233

Chapter 8
Supporting
High-Quality
Physical
Education

Classroom Management Policies

School administrators support physical educators in their efforts to develop effective classroom management policies. By working together with the physical education staff, school administrators demonstrate their support for the physical education program. This collaboration also helps administrators and teachers define their roles in the student discipline process.

The following considerations are important for classroom management policies:

- Classroom and schoolwide discipline plans and procedures are implemented by all staff members.
- Discipline is appropriate to the infraction and consistent with expectations of classroom behavior for other programs and subject areas.
- Discipline practices are fair and consistent and encourage students to take responsibility for their own behavior.
- Physical education is not withheld as a punishment or earned as a reward.
- Physical exercise is not used as punishment.
- Teachers believe that every student can behave properly and achieve the content standards.

Instructional Time

Physical education is the only subject area in which schools are required by the state to provide a minimum number of instructional minutes. California *Education Code (EC)* Section 51210 states that district-adopted courses of study for grades one to six shall include physical education for not less than 200 minutes every 10 school days. Statutory language on physical education for students in grades one through six (*EC* 51210[g]) further states that physical education instructional minutes are exclusive of recesses and the lunch period.[1] According to the United States Department of Health and Human Services, it is best practice for elementary physical education to be conducted daily (*Healthy People 2010* 2000).

Schools are required to provide a minimum of 400 minutes of physical education instruction every 10 school days for students in grades seven through twelve (*EC* 51222 and 51223).

However, local school boards or the office of the county superintendent of schools may exempt students from physical education under certain circumstances. Under *EC* 51241(a), students can be temporarily exempted from physical education if the student is injured or ill and a modified program to meet the needs of the student cannot be provided or the student is enrolled for one-half or less of the work normally required of a full-time student.

High school students must pass the physical performance test administered in grade nine to receive the temporary two-year exemption under *EC* 51241(b) that allows districts to exempt students from physical education any two years in grades ten, eleven, or twelve. State statute defines "passing" as meeting satisfactorily (scoring in the Healthy Fitness Zone) at least five of the six standards of the current (2008) physical performance test, the FITNESSGRAM®. Information on the

---

[1] *Education Code* sections cited are current as of January 2009.

234

Chapter 8
Supporting
High-Quality
Physical
Education

statewide physical performance test is available online at http://www.cde.ca.gov/ta/tg/pf.

EC 51222 requires schools that exempt students from physical education (under *EC* 51241[b]) to offer those students a variety of physical education elective courses of not less than 400 minutes each 10 school days.

School districts may grant permanent exceptions under *EC* 51241(c) for students who meet any of the following conditions:

- Sixteen years of age or older and have been enrolled in tenth grade for one academic year or longer;
- Enrolled as a postgraduate pupil; or
- Enrolled in a juvenile home, ranch, camp, or forestry camp school

To ensure that students are provided with adequate opportunities for physical education and physical activity, schools provide classes in physical education daily or through a block schedule whereby the class meets every other day for a double instructional period instead of schedules where classes meet less frequently. Under a block schedule, schools need to consider how the physical education classes will address the physical education model content standards that call for students to participate in moderate to vigorous physical activity for a minimum of four days a week. One example is where an elective class and a physical education class share a block, and each class meets daily.

Students are assigned to physical education classes in the same manner as they are assigned to other classes. Students with special needs are placed in the least restrictive physical education class where both the students with special needs and other students will be most successful at attaining the standards. For all grade levels and course levels, activities that interfere with regularly scheduled physical education are limited. For example, school events such as assemblies, school pictures, and vision screenings are not held during physical education classes more frequently than during other classes. Physical education should not be scheduled during recess or lunch time to ensure the availability of adequate space, sufficient equipment, and other resources necessary for physical education instruction, including students' attention and teacher focus. (Recess and lunch time must not be counted as physical education instructional minutes, pursuant to *EC* 51210[g] and 51223.[2])

Providing Instructional Aides

Physical education classes, like other academic classes, benefit from the addition of an instructional aide. As school and district administrators develop their physical education program, the hiring of instructional aides should be considered. Physical education classes tend to be heterogeneous, consisting of English learners, special-needs students, and students with a wide range of intellectual and physical abilities. Instructional aides can be used in physical education as language interpreters or translators, one-on-one tutors for special-needs students,

---

[2]Ibid.

235

Chapter 8
Supporting
High-Quality
Physical
Education

and tutors for small-group instructional assistance. Instructional aides are not solely responsible for instruction; they assist the teacher.

Instructional aides can have a positive impact on student success when trained to provide appropriate support and assistance. Training for physical education instructional aides focuses on the aide's role in the physical education instructional process. Additionally, opportunities for planning, communication, and collaboration with physical education teachers are critical for all instructional aides.

Physical education programs also benefit from the use of locker room attendants. One attendant should be hired for the boys locker room, and one attendant should be hired for the girls locker room. The responsibilities of locker room attendants include locker room supervision, distribution of loaner clothes and shower towels to students, organization and maintenance of sporting goods equipment, and the assignment of lockers to students.

Teacher Leaders

The role of the teacher leader is especially important in physical education, because many county offices of education and school districts do not have an administrator or coordinator whose primary responsibility is physical education. The lack of a district leader focusing solely on physical education is unfortunate because the research shows physical education leaders play a key role in the success of physical education programs (Evaul 2007). Teacher leaders, therefore, assume the responsibility for training other teachers, mentoring beginning teachers, representing physical education on various committees and in various situations, advocating support, and working on curriculum development. In their role as mentors for beginning teachers, teacher leaders provide demonstration lessons, observe and coach teachers, and assist in the development of teacher improvement plans.

Teacher leaders are first and foremost good teachers. They understand standards-based curriculum, assessment, and instruction. They understand physical education content, have good classroom management skills, and know how to provide a safe and supportive physical and psychological environment. In addition, they are effective listeners and communicators both orally and in writing. Teacher leaders are most successful when they receive specific training on being an effective leader.

Two other important characteristics of a teacher leader are passion and a vision for the field of physical education. Teacher leaders have a desire, love, and enthusiasm for creating exemplary physical education instructional programs. Teacher leaders also have a vision, a picture they carry around with them of an ideal physical education program. Leaders use their vision to clarify the purpose and direction they are taking, and they articulate this vision to others.

Becoming a teacher leader begins with a commitment to making the vision of high-quality, standards-based physical education a reality. It involves:

- Joining and actively participating in professional organizations (see Appendix L)
- Asking for more responsibility both within the school and the district

- Being a lifelong learner and engaging in long-term professional development opportunities
- Being an advocate of quality physical education for every student in every school

College and University Support

The support of college and university personnel for high-quality physical education programs is also crucial. Personnel from institutions of higher education support K–12 physical education by joining in partnership with their local schools. By becoming more involved with these other institutions of learning, college and university personnel become more aware of the research that needs to be done in the school settings. Armed with research derived from the local community, college and university personnel can be strong advocates of high-quality physical education programs and the use of only credentialed teachers in the teaching of K–12 physical education.

Teachers well prepared to teach physical education are vital to the success of physical education instruction. Most teachers are credentialed through the state colleges and universities. In addition, adoption of physical education model content standards and recent changes in assessment require teachers to gain new knowledge and alter classroom practices. Experienced teachers need support in learning and instituting new curriculum and instructional strategies, and new teachers and teacher candidates need even greater support in learning to teach physical education as they acquire the fundamentals of teaching. Colleges and university personnel provide support for those teachers through school visits and through the learning opportunities offered by higher education.

Community and Parent Support

Physical education is everybody's business. Business leaders, community members, and parents can all make significant contributions to the school's physical education program. The more knowledgeable these individuals are about physical education, the more they will be able to support physical education programs. Physical education departments can do much to influence the physical activity levels of business partners, community members, and parents.

Although the school is the primary learning environment for physical education, the home and community also play significant roles. Only through the cooperation of the school, the home, and the community can students become fully prepared for lifelong participation in physical activity and effective social interaction. For example, the interaction between school and family can help to promote an acceptance of physically active and healthier, happier, more productive lifestyles throughout the community. Schools can establish wellness centers that provide assessment of physical well-being, individual counseling, and a variety of fitness activities. They can also involve families in extracurricular activities at the school site and coordinate school and community recreational

237

Chapter 8
Supporting
High-Quality
Physical
Education

programs. The community, working closely with the school, can play an active role in promoting fitness and wellness by providing opportunities for physical activity for families and individuals. Through participation in a variety of physical activities at school, students will be better prepared to take advantage of opportunities for physical activity provided in the home or in the community.

Schools create partnerships with a variety of public and private organizations, agencies, and businesses to seek support and participation in the physical education of California's children. Many private companies and organizations have education departments that seek opportunities to work with youngsters. Schools are encouraged to (1) use community resources to provide the additional adult support and instructional materials that students need to meet their physical education requirements and (2) start to develop students' ideas about the workforce, careers, and their relationships to their communities. (See Appendix K, "Careers in Physical Education.") Some governmental agencies, health organizations, sports and recreation associations, and youth and community service groups supply schools with physical education instructional materials free of charge. Many professional sports teams also work with schools, so checking with local teams is a good idea. Approaching local sports and recreational agencies with the idea of sharing facilities may also be considered.

Parental involvement in the physical education of their children can take many different forms. Some parents may show their support by voicing to their children consistent respect for the value of education in general and physical education specifically. Other parents may volunteer in the classroom or serve in an advisory capacity on a school wellness committee. Regardless of how parents or family members support education, they are always made to feel welcome at their children's schools and know that their contributions are valued and appreciated.

Parents and families are advised of school district goals and plans for physical education programs. Additionally, they are informed about the physical education model content standards and the grade- or course-level expectations for their children and how to support their children's achievement of the standards. Program materials are organized such that students take home family fitness activities to promote family and community fitness. Children and youths who have physically active parents and family members and regularly participate in physical activities with them are more likely to be active than those who are inactive in the family setting (Kalakanis and others 2001; Brustad 1996; Brustad 1993). Just as children and youths can learn the habit of regular physical activity, they may also learn to be inactive if they are not given opportunities to be active when young.

9

Instructional
Resources

Instructional resources for physical education include instructional materials, equipment and supplies, technology, and facilities. The selection and maintenance of high-quality instructional resources help teachers to instruct and students to achieve the physical education model content standards. The selection process for instructional resources described in this chapter is suggested for use in the review and evaluation processes to ensure that instructional resources are aligned with the California physical education model content standards and are of high quality.

Evaluation Process

The evaluation process for the selection of all instructional resources is similar. A district-level or school-level committee may be appointed to review and select instructional resources. It is imperative that prior to any work the committee is trained in the physical education model content standards as well as the process and procedures for selecting instructional resources.

The committee's first responsibility is to create a list, based on the physical education model content standards and the needs of the students, of the evaluation criteria and the specific measures that will be used to select instructional resources for the school district or school. A comprehensive list of instructional resources needed to implement a standards-based physical education program is then developed. Next the committee reviews current instructional resources to determine the appropriateness of those resources for use with the new physical education model content standards and the instructional needs of their students. Then the committee creates a list of the instructional resources not currently available in the school or district.

Finally, the committee starts the selection process. The selection process consists of (1) creating a list of potential instructional resources for review; (2) evaluating the potential instructional resources based on the specifications developed by the committee and their alignment to the physical education model content standards; and (3) selecting the most appropriate standards-aligned instructional resources. When this is done on a districtwide basis, the teachers and students benefit from well-designed instructional resources.

Evaluation of Instructional Materials

Because the state does not adopt instructional materials for physical education, each district is responsible for conducting its own evaluation of instructional materials for physical education. "Instructional materials" refer to student textbooks, teacher's editions, workbooks/work sheets, task cards, and activity sheets, as well as technology-based instructional materials such as DVDs, CDs, video clips, and software. All teachers need high-quality instructional materials, but new teachers especially depend on well-designed instructional materials that are aligned with the model content standards. The instructional materials should present physical education as a comprehensive, sequential curriculum that promotes the physical, mental, emotional, and social well-being of each student.

Instructional materials are to be selected with great care because they play a major role in determining the content that students learn. The considerations for evaluating instructional materials are organized into five categories.

1. **Physical education content**

    The content in the instructional materials aligns with the physical education model content standards specified for kindergarten through grade twelve and described in detail in Chapter 2 through Chapter 4. The content also reflects the information presented throughout this framework and current and confirmed research in physical education instruction. Instructional materials reviewers consider whether the materials meet such specifications as the following ones:

    - Content is scientifically accurate and current (e.g., no contraindicated exercises).
    - The authors are credible experts in physical education.
    - Instructional materials are designed to meet the needs and interests of students and are age-appropriate.
    - There is comprehensive teaching of all standards. The materials include motor learning principles, biomechanics principles, fitness principles, social and psychological principles, and other cognitive understanding, as well as physical activity. (When purchasing a commercial curriculum, schools may need to supplement those materials to ensure comprehensive coverage of all standards.)
    - Instructional materials address the *why* as well as the *how*.

2. **Program organization**

    Sequential organization of the physical education curriculum provides structure for what students should learn each year. It allows teachers to convey the physical education instruction efficiently and effectively. The content is organized logically and presented so that every student has an opportunity to acquire the essential knowledge and skills described in the standards. Reviewers consider whether:

    - All content standards for the grade level or course level are addressed in a coherent fashion.
    - Instructional materials address the development of skills and knowledge that build throughout the grade or course levels.
    - The organization of instructional materials provides structure to what students should learn each year and allows teachers to teach efficiently and effectively by providing:
        a. Learning structure: lesson, unit, year
        b. Specific instructional objectives
        c. Clearly stated student outcomes showing both scope and sequence
        d. Assessments
        e. Support materials (audiotapes, videotapes, DVDs, CDs, etc.)

- Instructional materials include interdisciplinary suggestions aligned to grade-level or course-level standards for each discipline when appropriate.
- The relationship of lessons to standards or skills within standards is explicit.
- Details are provided regarding the instructional time (pacing) necessary for all instruction and physical activities.
- Suggestions for organizing resources are provided.
- Critical components of lessons are prioritized.
- Learning objectives and instruction are explicit.
- Clear, grade-appropriate explanations of physical education concepts, principles, and theories are presented in a form that teachers can easily adapt for instructional use.

3. **Assessment**

   Assessment strategies, procedures, and tools in the instructional materials align with the physical education model content standards. The assessment tools measure what students know and can do and reflect the information in Chapter 5. The assessment strategies and procedures assist teachers in using the assessment results to design and modify instruction to help all students meet or exceed the standards. Reviewers consider the following points:

   - Materials provide tools for continually measuring student achievement.
   - Materials provide "Guiding Questions" to monitor student comprehension.
   - Multiple measures of student progress are available.
   - Entry-level assessments are included to determine the background knowledge and skills of students.
   - Progress-monitoring assessments provide strategies to address and correct common student errors and misconceptions and include suggestions for checking for understanding.
   - Summative assessments for end-of-term and end-of-course administration are provided.

4. **Universal Access**

   Instructional materials present comprehensive guidance for teachers in providing effective, efficient instruction for every student, including special education students; students whose proficiency in English is significantly lower than that typical for the age, classroom, or grade level; students whose achievement is significantly below or above that typical for the age, classroom, or grade level; and other students with special needs. Suggestions and procedures for meeting the instructional needs of students with special learning needs must not be superficial or be mere afterthoughts to the main focus of instruction. Materials are constructed so that extensive modifications are not necessary for the teacher to meet the learning needs of a full range of students. When considering the accessibility of instructional materials, reviewers look for:

- Suggestions to assist English learners in vocabulary and concepts
- Culturally sensitive instructional materials
- Multicultural examples to promote respect for others
- Instructional materials that are adaptable for students with special needs
- Use of considerate text (for example, clear headings and subheadings; clearly labeled charts, graphs, illustrations, and photographs; and identification and highlighting of important terms)
- Gender-neutral instructional materials

5. **Instructional Planning and Support**

Instructional materials include materials specifically designed for use by the teacher. The teacher's materials include instructional planning and support information as well as materials needed for successful implementation of the physical education program. The application of instructional design principles in constructing instructional materials is evident. Materials are formatted so that additional examples of a skill or strategy are easy to locate. Examples are easily accessible to the teacher for moment-to-moment adjustments in response to learner performance so that all students can be assisted to meet or exceed the standards as efficiently as possible. The following list provides guidance for reviewers:

- Materials provide a clear road map for teachers in planning instruction.
- A variety of instructional approaches and strategies are included in the instructional materials.
- Materials have ample and useful annotations and suggestions on how to present the content in the student materials.
- Materials contain full, adult-level explanations and examples of the more advanced physical education concepts, principles, and theories that appear in the lessons so that teachers can refresh or enhance their own knowledge of the topics being covered.
- Materials include lists of necessary equipment, supplies, and materials for activities, guidance on obtaining those materials inexpensively, and explicit instructions for organizing and safely conducting the instruction.
- Technical support and suggestions are provided for appropriate use of audiovisual, multimedia, and information technology resources associated with a unit.
- Blackline masters are accessible in print and in digitized formats and are easily reproduced. Dark areas are minimized to conserve toner.
- Instructional materials include suggestions for involving families and the community.
- Strategies are suggested for informing parents and guardians about the physical education program and how they can help to support student achievement.

Materials Free of Charge

Because funding for the purchase of instructional materials is often limited, teachers may be tempted to depend upon materials that are available free of charge to augment their instruction. Although such materials may be of use in the classroom, they should be subject to the same type of scrutiny as other instructional materials used in the school.

It is important to know who produced the materials and to determine whether the materials advocate a particular point of view. Governmental agencies, professional associations, and many nonprofit organizations produce and distribute materials free of charge for educational and promotional purposes. However, many of the free materials offered to schools are little more than advertisements for particular commercial products or brand names with little to no instructional content. All free materials need to be reviewed to determine whether they align with the content that students are expected to learn and whether the materials are prepared at the appropriate level for the intended students.

All materials, especially those prepared by corporations or commercial entities, must be reviewed to determine whether there is unnecessary exposure to brand names or corporate logos. In the *Standards for Evaluating Instructional Materials for Social Content* (2000, 10) it states:

> Instructional materials shall not contain illustrations of any identifiable commercial brand names, products, or corporate or company logos unless such illustrations are necessary to the educational purpose of the instructional material and that purpose cannot be achieved without using such illustrations, or unless such illustrations are incidental to a scene of general nature (example: Times Square, New York City).

Evaluation of Equipment and Supplies

The instructional needs of the physical education curriculum dictate the equipment and supplies to be purchased. Equipment and supply purchases are made with an emphasis on quality instruction. The equipment should be separate from equipment that is purchased for recess, intramural, or athletic activities to ensure that the equipment required for physical education class is always available when needed. The equipment and supplies are sufficient in quantity (e.g., one jump rope per student, one ball per student) and quality to provide all students with opportunities to enjoy maximum participation. No student should have to wait for the opportunity to practice a skill simply because there is not enough equipment.

A wide variety of equipment and supplies is necessary to implement the physical education model content standards. All equipment and supplies should be made from high-quality durable materials. "Equipment" refers to those items that are not considered expendable but are used for a period of years, such as heart rate monitors and tumbling mats. "Supplies" are those materials that are expendable and that typically last less than one year. Some examples include chalk, journal notebooks, videotapes for recording, reference books, tennis balls, basketballs, and playground balls.

Different types of equipment and supplies are purchased to accommodate the size, confidence, and skill levels of every student. Softer balls encourage younger and less-skilled students to practice skills. Balls in different sizes with color variations can be easier to track and help students who are having difficulty with catching and trapping skills.

All equipment and supplies are safely stored, well maintained, and readily accessible. An inventory is routinely conducted, and equipment and supplies are formally inspected throughout the school year. Purchased storage bins can store the physical education equipment in one or more central locations. Regardless of where it is stored, equipment should be inspected prior to use to ensure that it is in working order and safe for student use.

When new equipment and supplies are purchased, the physical education program drives purchasing decisions. Equipment and supplies need to be appropriate for the standard(s) being taught and the developmental level of the students. Similar products should be compared for quality, durability, safety, and warranties. Commercial versions of equipment, if available, are considered for purchase.

Evaluation of Technology

Instructional technology in physical education can be used to improve the instructional process and prepare students for the sport and fitness experiences they will encounter as adults. Technology can be used to increase access to physical activity for students with special needs. Beeper balls, sports wheelchairs, switch-activated ramps for bowling or bocce ball, and software for animated demonstrations are examples of adaptations that may assist students. Technology can also be an effective tool for motivating students. Heart rate monitors provide feedback on heart rates as students perform cardiovascular exercises; pedometers and accelerometers provide feedback on physical activity levels; electronic blood pressure devices and spirometers relay information about students' personal health; and body composition devices inform students about their percent of body fat. Digital photos and videos, along with video-analysis software, enhance students' opportunities to learn and improve movement skills. A variety of interactive software programs and Web sites are available to provide students with information on various sports and fitness concepts. Finally, virtual reality–based exercise equipment motivates students to engage in continuous physical activity.

Specific technologies can be used to support the model content standards. Table 9.1 shows the relationship between each technology and some of the standards that it can support. There are other standards where technology can be used to support standards.

Table 9.1 Uses of Technology for Standards-Based Physical Education

Standard	Technology
Grade 2, Standard 4.6: Compare and contrast the function of the heart during rest and during physical activity. **Grade 5, Standard 4.10:** Compare target heart rate and perceived exertion during physical activity. **Grade 6, Standard 3.6:** Monitor the intensity of one's heart rate during physical activity. **High School Course 1, Standard 2.5:** Improve and maintain physical fitness by adjusting physical activity levels according to the principles of exercise.	Heart rate monitors
Grade 5, Standard 4.12: Explain how technology can assist in the pursuit of physical fitness.	Pedometers Electronic blood pressure devices Spirometers
Grade 1, Standard 3.2: Participate three to four times each week, for increasing periods of time, in moderate to vigorous physical activities that increase breathing and heart rate. **Grade 6, Standard 3.4:** Participate in moderate to vigorous physical activity a minimum of four days each week. **High School Course 2, Standard 2.1:** Participate in moderate to vigorous physical activity at least four days each week.	Accelerometers
High School Course 1, Standard 2.3: Meet health-related physical fitness standards established by a scientifically based health-related fitness assessment.	Body composition analyzers
Grade 1, Standard 1.22: Create or imitate movement in response to rhythms and music. **Grade 5, Standard 1.19:** Design and perform a routine to music that involves manipulation of an object. **Grade 8, Standard 1.1:** Identify and demonstrate square-dance steps, positions, and patterns set to music. **High School Course 3D, Standard 1.1:** Demonstrate advanced knowledge and skills in two or more dance activities, selecting one or more from each of the following categories: Category 1: ballet, folk, jazz; Category 2: modern, social, square.	Sound system

Table 9.1 (continued)

Standard	Technology
Grade 1, Standard 1.13: Catch, showing proper form, a gently thrown ball. **Grade 5, Standard 1.3:** Jump for distance, using proper takeoff and landing form. **Grade 7, Standard 1.1:** Demonstrate mature techniques for the following patterns: overhand, sidearm, and underhand throwing; catching; kicking/punting; striking, trapping, dribbling (hand and foot); and volleying. **Grade 7, Standard 2.6:** Diagram and demonstrate basic offensive and defensive strategies for individual and dual physical activities. **High School Course 1, Standard 1.4:** Explain and demonstrate advanced offensive, defensive, and transition strategies in aquatics and individual and dual activities.	Video system
Kindergarten, Standard 2.1: Explain the difference between under and over, behind and in front of, next to and through, up and down, forward and backward, and sideways. **Grade 2, Standard 4.10:** Identify muscles being strengthened during the performance of particular physical activities. **Grade 3, Standard 4.11:** Name and locate the major muscles of the body. **Grade 4, Standard 4.7:** Explain the purpose of warm-up and cool-down periods. **Grade 6, Standard 2.1:** Explain how to increase force based on principles of biomechanics. **Grade 7, Standard 2.5:** Compare and contrast the effectiveness of practicing skills as a whole and practicing skills in smaller parts. **High School Course 1, Standard 2.9:** Explain the inherent risks associated with physical activity in extreme environments. **High School Course 2, Standard 1.5:** Explain the use of the principles of biomechanics (leverage, force, inertia, rotary motion, and opposition); apply the principles to achieve advanced performance in combative, gymnastic/tumbling, and team activities; and evaluate the performance based on use of the principles.	Instructional software and Web resources

Table 9.1 (continued)

Standard	Technology
Grade 1, Standard 3.7: Sustain continuous movement for increasing periods of time while participating in moderate to vigorous physical activity. **Grade 4, Standard 3.7:** Sustain continuous movement for increasing periods of time while participating in moderate to vigorous physical activity. **Grade 6, Standard 3.6:** Monitor the intensity of one's heart rate during physical activity. **Grade 8, Standard 3.4:** Participate in moderate to vigorous physical activity a minimum of four days each week. **High School Course 2, Standard 2.1:** Participate in moderate to vigorous physical activity at least four days each week.	Virtual reality–based exercise equipment
Grade 2, Standard 1.6: Skip and leap, using proper form. **Grade 5, Standard 1.2:** Jump for height, using proper takeoff and landing form. **Grade 6, Standard 2.3:** Analyze and correct errors in movement patterns. **High School Course 1, Standard 1.7:** Analyze and evaluate feedback from proprioception, from others, and from the performance of complex motor (movement) activities to improve performance in aquatics, rhythms/dance, and individual activities and dual activities. **High School Course 1, Standard 1.10:** Analyze situations and determine appropriate strategies for improved performance in aquatic, rhythms/dance, and individual and dual activities.	Digital cameras and camcorders

Heart Rate Monitors

There are three basic types of pulse meters or heart rate monitors, depending on the body site where the monitor attaches. The first type attaches to the hand or is held in the palm, the second type attaches to the index finger or earlobe, and the third type attaches to the chest. The first and second types—pulse meters—use small infrared sensors to detect changes that result from the pulsing of the blood through the capillaries. However, head motion and changing light conditions can cause errors in readings. The third type—the actual heart rate monitor—is the model of choice for accuracy, but privacy and sanitation issues must be considered. The transmitter and strap need to be cleaned between uses.

The heart rate monitor consists of a transmitter and a receiver. The transmitter is positioned directly below the chest muscle where it picks up the ECG (electrocardiogram) signal. It is held in place by a strap that goes around the chest. The

ECG signal is transmitted to the receiver, which is typically located in a watch worn on the wrist. The receiver processes the information and displays the beats per minute. The receiver picks up any signal that is within approximately one meter or less. When several students are wearing heart rate monitors, one receiver can inadvertently pick up a signal from another student's transmitter. Purchasing heart rate monitors designed to eliminate cross-talk helps resolve this problem.

The batteries used in heart rate monitor receivers typically last one year, while the batteries in the chest straps typically last three to four years with average use. Purchasing heart rate monitors that allow the user to change both the receiver and transmitter battery will allow for long-term use. However, all sensors—earlobe, finger, and chest transmitters—will deteriorate over time and will need to be replaced.

Pedometers

Pedometers measure the number of steps that an individual takes. The industry standard for pedometer accuracy is within 3 percent. Several research studies (Bassett et al. 2000; Schneider et al. 2003; Welk 2002; Crouter et al. 2003) provide information on the reliability of various pedometer models. Continuous errors greater than 3 percent indicate a low-quality pedometer or that the batteries need to be replaced. Batteries typically last between one and a half to two years. It is most cost-effective to purchase large quantities of batteries.

Pedometers are worn on the waistband, positioned directly above the midline of the thigh on either side of the body (Bassett et al. 2000). However, for 20–30 percent of the users this is not the best location. Instruct students to walk 100 steps and check the pedometer. If the device is not within 3 percent (97–103 steps), then have the students move the device laterally and try again. Repeat the process until there is no more than a 3 percent error. A pedometer records steps anytime it moves or is shaken, so students need to be monitored to ensure accuracy.

Accelerometers

Accelerometers are accurate (Metcalf et al. 2002) electronic devices used to measure the quantity and intensity of movement in one or more dimensions. Welk (2002, 125) has concluded, "Accelerometers provide a valid indicator of overall physical activity, but a less accurate prediction of energy expenditure." Accelerometers require periodic calibration. Check the user's guide for more details. Batteries typically last between one and a half to two years; the cost for replacement should be factored into the physical education budget. It is most cost-effective to purchase large quantities of batteries.

Accelerometers are typically attached at the right or left hip of the user, although Bouten et al. (1997) concluded that monitor placement position does not influence the results. The device contains a motion sensor and a very small computer programmed to convert acceleration to activity counts or energy expenditure (kcal).

Electronic Blood Pressure Devices

Electronic blood pressure devices measure blood pressure. These devices allow students to take each other's blood pressure with very little training. Some machines take readings on the index finger or wrist; however, the most accurate models employ a cuff around the upper arm and inflate automatically to a reading of 180. Once inflated to 180, these devices automatically deflate the cuff and read and display the systolic and diastolic blood pressure. Because it is important to use the correct cuff size for each participant to ensure an accurate reading, cuffs should be purchased that fit the arm sizes of students who will be using the devices. Measurements should be taken at least 30 minutes after eating, drinking caffeinated beverages, or exercising. Electronic blood pressure devices require batteries.

Spirometers

A spirometer measures forced vital capacity (FVC). The FVC is the total amount of air that an individual is capable of exhaling at one time. Spirometers are used to help estimate an individual's cardiorespiratory fitness. The little evidence that exists suggests that endurance training may affect lung structure, volume, and capacity. Spirometers do not require batteries, but they do require plastic or cardboard mouthpieces. Plastic mouthpieces are more expensive but cost-effective in the long term since they can be cleaned with bleach and water for reuse.

Body Composition Analyzers

Body composition analyzers measure body composition, the ratio of fat-free mass to fat mass. There are a variety of ways to measure body composition, including bioelectrical impedance, skinfold, and hydrostatic weighing. Body mass index (BMI) is sometimes used as a measure of body composition. However, BMI is not an estimate of body composition; it is a ratio between height and weight. According to Hager and Vehrs (2006),

> Even though the correlation between BMI and % BF (percent of body fat) is modest, and high BMI values are generally associated with greater % BF, BMI is a poor predictor of % BF. It is very common for children and adolescents who have not yet reached their growth spurt to have high BMI values. As many of these children reach puberty and grow in height and increase muscle mass, BMI values may eventually normalize.

Skinfold measurements are accurate, but they require some expertise and practice. Teachers often look to electronic-based devices. The four contact bioelectrical impedance devices are accurate and reliable if the administration protocol is followed. The segmental bioelectrical impedance devices (hand-to-hand or foot-to-foot) have two important disadvantages: the variability of results from day to day and the accuracy of the results depends on the students' providing correct information (Hager and Vehrs 2006).

Sound Systems

A sound system for physical education should consist of a wireless microphone and receiver, media player, mixer, amplifier, and speakers. A microphone is essential for teachers who must project their voices in a noisy gymnasium or over music. A wireless microphone transmits sound using VHF (very high frequency) or UHF (ultra high frequency) bands. The VHF band of frequencies is more crowded and therefore makes VHF wireless microphone systems more susceptible to interference. Therefore, a UHF wireless microphone system is recommended.

Amplifiers play a role in adjusting the sound volume. Stronger amplifiers are capable of generating greater volume. Power output for an amplifier is measured in wattage. Two hundred watts is a minimum for indoor needs, while outdoor areas require higher wattage. Mixers allow individual adjustment and combination of sounds (i.e., voice and music). A good mixer will help compensate for poor room acoustics and audio feedback.

Speakers convert the signals from the audio source into sound waves. Some speaker systems contain one full-range speaker cone designed to handle the entire frequency spectrum, while others contain two or three drivers for each channel. Although a two-way system (one for low frequencies and one for high frequencies) is almost always better than a single full-range speaker, a three-way system (a woofer for low frequencies, a tweeter for high frequencies, and a third for mid-range) is not necessarily better than a two-way system. The most important specification is frequency response (the highest and lowest frequencies of sound that a speaker can reproduce). The ideal range is 20 Hz (hertz) to 20 Khz (kilohertz).

Video Systems

Still images show students key positions for different phases of a motor skill. Video clips, however, provide students with demonstrations of motor skills and strategic play. In addition, there are instructional videos that are aligned to the model content standards for physical education. Still images and videos are viewed on a monitor or through a projection system. If a projection system is used, it can be bracketed to the ceiling so that it does not interfere with any physical activity that may take place in the same location. Large screen monitors can be attached to walls; however, they will need to be protected from any activities that take place in the same location.

The recording of students' performances is an effective approach to helping students master skills and analyze strategy. Students learn to record each other performing motor skills or participating in a scrimmage so that they can immediately view their performances.

The California Learning Resource Network (CLRN) provides a list of standards-aligned videos that meet legal and social content requirements. Instructional materials approved by CLRN are listed in a searchable database at http://clrn.org.

Instructional Software/Web Resources

Instructional software and Web resources can provide students with information at a rate that is appropriate and meaningful to them. Software and Web resources can be used for full-class presentations, small-group tutorials, problem-solving activities, simulations, and student projects. There are several different types of instructional software on the market, including drill-and-practice programs, tutorials, analysis, reference, mind mapping, educational games, and simulations. When selecting software, be sure that it runs on the type of computer operating system available. The physical education facility will need a wireless connection or computer ports for both indoor and outdoor access to Web resources. In the physical education environment, mobile computers are most efficient. However, larger computers may be used if they are placed in wall pockets so that they do not interfere with physical activity.

The Internet provides students with access to numerous Web resources and online physical education courses. All Web resources and online courses must be reviewed and selected based on accuracy and alignment to the California grade- and course-level physical education model content standards. In addition, the following questions should be considered before selection of an online course:

- Are all or some grade- and course-level physical education model content standards addressed?
- Is the author/teacher a physical education expert?
- Does the teacher have the proper licensing to teach physical education in California?
- Is the course accredited?
- Are the students provided with opportunities for physical activity?
- Are course materials and equipment provided for each student?
- Have adaptations been made for students with special needs?
- Are a variety of instructional strategies used in the delivery of content?
- Are students assessed on every grade- and course-level physical education standard?

Once an online course is selected, then the local board of education has to decide whether to approve the course for physical education credit in its district.

Virtual Reality–Based Exercise Equipment

Virtual reality–based exercise equipment combines computer hardware and software to give the user the sensory illusion of being in a different environment. These devices may motivate students to start and continue exercise programs. Components of a virtual reality system include a computer or gaming console, special user interfaces (fitness equipment, sport equipment, gloves), and a monitor. The interface and monitor are connected to the computer-based device, and the software controls the visual images on the monitors. Users interact with the "virtual" environment by manipulating fitness equipment, wireless remotes, or their body. While technology is constantly changing, specific interfaces today include exercise bikes and isometric resistance devices. Staying current with new technologies will help teachers and districts make better decisions about virtual reality-based equipment. Whenever available, commercial quality interfaces should be purchased.

Virtual reality–based exercise equipment can be used as a whole-class activity where each student has an interface or in a station approach in which a few students use the interactive activity at one time while other students participate at other task stations. The latter is a less expensive alternative that still affords access to the equipment.

Facilities

Physical education facilities are planned, updated, monitored, and maintained to ensure functionality and safety. Emphasis is placed upon student needs and what is necessary to implement a high-quality standards-based physical education program. Administrators and physical educators work with risk-management coordinators to minimize liability issues and to create optimum environments for learning.

Indoor and outdoor facilities are adequate for the number of students in a school, free from obstacles, appropriate to the needs of all students (e.g., acoustics such that all students can clearly hear instruction), accessible to students with special needs, and supportive of student mastery of the physical education model content standards. Dressing rooms are clean and safe, adequate for the number of students served, and appropriately supervised without requiring physical education instructors to lose instructional time to supervision. School and community facilities are planned and used to supplement and complement each other in meeting the needs of the students and community. The California Department of Education's publications, *Guide to School Site Analysis and Development* (2000) and *Healthy Children Ready to Learn: Facilities Best Practices* (2007), provide guidelines and recommendations regarding space requirements based on courses of instruction.

Healthy Children Ready to Learn: Facilities Best Practices (2007, 12–28) recommends the following practices in the design, renovation, reconfiguration, and remodel of school facilities:

1. Develop educational specifications and involve end users in the planning process.
2. Have schools and communities collaborate as partners in developing physical activity facilities.
3. Incorporate technology opportunities in physical education facilities.
4. Designate physical education teaching stations in small spaces for high-quality instruction in a challenging environment.
5. Create flexible-use spaces and layouts (at least one large turf field and one large hardcourt area, without poles and standards).
6. Remodel athletic weight rooms into fitness rooms (for physical education).
7. Convert locker areas to other uses.
8. Provide landscaping maintenance.

9. Allow enough space to provide for both physical education and recess space.

10. Ensure proper planning for placement of utilities—especially proper grading and drainage.

11. Consider artificial turf.

12. Maintain a clean, well-organized, and bright environment.

13. Plan appropriate equipment storage.

14. Provide sufficient equipment for maximum student participation.

15. Plan for future growth.

16. Provide adequate drinking water.

17. Maximize usable square footage by design.

18. Apply striping on hard play surfaces.

19. Meet state minimum site-size standards for the student body.

20. Look beyond the traditional (play areas on the roof; off-campus facilities—golf course/driving range, tennis courts, bowling alleys).

The physical education model content standards establish the need for a variety of facilities for physical education: playfields, gymnasiums, multipurpose rooms, classrooms with desks and chairs (for cognitive work), alternative spaces for inclement weather, and fitness labs. The *California Code of Regulations, Title 5,* sets minimum standards for playfields, gymnasiums, multipurpose rooms, and classrooms in new schools. (See Appendix A for selected regulations.)

Table 9.2 Types of Teaching Stations for High School Physical Education

Teaching station needs	Aquatics	Body mechanics	Combatives	Gymnastics/tumbling	Individual/dual sports	Health and physical activity	Rhythms/dance	Team sports
Courts Area		X			X	X		X
Field					X	X		X
Gymnasium		X	X	X	X	X	X	X
Dance/ Wrestling Room		X	X	X	X	X	X	X
Fitness Room	X	X	X	X	X	X	X	X
Pool	X				X			X
Classroom	X	X	X	X	X	X	X	X

Source: Appendix A (*Healthy Children Ready to Learn: Facilities Best Practices* 2007).

The *Guide to School Site Analysis and Development* (2000) (at http://www.cde. ca.gov/ls/fa/sf/schoolsiteguide.asp) defines a physical education teaching station as "a play area adequate for one class to be taught by one teacher at one time so that pupils waste no time waiting turns because of lack of space and facilities." Table 9.2 provides suggestions on the types of teaching stations that support instruction in the high school course content areas. The numbers and types of teaching stations should be based on the high school's student enrollment and its physical education program.

Similarly, sufficient space and teaching stations for middle and elementary schools are determined by the number of students enrolled and the school's physical education program. Planning for the implementation of standards-based physical education at all grade and course levels includes careful consideration of space, teaching stations, and equipment. And, at all levels, indoor facilities should be provided to meet the state-mandated minimum number of physical education instructional minutes for instruction during periods of adverse environmental conditions, such as rain, snow, excessive heat, and poor air quality.

All facilities must meet the guidelines set forth in the Americans with Disabilities Act for barrier-free, accessible environments, including play areas, recreational facilities, outdoor areas, and public rights-of-ways. Additionally, motor labs (Seaman et al. 2007) support adapted physical education instruction. A motor lab is:

> a room containing specialized equipment necessary for individuals with a disability, but that can and is used by all students. Such equipment might include mirrors (that can be covered), stall bars, wall-pulley weights, a scale for measuring body weight, hanging and chinning bars, a ramp for riding scooter boards, large crash pads, wedge mats, physio-balls, suspended equipment (e.g., swing, soft balls on a rope), parallel bars for gait training, gymnastics and arm upper body development, and perhaps a bicycle ergometer. (Seaman et al. 2007, 314)

Teachers should report, in writing, unsafe conditions to the administrator and follow up on the resolution of the unsafe situation. Teachers should keep copies of all documents submitted to the administration. If the facility is not safe, then it is the teacher's responsibility to avoid the hazard. For example, if there are cracks on the basketball court that make a particular activity unsafe, then the teacher should notify the administrator in writing and conduct the activity in a different location.

The guidelines below are intended to provide district and school personnel with suggestions for the evaluation of current facilities and a beginning checklist for designing, renovating, reconfiguring, and remodeling facilities. The guidelines are not a comprehensive list and will not apply in all circumstances. Additional guidelines are provided in Appendix M.

Special Guidelines for Playgrounds

Parts or portions of playground structures are often used in teaching the physical education model content standards. Playground structures are also frequently used during recess and for other purposes; therefore, when calculating the total number of teaching stations at a school site, the availability of playground structures solely for physical education instruction must be considered. If playground structures are used for physical education instruction, they should not be used for any other purpose at the same time. Because the play structure area is where the majority of injuries—and the most severe ones—occur, it is necessary for the administrators and teachers to be familiar with the Consumer Product Safety Commission Guidelines (see the *Handbook for Public Playground Safety*) that all playground structures are required to meet under California *Health and Safety Code* Section 115725.

Some important guidelines related to student safety are as follows:

- Proper surfacing should be installed and maintained under playground structures; a minimum depth of 12 inches of loose fill is recommended.
- Proper installation of loose fill surfacing will help in the maintenance of fill materials. For instance, if no allowance is made for proper drainage of the playground surface, water may wash away loose fill materials or may pool under the equipment and erode the equipment. Slope, drainage, and placement of concrete footers are critical to the proper installation of loose fill surfacing (Thompson, Hudson, and Olsen 2007).
- Annual playground audits are to be conducted by certified playground safety inspectors.

Especially in joint-use situations when schools share uses with the community (e.g., students and the general public), daily inspection of playgrounds should be conducted to verify the safety of the facilities prior to student use. Trash, glass, and other hazards should be removed, and unsafe areas should be properly marked to restrict student access.

Designing facilities for a new school provides the best possible scenario for supporting standards-based physical education. However, many schools are faced with limited facilities and are not currently in line for capital improvements. The following guidelines were designed to assist those schools with the implementation of a standards-based physical education program:

- Do not schedule physical education classes during times when facilities are used for other purposes such as recess and lunch.
- Use alternative areas (e.g., cafeteria, auditorium, classrooms) for teaching stations.
- Design outdoor spaces to maximize use and spread students across available areas.
- Limit the number of classes using the facilities at one time by creating a schedule that maximizes use of available space throughout the day.
- Use portable equipment to maximize use of limited space (e.g., portable basketball hoops, backstops, soccer goals, etc.).
- Modify (for example, subdivide into smaller areas using cones) regulation-sized spaces (e.g., soccer field) to maximize participation in activity.

Some schools have experienced success working with community partners to optimize resources by designing and developing facilities that meet the physical activity needs of children, youths, and adults. For example, during the school day students learn and practice new movement skills in the gymnasium, using colorful equipment sized just for them. After school ends, the gymnasium becomes a hub of physical activity for youths and adults who join in classes, participate in community leagues, and enjoy other opportunities offered at an indoor facility. Partnerships between schools and community entities help spread the financing and maintenance costs of these facilities among the partners. A less tangible benefit, but one noted by districts that use these partnerships, is the decrease in vandalism. Administrators and teachers attribute this benefit to both increased community pride in the facility and, because the facility is used more often, greater supervision.

A difficult task in any partnership is balancing the need for public access to the site and the need for student safety. Placement of a joint-use pool, gym, or other facility on the edge of the campus and fences in strategic locations ensure controlled and safe access to the site. The facility can be available on the weekend or after school while the rest of the campus is secure from vandalism. The CDE publication *Guide to School Site Analysis and Development* offers a number of practical tips on a joint-use agreement. This document is available for download at http://www.cde.ca.gov/ls/fa/sf/guideschoolsite.asp.

Appendixes

Appendix A
Selected Laws and Regulations

(Current as of January 1, 2009)

California *Education Code*

Selected Non-Discrimination Statutes

200. It is the policy of the State of California to afford all persons in public schools, regardless of their disability, gender, nationality, race or ethnicity, religion, sexual orientation, or any other characteristic that is contained in the definition of hate crimes set forth in Section 422.55 of the Penal Code, equal rights and opportunities in the educational institutions of the state. The purpose of this chapter is to prohibit acts that are contrary to that policy and to provide remedies therefor.

201. (a) All pupils have the right to participate fully in the educational process, free from discrimination and harassment.

(b) California's public schools have an affirmative obligation to combat racism, sexism, and other forms of bias, and a responsibility to provide equal educational opportunity.

(c) Harassment on school grounds directed at an individual on the basis of personal characteristics or status creates a hostile environment and jeopardizes equal educational opportunity as guaranteed by the California Constitution and the United States Constitution.

(d) There is an urgent need to prevent and respond to acts of hate violence and bias-related incidents that are occurring at an increasing rate in California's public schools.

(e) There is an urgent need to teach and inform pupils in the public schools about their rights, as guaranteed by the federal and state constitutions, in order to increase pupils' awareness and understanding of their rights and the rights of others, with the intention of promoting tolerance and sensitivity in public schools and in society as a means of responding to potential harassment and hate violence.

(f) It is the intent of the Legislature that each public school undertake educational activities to counter discriminatory incidents on school grounds and, within constitutional bounds, to minimize and eliminate a hostile environment on school grounds that impairs the access of pupils to equal educational opportunity.

(g) It is the intent of the Legislature that this chapter shall be interpreted as consistent with Article 9.5 (commencing with Section 11135) of Chapter 1 of Part 1 of Division 3 of Title 2 of the Government Code, Title VI of the federal Civil Rights Act of 1964 (42 U.S.C. Sec. 1981, et seq.), Title IX of the Education Amendments of 1972 (20 U.S.C. Sec. 1681, et seq.), Section 504 of the federal Rehabilitation Act of 1973 (29 U.S.C. Sec. 794(a)), the federal Individuals with Disabilities Education Act (20 U.S.C. Sec. 1400 et seq.), the federal Equal Educational Opportunities Act (20 U.S.C. Sec. 1701, et seq.), the Unruh Civil Rights Act (Secs. 51 to 53, incl., Civ. C.), and the Fair Employment and Housing Act (Pt. 2.8 (commencing with Sec. 12900), Div. 3, Gov. C.), except where this chapter may grant more protections or impose additional obligations, and that the remedies provided herein shall not be the exclusive remedies, but may be combined with remedies that may be provided by the above statutes.

210.1. "Disability" includes mental and physical disability as defined in Section 12926 of the Government Code.

210.7. "Gender" means sex, and includes a person's gender identity and gender related appearance and behavior whether or not stereotypically associated with the person's assigned sex at birth.

212. "Nationality" includes citizenship, country of origin, and national origin.

212.1. "Race or ethnicity" includes ancestry, color, ethnic group identification, and ethnic background.

212.3. "Religion" includes all aspects of religious belief, observance, and practice and includes agnosticism and atheism.

212.6 "Sexual orientation" means heterosexuality, homosexuality, or bisexuality.

219. Disability, gender, nationality, race or ethnicity, religion, sexual orientation, or any other characteristic contained in the definition of hate crimes set forth in Section 422.55 of the Penal Code includes a perception that the person has any of those characteristics or that the person is associated with a person who has, or is perceived to have, any of those characteristics.

220. No person shall be subjected to discrimination on the basis of disability, gender, nationality, race or ethnicity, religion, sexual orientation, or any other characteristic that is contained in the definition of hate crimes set forth in Section 422.55 of the Penal Code in any program or activity conducted by an educational institution that receives, or benefits from, state financial assistance or enrolls pupils who receive state student financial aid.

221.5. (a) It is the policy of the state that elementary and secondary school classes and courses, including nonacademic and elective classes and courses, be conducted, without regard to the sex of the pupil enrolled in these classes and courses.

(b) A school district may not prohibit a pupil from enrolling in any class or course on the basis of the sex of the pupil, except a class subject to Chapter 5.6 (commencing with Section 51930) of Part 28.

(c) A school district may not require a pupil of one sex to enroll in a particular class or course, unless the same class or course is also required of a pupil of the opposite sex.

(d) A school counselor, teacher, instructor, administrator, or aide may not, on the basis of the sex of a pupil, offer vocational or school program guidance to a pupil of one sex that is different from that offered to a pupil of the opposite sex or, in counseling a pupil, differentiate career, vocational, or higher education opportunities on the basis of the sex of the pupil counseled. Any school personnel acting in a career counseling or course selection capacity to a pupil shall affirmatively explore with the pupil the possibility of careers, or courses leading to careers, that are nontraditional for that pupil's sex. The parents or legal guardian of the pupil shall be notified in a general manner at least once in the manner prescribed by Section 48980, in advance of career counseling and course selection commencing with course selection for grade 7 so that they may participate in the counseling sessions and decisions.

(e) Participation in a particular physical education activity or sport, if required of pupils of one sex, shall be available to pupils of each sex.

221.7. (a) The Legislature finds and declares that female pupils are not accorded opportunities for participation in school-sponsored athletic programs equal to those accorded male pupils. It is the intent of the Legislature that opportunities for participation in athletics be provided equally to male and female pupils.

(b) Notwithstanding any other provisions of law, no public funds shall be used in connection with any athletic program conducted under the auspices of a school district governing board or any student organization within the district, which does not provide equal opportunity to both sexes for participation and for use of facilities. Facilities and participation include, but are not limited to, equipment and supplies, scheduling of games and practice time, compensation for coaches, travel arrangements, per diem, locker rooms, and medical services.

(c) Nothing in this section shall be construed to require a school district to require competition between male and female pupils in school-sponsored athletic programs.

233. (a) At the request of the Superintendent of Public Instruction, the State Board of Education shall do all of the following as long as the board's actions do not result in a state mandate or an increase in costs to a state or local program:

(1) Adopt policies directed toward creating a school environment in kindergarten and grades 1 to 12, inclusive, that is free from discriminatory attitudes and practices and acts of hate violence. [*statute continues*]

235. There shall be no discrimination on the basis of the characteristics listed in Section 220 in any aspect of the operation of alternative schools or charter schools.

260. The governing board of a school district shall have the primary responsibility for ensuring that school district programs and activities are free from discrimination based on age and the characteristics listed in Section 220 and for monitoring compliance with any and all rules and regulations promulgated pursuant to Section 11138 of the Government Code.

Physical Education Data Required on the School Accountability Report Card

33126. (a) The school accountability report card shall provide data by which a parent can make meaningful comparisons between public schools that will enable him or her to make informed decisions on the school in which to enroll his or her children.

(b) The school accountability report card shall include, but is not limited to, assessment of the following school conditions:

(1) (A) Pupil achievement by grade level, as measured by the standardized testing and reporting programs pursuant to Article 4 (commencing with Section 60640) of Chapter 5 of Part 33.

(B) After the state develops a statewide assessment system pursuant to Chapter 5 (commencing with Section 60600) and Chapter 6 (commencing with Section 60800) of Part 33, pupil achievement by grade level, as measured by the results of the statewide assessment. *(statute continues)*

Establishment of Courses in Physical Education

33350. The State Department of Education shall do all of the following:

(a) Adopt rules and regulations that it deems necessary and proper to secure the establishment of courses in physical education in the elementary and secondary schools.

(b) Compile or cause to be compiled and printed a manual in physical education for distribution to teachers in the public schools of the state.

(c) Encourage school districts offering instruction in kindergarten and any of grades 1 to 12, inclusive, to the extent that resources are available, to provide quality physical education that develops the knowledge, attitudes, skills, behavior, and motivation needed to be physically active and fit for life; to provide daily recess periods for elementary school pupils, featuring time for unstructured but supervised play; to provide extracurricular physical activity and fitness programs and physical activity and fitness clubs; and to encourage the use of school facilities for physical activity and fitness programs offered by the school, public park and recreation districts, or community-based organizations outside of school hours.

33351. The Department of Education may employ the necessary expert and clerical assistants in order to carry out the provisions of this article.

Monitoring of Provision of Physical Education Instruction

33352. (a) The department shall exercise general supervision over the courses of physical education in elementary and secondary schools of the state; advise school officials, school boards, and teachers in the development and improvement of their physical education and activity programs; and investigate the work in physical education in the public schools.

(b) The department shall ensure that the data collected through the categorical program monitoring indicates the extent to which each school within the jurisdiction of a school district or county office of education does all of the following that are applicable to the school:

(1) Provides instruction in physical education for a total period of time of not less than 200 minutes each 10 schooldays to pupils in grades 1 to 6, inclusive, as required pursuant to subdivision (g) of Section 51210.

(2) Provides instruction in physical education for a total period of time of not less than 400 minutes each 10 schooldays to pupils in grades 7 to 12, inclusive, as required pursuant to subdivision (a) of Section 51222.

(3) Provides instruction in physical education for a total period of time of not less than 200 minutes each 10 schooldays to pupils in an elementary school maintaining grades 1 to 8, inclusive, as required pursuant to Section 51233.

(4) Conducts physical fitness testing of pupils as required pursuant to Chapter 6 (commencing with Section 60800) of Part 33.

(5) Includes the results of physical fitness testing of pupils in the school accountability report card as required pursuant to subparagraph (C) of paragraph (1) of subdivision (b) of Section 33126.

(6) Offers pupils exempted from required attendance in physical education courses pursuant to paragraph (1) of either subdivision (b) or (c) of Section 51241 a variety of elective physical education courses of not less than 400 minutes every 10 schooldays.

(7) Provides a course of study in physical education to pupils in any of grades 9 to 12, inclusive, that includes a developmentally appropriate sequence of instruction, including the effects of physical activity upon dynamic health, the mechanics of body movement, aquatics, gymnastics and tumbling, individual and dual sports, rhythms and dance, team sports, and combatives.

(8) Provides instruction in physical education to pupils that provides equal opportunities for participation regardless of gender.

(9) Provides instruction in physical education to pupils in any of grades 1 to 12, inclusive, by physical education teachers who hold appropriate teaching credentials issued by the Commission on Teacher Credentialing.

(c) The department annually shall do both of the following:

(1) Submit a report to the Governor and the Legislature that summarizes the data collected through categorical program monitoring regarding the items described in paragraphs (1) to (9), inclusive, of subdivision (b).

(2) Post a summary of the data collected through categorical program monitoring regarding the items described in paragraphs (1) to (9), inclusive, of subdivision (b) on the Internet Web site of the department.

51210.1. (a) (1) The Legislature finds and declares all of the following:

(A) The Education Code currently mandates 200 minutes of physical education every 10 schooldays for pupils in elementary school. Recent studies have shown that the vast majority of children and youth are not physically fit.

(B) According to a March 1997 report by the Centers for Disease Control, the percentage of children and adolescents who are overweight has more than doubled in the last 30 years. Most of this increase occurred within the last 10 years.

(C) Nearly 40 percent of children of ages five to eight years have health conditions that significantly increase their risk of early heart disease.

(D) Some 70 percent of girls, and 40 percent of boys, who are from 6 to 12 years of age do not have enough muscle strength to do more than one pull up.

(E) Most children lead inactive lives. On the average, first through fourth graders spend two hours watching television on schooldays and spend close to three and one-half hours watching television on weekend days.

(2) It is, therefore, the intent of the Legislature that all children shall have access to a high-quality, comprehensive, and developmentally appropriate physical education program on a regular basis.

(b) (1) Each school district selected by the Superintendent of Public Instruction pursuant to paragraph (2) shall report to the Superintendent of Public Instruction in the Coordinated Compliance Review as to the extent of its compliance with subdivision (g) of Section 51210 for grades 1 to 6, inclusive, during that school year.

(2) The Superintendent of Public Instruction shall select not less than 10 percent of the school districts of the state to report compliance with the provisions set forth in paragraph (1). The school districts selected shall provide a random and accurate sampling of the state as a whole.

(c) For purposes of determining compliance with paragraphs (1) and (2) of subdivision (b), the Superintendent of Public Instruction shall not count the time spent in recesses and the lunch period.

(d) A school district that fails to comply with the existing statutory requirements shall issue a corrective action plan to the state Department of Education in accordance with the Coordinated Compliance Review process.

(e) This section shall not be applicable to high schools.

Physical Education in Continuous School Programs

37631. The courses of instruction offered at a school maintained pursuant to this chapter shall meet all applicable requirements of law, including the requirements prescribed by Chapter 2 (commencing with Section 51200) of Part 28 relating to physical education and Chapter 5.6 (commencing with Section 51930) of Part 28. For these purposes the instructional program shall be designed to provide at least the overall equivalent in instruction in each course of study required by law to be provided in kindergarten and grades 1 to 12, inclusive, upon the completion by a pupil of the work prescribed for any particular grade.

Grading in Physical Education Classes

49066. (a) When grades are given for any course of instruction taught in a school district, the grade given to each pupil shall be the grade determined by the teacher of the course and the determination of the pupil's grade by the teacher, in the absence of clerical or mechanical mistake, fraud, bad faith, or incompetency, shall be final.

(b) The governing board of the school district and the superintendent of such district shall not order a pupil's grade to be changed unless the teacher who determined such grade is, to the extent practicable, given an opportunity to state orally, in writing, or both, the reasons for which such grade was given and is, to the extent practicable, included in all discussions relating to the changing of such grade.

(c) No grade of a pupil participating in a physical education class, however, may be adversely affected due to the fact that the pupil does not wear standardized physical education apparel where the failure to wear such apparel arises from circumstances beyond the control of the pupil.

Summary of Nutrition and Physical Activity Laws and Regulations

49432. By January 1, 2004, every public school may post a summary of nutrition and physical activity laws and regulations, and shall post the school district's nutrition and physical activity policies, in public view within all school cafeterias or other central eating areas. The State Department of Education shall develop the summary of state law and regulations.

Courses of Study, General Provisions

51206. The Legislature hereby finds and declares that the physical fitness and motor development of children in the public elementary schools is of equal importance to that of other elements of the curriculum.

The Legislature further finds that, in order to improve the level of physical education in the elementary grades, the Superintendent of Public Instruction shall, through the regular budget process, employ an elementary physical education specialist to develop model curriculum standards in physical education for grades 1 to 8, inclusive, provide technical assistance to teachers, and assist school districts in the development of their physical education programs.

Course of Study for Grades 1 to 6

51210(g) *[The adopted course of study for grades 1 to 6, inclusive, shall include instruction, beginning in grade 1 and continuing through grade 6, in the following areas of study:]* Physical education, with emphasis upon the physical activities for the pupils that may be conducive to health and vigor of body and mind, for a total period of time not less than 200 minutes each 10 schooldays, exclusive of recesses and the lunch period.

51210.2. (a) The Legislature hereby finds and declares that the physical fitness and motor development of children in the public elementary schools is of equal importance to that of other elements of the curriculum.

(b) It is, therefore, the intent of the Legislature to encourage each school district maintaining an elementary school composed of any of grades 1 to 6, inclusive, to do one of the following:

(1) Employ a credentialed physical education teacher to provide instruction in physical education for each class of grades 1 to 6, inclusive, within any elementary school in the district for a total period of time of not less than 200 minutes each 10 schooldays, exclusive of recesses and the lunch period.

(2) Provide each teacher providing instruction in physical education to any of grades 1 to 6, inclusive, within any elementary school in the district with yearly theoretical practical training in developmental physical education, as set forth in the Physical Education Framework adopted by the State Department of Education pursuant to Section 33350, except that any teacher who has successfully completed one college level course in elementary physical education shall not be subject to this paragraph.

Instructional Minutes for Elementary School Maintaining Any of Grades 1 to 8

51223. Notwithstanding the provisions of Sections 51210 and 51222, instruction in physical education in an elementary school maintaining any of grades 1 to 8 shall be for a total period of time of not less than 200 minutes each 10 schooldays, exclusive of recesses and the lunch period.

Course of Study for Grades 7 to 12

51220(d) *[The adopted course of study for grades 7 to 12, inclusive, shall offer courses in the following areas of study:]* Physical education, with emphasis given to physical activities that are conducive to health and to vigor of body and mind, as required by Section 51222.

High School Graduation Requirement for Courses in Physical Education

51225.3(a)(1)(F) *[Commencing with the 1988-89 school year, no pupil will receive a diploma of graduation from high school who, while in grades 9 to 12, inclusive, has not completed all of the following:]* Two courses in physical education, unless the pupil has been exempted pursuant to the provisions of this code.

Physical Education Exemptions

51222. (a) All pupils, except pupils excused or exempted pursuant to Section 51241, shall be required to attend upon the courses of physical education for a total period of time of not less than 400 minutes each 10 schooldays. Any pupil may be excused from physical education classes during one of grades 10, 11, or 12 for not to exceed 24 clock hours in order to participate in automobile driver training. Such pupil who is excused from physical education classes to enroll in driver training shall attend upon a minimum of 7,000 minutes of physical education instruction during such school year.

(b) The governing board of each school district that maintains a high school and that elects to exempt pupils from required attendance in physical education courses pursuant to paragraph (1) or (2) or both of subdivision (b) of Section 51241 shall offer those pupils so exempted a variety of elective physical education courses of not less than 400 minutes each 10 schooldays.

51241. (a) The governing board of a school district or the office of the county superintendent of schools of a county may grant a temporary exemption to a pupil from courses in physical education, if the pupil is one of the following:

(1) Ill or injured and a modified program to meet the needs of the pupil cannot be provided.

(2) Enrolled for one-half, or less, of the work normally required of full-time pupils.

(b) (1) The governing board of a school district or the office of the county superintendent of schools of a county, with the consent of a pupil, may grant a pupil an exemption from courses in physical education for two years any time during grades 10 to 12, inclusive, if the pupil has met satisfactorily at least five of the six standards of the physical performance test administered in grade 9 pursuant to Section 60800.

(2) Pursuant to Sections 51210, 51220, and 51222, physical education is required to be offered to all pupils, and, therefore, schools are required to provide adequate facilities and instructional resources for that instruction. In this regard, paragraph (1) shall be implemented in a manner that does not create a new program or impose a higher level of service on a local educational agency. Paragraph (1) does not mandate any overall increase in staffing or instructional time because, pursuant to subdivision (d), pupils are not permitted to attend fewer total hours of class if they do not enroll in physical education. Paragraph (1) does not mandate any new costs because any additional physical education instruction that a local educational agency provides may be accomplished during the existing instructional day, with existing facilities. Paragraph (1) does not prevent a local educational agency from implementing any other temporary or permanent exemption authorized by this section.

(c) The governing board of a school district or the office of the county superintendent of a county may grant permanent exemption from courses in physical education if the pupil complies with any one of the following:

(1) Is 16 years of age or older and has been enrolled in grade 10 for one academic year or longer.

(2) Is enrolled as a postgraduate pupil.

(3) Is enrolled in a juvenile home, ranch, camp, or forestry camp school where pupils are scheduled for recreation and exercise pursuant to the requirements of Section 4346 of Title 15 of the California Code of Regulations.

(d) A pupil exempted under paragraph (1) of subdivision (b) or paragraph (1) of subdivision (c) shall not attend fewer total hours of courses and classes if he or she elects not to enroll in a physical education course than he or she would have attended if he or she had elected to enroll in a physical education course.

(e) Notwithstanding any other law, the governing board of a school district also may administer to pupils in grades 10 to 12, inclusive, the physical performance test required in grade 9 pursuant to Section 60800. A pupil who meets satisfactorily at least five of the six standards of this physical performance test in any of grades 10 to 12, inclusive, is eligible for an exemption pursuant to subdivision (b).

51242. The governing board of a school district may exempt any four-year or senior high school pupil from attending courses of physical education, if the pupil is engaged in a regular school-sponsored interscholastic athletic program carried on wholly or partially after school hours.

51246. The governing board of a school district may exempt any pupil enrolled in his last semester or quarter, as the case may be, of the 12th grade who, pursuant to Section 46145 or 46147, is permitted to attend school less than 240 or 180 minutes per day, from attending courses of physical education; provided, however, that such pupil may not be exempted pursuant to this section from attending courses of physical education if such pupil would, after such exemption, attend school for 240 minutes or more per day.

Independent Study

51745. (a) Commencing with the 1990-91 school year, the governing board of a school district or a county office of education may offer independent study to meet the educational needs of pupils in accordance with the requirements of this article. Educational opportunities offered through independent study may include, but shall not be limited to, the following:

(1) Special assignments extending the content of regular courses of instruction.

(2) Individualized study in a particular area of interest or in a subject not currently available in the regular school curriculum.

(3) Individualized alternative education designed to teach the knowledge and skills of the core curriculum. Independent study shall not be provided as an alternative curriculum.

(4) Continuing and special study during travel.

(5) Volunteer community service activities that support and strengthen pupil achievement.

(b) Not more than 10 percent of the pupils participating in an opportunity school or program, or a continuation high school, calculated as specified by the State Department of Education, shall be eligible for apportionment credit for independent study pursuant to this article. A pupil who is pregnant or is a parent who is the primary caregiver for one or more of his or her children shall not be counted within the 10 percent cap.

(c) No individual with exceptional needs, as defined in Section 56026, may participate in independent study, unless his or her individualized education program developed pursuant to Article 3 (commencing with Section 56340) of Chapter 4 of Part 30 specifically provides for that participation.

(d) No temporarily disabled pupil may receive individual instruction pursuant to Section 48206.3 through independent study.

(e) No course included among the courses required for high school graduation under Section 51225.3 shall be offered exclusively through independent study.

Physical Education Model Content Standards

60605.2 (a) No later than December 1, 2004, the State Board of Education shall adopt model content standards, pursuant to recommendations developed by the Superintendent of Public Instruction, in the curriculum area of physical education.

(b) The model content standards are intended to provide a framework for programs that a school may offer in the instruction of physical education. Nothing in this section shall be construed to require a school to follow the model content standards.

Physical Performance Test

60800. (a) During the month of February, March, April, or May, the governing board of each school district maintaining any of grades 5, 7, and 9 shall administer to each pupil in those grades the physical performance test designated by the state board. Each pupil with a physical disability and each pupil who is physically unable to take all of the physical performance test shall be given as much of the test as his or her condition will permit.

(b) Upon request of the department, a school district shall submit to the department, at least once every two years, the results of its physical performance testing.

(c) The department shall compile the results of the physical performance test and submit a report every two years, by December 31, to the Legislature and Governor that standardizes the data, tracks the development of high-quality fitness programs, and compares the performance of California's pupils with national performance, to the extent that funding is available.

(d) Pupils shall be provided with their individual results after completing the physical performance testing. The test results may be provided orally as the pupil completes the testing.

(e) The governing board of a school district shall report the aggregate results of its physical performance testing administered pursuant to this section in their annual school accountability report card required by Sections 33126 and 35256.

California Code of Regulations, Title 5, Education

3051.5. Adapted Physical Education for Individuals with Exceptional Needs.

(a) Adapted physical education is for individuals with exceptional needs who require developmental or corrective instruction and who are precluded from participation in the activities of the general physical education program, modified general physical education program, or in a specially designed physical education program in a special class. Consultative services may be provided to pupils, parents, teachers, or other school personnel for the purpose of identifying supplementary aids and services or modifications necessary for successful participation in the regular "D" Physical education program or specially designed physical education programs.

(b) The person providing instruction and services shall have a credential authorizing the teaching of adapted physical education as established by the Commission on Teacher Credentialing.

4930. General Provisions

(a) Local agency or educational institution or counselor shall not discriminate against any person on the basis of sex, sexual orientation, gender, ethnic group identification, race, ancestry, national origin, religion, color, or mental or physical disability in the counseling or guidance of pupils.

(b) Nothing in this section shall be construed as prohibiting a local agency from encouraging members of one sex to enter courses, programs, activities or occupations which are traditionally entered by the other sex.

(c) Counseling includes, but is not limited to, academic, vocational, career, social or psychological counseling which is conducted or sponsored by, through, or at an educational institution whether in an informal or formal program, workshop or other activity, or whether conducted or sponsored on a routine or sporadic basis.

(d) Counseling includes, but is not limited to, any person, group, or sub-group, regardless of title or job description, who engages in counseling of any pupil.

4940. General Provisions.

(a) A local agency and its educational institutions shall not provide any course or otherwise carry out any of its educational programs or activities separately on the basis of sex, sexual orientation, gender, ethnic group identification, race, ancestry, national origin, religion, color, or mental or physical disability or require or refuse participation therein by any of its students on such basis, including but not limited to, agriculture, health, physical education, industrial technology, business, career, vocational and emerging technical educational programs, home economics, work experience programs, occupational training programs, research opportunities, visual and performing arts, and adult education courses.

(b) Portions of classes which deal with human sexuality may be conducted in separate sessions for males and females.

(c) Local agencies and their educational institutions may make requirements based on vocal range or quality which may result in a chorus or choruses of one, or predominantly one, sex.

(d) A local agency and its educational institutions shall not permit any course or activity labeling and scheduling which results in the separation of students on the basis of sex, sexual orientation, gender, ethnic group identification, race, ancestry, national origin, religion, color, or mental or physical disability. In educational institutions where students have the opportunity to select a specific activity for a physical education course, the course title and description shall be gender neutral.

(e) While instruction in all physical education classes is coeducational, nothing in this section shall prohibit the grouping of students during physical education activities by ability when assessed by objective standards of individual performance without regard to sex and all students are involved in the same physical activity or conceptual learning experience at the same time.

(f) Recruitment. An educational institution may choose to undertake affirmative recruitment efforts to overcome the effect of conditions which resulted in limited participation in certain courses by a particular group of students including but not limited to math, science, emerging technologies, occupational training, and career vocational and technical educational program courses.

(g) Prerequisites. Nothing herein shall be construed to prohibit the use of prerequisites that have been demonstrated to be essential to success in a given program or course. If a prerequisite is not essential to success in a given course or program, it shall be abolished as a prerequisite.

(h) Required Courses. In determining required courses for any student, such determination shall be made without regard to sex, sexual orientation, gender, ethnic group identification, race, ancestry, national origin, religion, color, or mental or physical disability, except as otherwise provided in these regulations.

10060. Criteria for Physical Education Program

Each school district shall appraise the quality of the physical education program in each senior or four-year high school of the district by the following criteria:

(a) The course of study provides for instruction in a development sequence in each of the following areas:

    (1) Effects of physical activity upon dynamic health

    (2) Mechanics of body movement

    (3) Aquatics

    (4) Gymnastics and tumbling

    (5) Individual and dual sports

    (6) Rhythms and dance

    (7) Team sports

    (8) Combatives for boys

(b) Assignment of pupils to physical education courses is made on the basis of individual needs including such factors as health status, skill development, and/or grade level.

(c) Instruction is provided for pupils with physical limitations including those with inadequate skill development and the physically underdeveloped. Physical performance tests as required by Section 1041 are used to identify physically underdeveloped pupils and to appraise the motor aspects of physical fitness

(d) Each course includes activities of a vigorous nature adopted to individual capacities, and designed to permit maximum development of each individual pupil.

(e) Each class period includes the teaching of the fundamentals and techniques of each instructional area conducted during that period.

(f) Class size is consistent with the requirements of good instruction and safety.

(g) Reporting of pupil achievement is based upon all of the following:

    (1) Evaluation of the pupil's individual progress and the measure of his attainment of the goals specified in each area of instruction listed in subsection (a) of this section.

    (2) Tests designed to determine skill and knowledge.

    (3) Physical performance tests.

(4) Any other evaluation procedures required by local governing board regulations.

(h) Teaching stations are of sufficient number and suitability to provide instruction in activities conducted under subsection (a) of this section.

(i) Supplies and equipment of sufficient quantity and quality are provided to allow active participation of each pupil throughout the class period.

14001. Minimum Standards.

Educational facilities planned by school districts shall be:

(a) Evolved from a statement of educational program requirements which reflects the school district's educational goals and objectives.

(b) Master-planned to provide for maximum site enrollment.

(c) Located on a site which meets California Department of Education standards as specified in Section 14010.

(d) Designed for the environmental comfort and work efficiency of the occupants.

(e) Designed to require a practical minimum of maintenance.

(f) Designed to meet federal, state, and local statutory requirements for structure, fire, and public safety.

(g) Designed and engineered with flexibility to accommodate future needs.

Selected Sections of 14030. Standards for Development of Plans for the Design and Construction of School Facilities.

The following standards for new schools are for the use of all school districts for the purposes of educational appropriateness and promotion of school safety:

(a) Educational Specifications.

Prior to submitting preliminary plans for the design and construction of school facilities, and as a condition of final plan approval by CDE, school board-approved educational specifications for school design shall be prepared and submitted to the California Department of Education based on the school district's goals, objectives, policies and community input that determine the educational program and define the following:

(1) Enrollment of the school and the grade level configuration.

(2) Emphasis in curriculum content or teaching methodology that influences school design.

(3) Type, number, size, function, special characteristics of each space, and spatial relationships of the instructional area that are consistent with the educational program.

(4) Community functions that may affect the school design.

(c) Playground and Field Areas.

Adequate physical education teaching stations shall be available to accommodate course requirements for the planned enrollment, specifically:

(1) A variety of physical education teaching stations are available to provide a comprehensive physical education program in accordance with the district's adopted course of study (including hardcourt, field area and indoor spaces).

(2) The physical education teaching stations are adequate for the planned student enrollment to complete the minimum instruction and course work defined in Education Code Sections 51210(g), 51220(d) and 51225.3(a)(1)(F).

(3) Supervision of playfields is not obstructed by buildings or objects that impair observation.

(4) Joint use for educational purposes with other public agencies is explored. Joint use layout with parks is not duplicative and fulfills both agencies' needs.

(e) Future Expansion.

Site layouts shall have capability for expansion without substantial alterations to existing structures or playgrounds:

(1) Site layout designates area(s) for future permanent or temporary additions that are compatible with the existing site plans for playground layout and supervision.

(2) Utilities to the expansion area are included in the plans and have the capacity to accommodate anticipated growth.

(3) Exits, corridors, stairs, and elevators are located to accommodate capacity of additions, particularly in such buildings added as the multi-purpose/cafeteria, administration, gymnasium/or auditorium.

(f) Placement of Buildings.

Building placement shall consider compatibility of the various functions on campus and provide optimum patterns of foot traffic flow around and within buildings. Site layout of buildings, parking, driveways, and physical education areas shall be adequate to meet the instructional, security and service needs of the educational program:

(1) Building placement is compatible with other functions on campus; e.g., band room is not next to library.

(2) Physical relationship of classrooms, auxiliary, and support areas allows unobstructed movement of staff and students around the campus.

(3) Building placement has favorable orientation to wind, sun, rain, and natural light.

(4) Restrooms are conveniently located, require minimum supervision, and, to the extent possible, are easily accessible from playground and classrooms.

(5) Parking spaces are sufficient for staff, visitors, and students (where applicable).

(6) The campus is secured by fencing and electronic devices such as code entries, electronic monitoring or motion sensors when needed.

(j) Gymnasium, Shower/Locker shall be designed to accommodate multiple use activities in accordance with the planned enrollment:

(1) The gymnasium is secured from other parts of the campus for evening and weekend events or for public use purposes.

(2) The shower/locker area is of sufficient size to allow students enrolled in the physical education program to shower and dress each period.

(3) Toilets are available for the public in facilities intended for shared community use other than in shower/locker areas.

(4) Office space is provided for physical education teachers.

(5) Space is available for specialized age-appropriate physical education activities such as weight lifting, exercise equipment usage, aerobics.

(k) Auxiliary Areas.

(1) Multipurpose/cafeteria area (indoor or outdoor) shall be adequately sized and flexibly designed to protect students from the elements and to allow all students adequate eating time during each lunch period and to accommodate such uses as physical education activities, assemblies, and extracurricular activities:

(A) Tables and benches or seats are designed to maximize space and allow flexibility in the use of the space.

(B) The location is easily accessible for student and community use, but is close to street for delivery truck access

(C) Stage/platform may have a dividing wall to be used for instructional purposes but is not intended as a classroom.

(D) Area for the cafeteria line is designed for the flow of traffic for each lunch period.

(E) Design of kitchen reflects its planned function; e.g., whether for food preparation or warming only.

(F) Space is available for refrigeration and preparation of foods to accommodate maximum number of students planned for the school.

(G) Office, changing, and restroom area for food preparation staff is available and shall comply with local department of health requirements.

(H) Ceiling height allows for clearance of light fixtures for physical education activities

14034. Planning Guides

The latest edition of The Guide for Planning Educational Facilities, published by the Council of Educational Facility Planners, 29 West Woodruff Avenue, Columbus, Ohio, 43210, may be used as a guide in developing school building plans.

California *Health and Safety Code*

Playgrounds

115725. (a) All new playgrounds open to the public built by a public agency or any other entity shall conform to the playground-related standards set forth by the American Society foresting and Materials and the playground-related guidelines set forth by the United States Consumer Product Safety Commission.

(b) Replacement of equipment or modification of components inside existing playgrounds shall conform to the playground-related standards set forth by the American Society for Testing and Materials and the playground-related guidelines set forth by the United States Consumer Product Safety Commission.

(c) All public agencies operating playgrounds and all other entities operating playgrounds open to the public shall have playground safety inspector, certified by the National Playground Safety Institute, conduct an initial inspection for the purpose of aiding compliance with the requirements set forth in subdivision (a)or (b), as applicable. Any inspection report may serve as a reference when the upgrades are made, but is not intended for any other use.

(d) Playgrounds installed between January 1, 1994, and December 31, 1999, shall conform to the playground-related standards set forth by the American Society for Testing and Materials and the playground-related guidelines set forth by the United States Consumer Product Safety Commission not later than 15 years after the date those playgrounds were installed.

(e) For purposes of this section, all of the following shall apply:

(1) An "entity operating a playground open to the public" includes, but is not limited to, a church, subdivision, hotel, motel, resort, camp, office, hospital, shopping center, day care setting, and restaurant. An "entity operating a playground open to the public" shall not include a foster family home, certified family home, small family home, group home, or family day care home, which is licensed and regulated to meet child safety requirements enforced by the State Department of Social Services.

(2) "Playground" means an improved outdoor area designed, equipped, and set aside for children's play that is not intended for use as an athletic playing field or athletic court, and shall include any playground equipment, fall zones, surface materials, access ramps, and all areas within and including the designated enclosure and barriers.

(f) Operators of playgrounds in child care centers regulated by the California Department of Social Services (CDSS) pursuant to Title 22 of Division 12 of Chapter 1 of the California Code of Regulations and facilities operated for the developmentally disabled, shall comply with the requirements established in this section.

(g) (1) No state funding shall be available for the planning, development, or redevelopment of any playground, unless the playground, after completion of the state-funded project, will conform to the requirements of subdivision (a) or (b), as applicable.

However, where state funds have been appropriated to, or allocated for, a playground project prior to the effective date of this section but the section becomes effective prior to the completion of the project, that funding shall be maintained, as long as the playground is altered to conform to the requirements of subdivision (a) or (b), as applicable, to the extent the alterations can be made without adding significantly to the project cost.

(2) After the date by which an entity is required to conform its playground to satisfy requirements of this section, no state funding shall be available for the operation, maintenance, or supervision of the playground unless the playground conforms to the applicable requirements of the section.

115730. (a) The State Department of Social Services shall convene working group to develop recommendations for minimum safety requirements for playgrounds at child care centers.

(b) The working group shall include, but not be limited to, childcare center operators, including representatives of the Professional Association for Childhood Education, the California Child Care Health Program, the Children's Advocacy Institute, the State Department of Health Services, and certified playground inspectors.

(c) The working group shall use the national guidelines published by the United States Consumer Product Safety Commission and those regulations adopted pursuant to this article as a reference in developing its recommendations. However, the State Department of Social Services shall determine minimum safety requirements that are protective of child health on playgrounds at child care centers.

(d) The working group shall submit its playground safety recommendations to the State Department of Social Services by September 1, 2001.

(e) The working group shall submit its recommendations to the Legislature by November 1, 2001.

(f) This section shall be construed as a continuation of former Section 115736.

115735. This article shall become operative on January 1, 2008.

California *Penal Code*

Hate Crime

422.55. For purposes of this title, and for purposes of all other state law unless an explicit provision of law or the context clearly requires a different meaning, the following shall apply:

(a) "Hate crime" means a criminal act committed, in whole or in part, because of one or more of the following actual or perceived characteristics of the victim:

(1) Disability.

(2) Gender.

(3) Nationality.

(4) Race or ethnicity.

(5) Religion.

(6) Sexual orientation.

(7) Association with a person or group with one or more of these actual or perceived characteristics.

(b) "Hate crime" includes, but is not limited to, a violation of Section 422.6.

Federal Statutes

Selected Sections of the Individuals with Disabilities Education Improvement Act of 2004, Public Law 108–446—Dec. 3, 2004 118 Stat. 2647

In 2004, Congress passed the Individuals with Disabilities Education Improvement Act (IDEA 2004)

The stated purposes of IDEA 2004 are:
(d) PURPOSES
(1)(A) to ensure that all children with disabilities have available to them a free appropriate public education that emphasizes special education and related services designed to meet their unique needs and prepare them for further education, employment, and independent living;
(B) to ensure that the rights of children with disabilities and parents of such children are protected; and
(C) to assist States, localities, educational service agencies, and Federal agencies to provide for the education of all children with disabilities;
(2) to assist States in the implementation of a statewide, comprehensive, coordinated, multidisciplinary, interagency system of early intervention services for infants and toddlers with disabilities and their families;

(3) to ensure that educators and parents have the necessary tools to improve educational results for children with disabilities by supporting system improvement activities; coordinated research and personnel preparation; coordinated technical assistance, dissemination, and support; and technology development and media services; and

(4) to assess, and ensure the effectiveness of, efforts to educate children with disabilities

In the definitions section of IDEA 2004, instruction in physical education is specifically mentioned:

Sec. 602. Definitions

(29) Special Education.—The term 'special education' means specially designed instruction, at no cost to parents, to meet the unique needs of a child with a disability, including—

(A) instruction conducted in the classroom, in the home, in hospitals and institutions, and in other settings; and

(B) instruction in physical education.

Title 20, Chapter 33, Subchapter I, Sec. 1401, Definitions
(3) Child with a disability
(A) In general

The term "child with a disability" means a child—

(i) with mental retardation, hearing impairments (including deafness), speech or language impairments, visual impairments (including blindness), serious emotional disturbance (referred to in this chapter as "emotional disturbance"), orthopedic impairments, autism, traumatic brain injury, other health impairments, or specific learning disabilities; and

(ii) who, by reason thereof, needs special education and related services.

Federal Regulations

Title 34: Education, Chapter I—Office for Civil Rights, Department of Education

§106.34 Access to classes and schools. (34 CFR 106.34)

(a) *General standard.* Except as provided for in this section or otherwise in this part, a recipient shall not provide or otherwise carry out any of its education programs or activities separately on the basis of sex, or require or refuse participation therein by any of its students on the basis of sex.

(1) *Contact sports in physical education classes.* This section does not prohibit separation of students by sex within physical education classes or activities during participation in wrestling, boxing, rugby, ice hockey, football, basketball, and other sports the purpose or major activity of which involves bodily contact.

(2) *Ability grouping in physical education classes.* This section does not prohibit grouping of students in physical education classes and activities by ability as assessed by objective standards of individual performance developed and applied without regard to sex.

(3) *Human sexuality classes.* Classes or portions of classes in elementary and secondary schools that deal primarily with human sexuality may be conducted in separate sessions for boys and girls.

(4) *Choruses.* Recipients may make requirements based on vocal range or quality that may result in a chorus or choruses of one or predominantly one sex.

(b) *Classes and extracurricular activities*

(1) *General standard.* Subject to the requirements in this paragraph, a recipient that operates a nonvocational coeducational elementary or secondary school may provide nonvocational single-sex classes or extracurricular activities, if—

(i) Each single-sex class or extracurricular activity is based on the recipient's important objective—

(A) To improve educational achievement of its students, through a recipient's overall established policy to provide diverse educational opportunities, provided that the single-sex nature of the class or extracurricular activity is substantially related to achieving that objective; or

(B) To meet the particular, identified educational needs of its students, provided that the single-sex nature of the class or extracurricular activity is substantially related to achieving that objective;

(ii) The recipient implements its objective in an evenhanded manner;

(iii) Student enrollment in a single-sex class or extracurricular activity is completely voluntary; and

(iv) The recipient provides to all other students, including students of the excluded sex, a substantially equal coeducational class or extracurricular activity in the same subject or activity.

(2) *Single-sex class or extracurricular activity for the excluded sex.* A recipient that provides a single-sex class or extracurricular activity, in order to comply with paragraph (b)(1)(ii) of this section, may be required to provide a substantially equal single-sex class or extracurricular activity for students of the excluded sex.

(3) *Substantially equal factors.* Factors the Department will consider, either individually or in the aggregate as appropriate, in determining whether classes or extracurricular activities are substantially equal include, but are not limited to, the following: the policies and criteria of admission, the educational benefits provided, including the quality, range, and content of curriculum and other services and the quality and availability of books, instructional materials, and technology, the qualifications of faculty and staff, geographic accessibility, the quality, accessibility, and availability of facilities and resources provided to the class, and intangible features, such as reputation of faculty.

(4) *Periodic evaluations.* (i) The recipient must conduct periodic evaluations to ensure that single-sex classes or extracurricular activities are based upon genuine justifications and do not rely on overly broad generalizations about the different talents, capacities, or preferences of either sex and that any single-sex classes or extracurricular activities are substantially related to the achievement of the important objective for the classes or extracurricular activities.

(ii) Evaluations for the purposes of paragraph (b)(4)(i) of this section must be conducted at least every two years.

(5) *Scope of coverage.* The provisions of paragraph (b)(1) through (4) of this section apply to classes and extracurricular activities provided by a recipient directly or through another entity, but the provisions of paragraph (b)(1) through (4) of this section do not apply to interscholastic, club, or intramural athletics, which are subject to the provisions of §§106.41 and 106.37(c) of this part.

(c) *Schools*

(1) *General Standard.* Except as provided in paragraph (c)(2) of this section, a recipient that operates a public nonvocational elementary or secondary school that excludes from admission any students, on the basis of sex, must provide students of the excluded sex a substantially equal single-sex school or coeducational school.

(2) *Exception.* A nonvocational public charter school that is a single-school local educational agency under State law may be operated as a single-sex charter school without regard to the requirements in paragraph (c)(1) of this section.

(3) *Substantially equal factors.* Factors the Department will consider, either individually or in the aggregate as appropriate, in determining whether schools are substantially equal include, but are not limited to, the following: The policies and criteria of admission, the educational benefits provided, including the quality, range, and content of curriculum and other services and the quality and availability of books, instructional materials, and technology, the quality and range of extracurricular offerings, the qualifications of faculty and staff, geographic accessibility, the quality, accessibility, and availability of facilities and resources, and intangible features, such as reputation of faculty.

(4) *Definition.* For the purposes of paragraph (c)(1) through (3) of this section, the term "school" includes a "school within a school," which means an administratively separate school located within another school.

Title 34: Education, Chapter III—Office of Special Education and Rehabilitative Services, Department of Education

§300.108 Physical education (34 CFR 300.108)

The State must ensure that public agencies in the State comply with the following:

(a) *General.* Physical education services, specially designed if necessary, must be made available to every child with a disability receiving FAPE, unless the public agency enrolls children without disabilities and does not provide physical education to children without disabilities in the same grades.

(b) *Regular physical education.* Each child with a disability must be afforded the opportunity to participate in the regular physical education program available to nondisabled children unless—

(1) The child is enrolled full time in a separate facility; or

(2) The child needs specially designed physical education, as prescribed in the child's IEP.

(c) *Special physical education.* If specially designed physical education is prescribed in a child's IEP, the public agency responsible for the education of that child must provide the services directly or make arrangements for those services to be provided through other public or private programs.

(d) *Education in separate facilities.* The public agency responsible for the education of a child with a disability who is enrolled in a separate facility must ensure that the child receives appropriate physical education services in compliance with this section.

§ 300.8 Child with a disability (34 CFR 300.8)

(a) *General.*

(1) *Child with a disability* means a child evaluated in accordance with §§300.304 through 300.311 as having mental retardation, a hearing impairment (including deafness), a speech or language impairment, a visual impairment (including blindness), a serious emotional disturbance (referred to in this part as "emotional disturbance"), an orthopedic impairment, autism, traumatic brain injury, an other health impairment, a specific learning disability, deaf-blindness, or multiple disabilities, and who, by reason thereof, needs special education and related services. [*regulation continues*]

§ 300.39 Special education (34 CFR 300.39).

(a) *General.*

(1) *Special education* means specially designed instruction, at no cost to the parents, to meet the unique needs of a child with a disability, including—

(i) Instruction conducted in the classroom, in the home, in hospitals and institutions, and in other settings; and

(ii) Instruction in physical education.

(2) *Special education* includes each of the following, if the services otherwise meet the requirements of paragraph (a)(1) of this section—

(i) Speech-language pathology services, or any other related service, if the service is considered special education rather than a related service under State standards;

(ii) Travel training; and

(iii) Vocational education.

(b) *Individual special education terms defined.* The terms in this definition are defined as follows:

(1) *At no cost* means that all specially-designed instruction is provided without charge, but does not preclude incidental fees that are normally charged to nondisabled students or their parents as a part of the regular education program.

(2) *Physical education* means—

(i) The development of—

(A) Physical and motor fitness;

(B) Fundamental motor skills and patterns; and

(C) Skills in aquatics, dance, and individual and group games and sports (including intramural and lifetime sports); and

(ii) Includes special physical education, adapted physical education, movement education, and motor development.

(3) *Specially designed instruction* means adapting, as appropriate to the needs of an eligible child under this part, the content, methodology, or delivery of instruction—

(i) To address the unique needs of the child that result from the child's disability; and

(ii) To ensure access of the child to the general curriculum, so that the child can meet the educational standards within the jurisdiction of the public agency that apply to all children.

(4) *Travel training* means providing instruction, as appropriate, to children with significant cognitive disabilities, and any other children with disabilities who require this instruction, to enable them to—

(i) Develop an awareness of the environment in which they live; and

(ii) Learn the skills necessary to move effectively and safely from place to place within that environment (e.g., in school, in the home, at work, and in the community).

(5) *Vocational education* means organized educational programs that are directly related to the preparation of individuals for paid or unpaid employment, or for additional preparation for a career not requiring a baccalaureate or advanced degree.

Appendix B

Content Areas of Standards, by Grade Level
(Kindergarten Through Grade Six)

Content Area	Kindergarten	Grade 1	Grade 2	Grade 3	Grade 4	Grade 5	Grade 6
Movement concepts	1.1 1.2 1.3 1.4 2.1 2.2	1.1 1.2 1.3 1.4 1.5 2.1 2.2	1.1 2.1 2.2	1.1 2.1	2.1 2.2	2.1 2.2	2.1 2.2 2.3 2.4 2.5
Body management	1.5 1.6 1.7 1.8 2.3 2.4	1.6 2.3	1.2 1.3 1.4 2.3 2.4	1.2 1.3 1.4	1.1 1.2 1.3 1.4 2.3 2.4	1.1 2.3	
Locomotor movement	1.9 1.10 1.11 2.5	1.7 1.8 1.9 2.4	1.5 1.6 2.5	1.5	1.5	1.2 1.3	
Manipulative skills	1.12 1.13 1.14 1.15 2.6 2.7 2.8	1.10 1.11 1.12 1.13 1.14 1.15 1.16 1.17 1.18 1.19 1.20 1.21 2.5 2.6 2.7 2.8 2.9 2.10 2.11 2.12 2.13	1.7 1.8 1.9 1.10 1.11 1.12 1.13 1.14 1.15 1.16 2.6 2.7 2.8 2.9 2.10 2.11 2.12 2.13 2.14	1.6 1.7 1.8 1.9 1.10 1.11 1.12 1.13 1.14 2.2 2.3 2.4 2.5	1.6 1.7 1.8 1.9 1.10 1.11 1.12 1.13 1.14 1.15 1.16 1.17 1.18 1.19 1.20 2.5 2.6 2.7 2.8 2.9	1.4 1.5 1.6 1.7 1.8 1.9 1.10 1.11 1.12 1.13 1.14 1.15 1.16 1.17 2.4	1.1 1.2 1.3 1.4 1.5 1.6 2.6 2.7 2.8 2.9

Content Area	Kindergarten	Grade 1	Grade 2	Grade 3	Grade 4	Grade 5	Grade 6
Rhythmic skills	1.16 1.17	1.22	1.17 1.18 1.19	1.15 2.6 2.7	1.21 1.22 2.10	1.18 1.19 2.5	1.7 1.8 2.10 2.11
Combinations of movement patterns and skills							1.9 1.10 1.11 2.12
Fitness concepts	3.1 4.1 4.2 4.3	3.1 4.1 4.2 4.3	3.1 4.1 4.2 4.3 4.4 4.5	3.1 3.2 4.1 4.2 4.3 4.4 4.5 4.6	3.1 3.2 4.1 4.2 4.3 4.4 4.5 4.6 4.7	3.1 3.2 4.1 4.2 4.3 4.4 4.5 4.6 4.7	
Aerobic capacity	3.2 4.4 4.5 4.6	3.2 4.4 4.5 4.6 4.7	3.2 4.6 4.7 4.8	3.3 4.7 4.8	3.3 4.8 4.9 4.10 4.11	3.3 4.8 4.9 4.10 4.11 4.12	
Muscular strength and endurance	3.3 3.4 4.7 4.8	3.3 3.4 3.5 4.8 4.9	3.3 3.4 4.9 4.10 4.11 4.12	3.4 3.5 4.9 4.10 4.11 4.12 4.13	3.4 3.5 4.12 4.13 4.14 4.15	3.4 3.5 4.13	
Flexibility	3.5 4.9	3.6 4.10 4.11	3.5 4.13 4.14	3.6 4.14 4.15	3.6 4.16	3.6 4.14	
Body composition	3.6 4.10	3.7 4.12	3.6 4.15	3.7 4.16	3.7 4.17	3.7 4.15 4.16	
Assessment	3.7	3.8	3.7	3.8	3.8 3.9	3.8 3.9	

Content Area	Kindergarten	Grade 1	Grade 2	Grade 3	Grade 4	Grade 5	Grade 6
Assessing and maintaining physical fitness (Standard 3)							3.1 3.2 3.3 3.4 3.5 3.6
Physical fitness concepts, principles, and strategies (Standard 4)							4.1 4.2 4.3 4.4 4.5 4.6 4.7
Self-responsibility	5.1 5.2	5.1 5.2	5.1 5.2	5.1 5.2 5.3	5.1 5.2 5.3 5.4	5.1 5.2 5.3 5.4	5.1 5.2
Social interaction	5.3 5.4	5.3 5.4	5.3 5.4 5.5 5.6	5.4 5.5	5.5	5.5 5.6	5.3
Group dynamics	5.5	5.5 5.6	5.7	5.6	5.6	5.7 5.8	5.4 5.5

Appendix C
The Movement Framework in Games, Gymnastics, and Dance

Body Aspect (What the body does)	**Space Aspect** (Where the body moves)
Actions of the body Curl, bend, stretch, twist, swing **Actions of body parts** Support body weight Lead action Apply/receive force or weight Flow—simultaneous/successive Symmetry/asymmetry **Activities of the body** *Locomotor*: Games: walk, run, jump, gallop, roll Dance: walk, run, gallop, jump, leap, hop, skip, step Gymnastics: jump/flight, rock, roll, slide, step, climb *Nonlocomotor*: Games: bend, stretch, twist, weight shift, pivot, alert stop-stillness Dance: gesture, curl, stretch, twist, spin, step and jump turns, rise, sink, open, close, stillness Gymnastics: balance/off balance, counterbalance, countertension, spin, step jump, circle turns, hang, curl, step, twist *Manipulative*: Games: throw, catch, strike, collect, carry, dribble, volley, kick **Shapes of the body** Straight, wide, round Narrow, twisted Symmetrical/asymmetrical **Symmetry/Asymmetry** Locomotion/phrasing Both sides/one side **Continuity** Continuous/noncontinuous	**Areas** General Personal (kinesphere) **Directions** Forward Backward Sideward Up Down **Levels** High Medium Deep-low **Pathways** (Air and Ground) Straight Curved Angular Twisted **Extensions** Large/far Small/near **Planes** Sagittal (wheel) Frontal (door) Horizontal (table)

Source: Terence W. Langton, "Applying Laban's Movement Framework in Elementary Physical Education," *Journal of Physical Education, Recreation, and Dance*, Vol. 78, No. 1 (January 2007), p. 20. Reprinted with permission.

Appendix C
The Movement
Framework
in Games,
Gymnastics,
and Dance

Effort Aspect (How the body moves)	**Relationships Aspect** (With whom or what the body is relating as it moves)
Time Student/fast/acceleration Sustained/slow/deceleration **Weight** Strong/firm Light/fine **Space** Straight/direct Flexible/indirect **Flow** Free/ongoing Bound/stoppable	**Body parts to each other** In front of/alongside/behind Far from/near to Above/below Meet/part Over/under **Individuals and Groups** (Dance and Gymnastics) In front of/alongside/behind Far from/near to Above/below Meet/mingle/part Lead/follow Around/between/through Toward/away Over/under Match/mirror/copy/contrast Unison/canon Simultaneous/successive Supporting/being supported **Individuals and Groups** (Games) In front of/alongside/behind Far from/near to Offense/defense Attack/defend spaces Pass to spaces (lead passes) Create spaces Cover spaces (guard) Player placement when receiving, sending, intercepting, or possessing an object Cooperation/competition **Other types** (Games) Rules/boundaries/goals **Other types** (Dance) Music/sound/rhythm/props Stories/poems/art Science/social studies **Other types** (Gymnastics) Rhythm **Apparatus** (Gymnastics) In front of/alongside/behind On/off/above/below Over/under Mount/dismount

Appendix D
Concepts and Principles of Biomechanics

Force

- A push or pull exerted on a body or an object.

External forces

- External forces include gravity, friction, air resistance, and the force exerted by a body when it collides with or rebounds from another.

Moving an object

- Force must be applied to change an object's motion.
- More force must be applied to make a large change in an object's motion than a small change.
- More force, or the same force applied over a longer time, must be applied to get a stationary object moving at a certain speed than to get the object up to that speed when it is already moving.
- More force must be applied to get the same change of motion in a heavy object than in a light one.

Absorbing impact force

- Impact force is absorbed by increasing the surface area and/or the distance or time over which it is absorbed.

Increasing balance

- Balance is improved by widening the base of support, lowering the center of gravity, or keeping the center of gravity over the base of support.
- Stepping forward on the opposite foot when throwing and kicking helps to keep the center of gravity over the base of support.
- When receiving an object, receive the force close to the center of gravity so that the force does not act to spin the receiver.

Increasing distance

- The stronger the action, the greater the reaction.
- The angle of release (45 degrees when the release is at ground level and progressively less as the height of the release increases) affects the distance an object or body travels.
- The higher the release above ground, with the angle of the release being constant, the greater the distance.
- Stabilizing the body segments involved in launching an object increases the distance the object travels.

Source: Bonnie Mohnsen, *Teaching Middle School Physical Education* (Second edition). Champaign, IL: Human Kinetics Publishers, 2003.

- Increasing the range of movement of the body segments that impart force increases the distance an object travels.
- Using sequential muscle movement increases the distance an object travels.
- Increasing the distance through which force is applied (putting the muscle on stretch, extending joints, using a longer lever) increases the distance an object travels.
- Using more muscles increases the distance an object travels.
- Using stronger muscles increases the distance an object travels.
- Using heavier implements increases the distance an object travels.
- Lengthening the striking element increases the distance an object travels.

Applying spin to a ball

- Spin results when a force applied to the surface of the ball does not point through the center of the ball.
- The ball will spin in the direction the force is applied.
  - Force applied below the center of gravity causes backward rotation (back spin), which results in the ball staying in the air longer, bouncing higher, and rolling a shorter distance along with a decrease in velocity after impact.
  - Force applied above the center of gravity causes forward rotation (top spin), which results in a quick drop with a longer but lower bounce and lengthened roll along with an increase in velocity after impact.

Rebounds

- A ball will rebound at an angle equal to that at which it strikes a surface unless the rebound is altered by the elasticity of the ball, the firmness of the surface, or spin.
- When two forces are applied, the result is a combination of the two forces in proportion to the strength of each force.
- Spin on rebound is altered by the rebound angle and the elasticity of the object.

Rotating an object

- Shortening the radius of rotation increases the angular velocity.
- To turn an object about an axis, a force must be exerted along a line that misses that axis. The greater the distance between the line and the axis, the greater a force's effect.

Increasing drag resistance

- Air and water resist any motion through them.
- As velocity increases, the resistance is increased (squared).
- A larger object has greater resistance than a smaller object.
- A streamlined position provides less resistance.
- A smoother surface provides less resistance.

Gravity

- Gravity decreases the speed of any object in free flight on its way up and increases the speed on its way down.
- Gravity causes objects dropped from the same height to fall at the same speed (discounting air resistance).

Levers

- There are three classes of levers:
  - First class—The fulcrum is between the effort arm and the resistance arm. First-class levers provide strength or speed depending on where the fulcrum is located.
  - Second class—The resistance arm is between the fulcrum and the effort arm. Second-class levers provide strength.
  - Third class—The effort arm is between the fulcrum and the resistance arm. Third-class levers provide speed.
- Levers have one of two functions:
  (1) They are used to exert a force greater than the force applied; or
  (2) They are used to increase the speed and range of motion through which an object can be moved.
- The mechanical advantage of a lever is represented by the ratio of the length of the force arm to the resistance arm.
- To be most effective, the force must be directed at right angles to the lever.

Appendix E
Concepts and Principles of Motor Learning

Feedback

- Feedback improves the learning of motor skills by providing error detection and motivation for the learner.
- Feedback should be based on the critical elements of each skill.
- Only one or two corrections should be identified for each performance.
- Feedback should be delayed for a few seconds after the performance to give the performer an opportunity to reflect on his or her own performance.
- Feedback should be given when the performer cannot see the result of the performance (e.g., technique).
- Feedback should not be given when the performer can see the result of the performance (e.g., accuracy, speed, or distance).
- Feedback is most helpful when it is specific and meaningful.
- Feedback should be given frequently in the early stages of learning and then taper off.

Stages of Learning

Stage One:

Consistent practice should be given for both open and closed skills.
Feedback should be provided on the intent of the skill.
Model demonstrations and information related to the skill should be provided.
Focus should be on success.

Stage Two:

Feedback should be provided on the refinement of the movement.
Focus should be on critical cues.
Numerous practice opportunities should be provided.
Distributed practice should be used.

Stage Three:

Focus should be on the use of the skill in performance situations (e.g., offensive/defensive strategies).
Focus should be on the refinement of skills.
Focus should be on consistency for closed skills and flexibility for open skills.
Variable practice should be used.

Source: Bonnie Mohnsen, *Teaching Middle School Physical Education* (Second edition). Champaign, IL: Human Kinetics Publishers, 2003.

Mental/Physical Practice

- Mental rehearsal can increase skill performance.
- Physical practice should be used before mental practice.
- Physical practice is better than mental practice.

Accuracy and Speed Practice

- When learners practice skills where both speed and accuracy are important, equal and simultaneous emphasis should be placed on speed and accuracy (e.g., moderate speed and moderate accuracy).

Goal Setting

- Setting goals based on current ability improves the learning of motor skills.
- Monitoring a change in motor skill development based on the type of improvement desired (e.g., accuracy, distance, technique) improves the learning of motor skills.
- Goals should be clear, measurable, and achievable.

Transfer of Learning

- Positive transfer occurs when previous learning has a favorable effect on new learning.
- Negative transfer occurs when prior learning interferes with learning new information or skills, or new skills interfere with previously learned tasks.
- The more closely related one skill is to another, the more likely the transfer of learning (e.g., throwing a variety of objects).
- Greater positive transfer occurs when the first task is well learned.
- Greater positive transfer occurs when similarities are pointed out to the learner.
- Transfer from practice to the game is subject to the same element issues as transfer from skill to skill.

Whole/Part Practice

- Most skills should be practiced as a whole to maintain the rhythm of the skill.
- If a skill is practiced in parts, it should be practiced as a whole as quickly as possible.
- Whole practice is used when the skill has highly dependent (integrated) parts, is simple, is not meaningful in parts, and/or is made up of simultaneously performed parts.
- Whole practice is used when the learner is highly skilled, is able to remember long sequences, and/or has a long attention span.
- Part practice is used when the skill has highly independent parts, is made up of individual skills, is very complex, and/or if limited work on certain parts is necessary.
- Part practice is used when the learner has a limited memory span, is unable to concentrate for a long period of time, is having difficulty with a particular part, and/or cannot succeed in the whole practice method.

Mass/Distributed Practice

- Mass practice is used when the skill is complex, has many elements, requires warm-up, and/or is a new skill for the learner.
- Distributed practice is used when the skill is simple, repetitive, boring, demands intense concentration, is fatiguing, and/or demands close attention to detail.
- Mass practice is used when the learner is older or more mature, is able to concentrate for long periods of time, and/or has good ability to focus attention.
- Distributed practice is used when the learner is young or immature, has a short attention span, has poor concentration skills, and/or tires quickly.

Constant/Variable Practice

- Variable practice involves practicing one skill in a variety of settings or conditions.
- Constant practice involves practicing one skill the same way for the entire practice session.
- Constant practice enhances the learning of open skills for beginners and closed skills.
- Variable practice enhances learning of open skills for intermediate and advanced learners.

Blocked/Random Practice

- Blocked practice refers to practicing one skill for a certain amount of time, then a second skill for the same amount of time, and then the third skills for the same amount of time.
- Random practice refers to practicing one skill for a few minutes, then a second skill for a few minutes, then the first skill again, and then the third skill (or some other random order).
- Blocked practiced leads to short-term success.
- Random practice leads to long-term success.

Appendix F

Contraindicated and Alternative Exercises

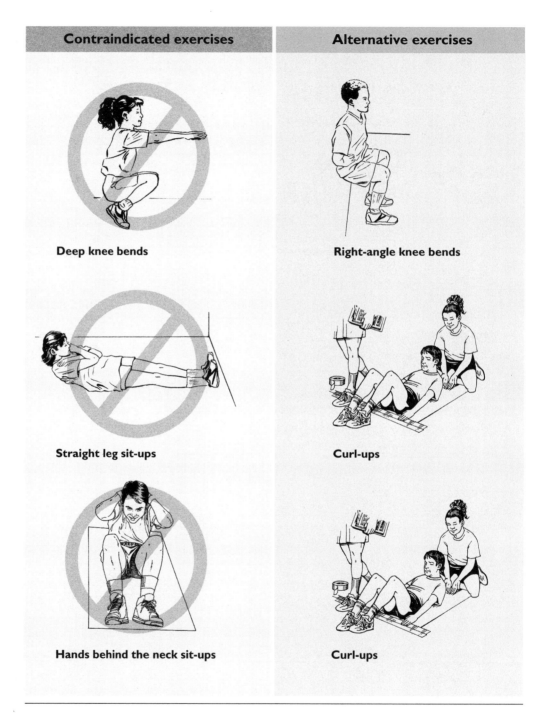

Contraindicated exercises	Alternative exercises
Deep knee bends	Right-angle knee bends
Straight leg sit-ups	Curl-ups
Hands behind the neck sit-ups	Curl-ups

ILLUSTRATION CREDITS

**DEEP KNEE BENDS
STRAIGHT LEG SIT-UPS
RIGHT-ANGLE KNEE BENDS**
Illustrations reprinted
with permission from
©Bonnie's Fitware, Inc.

CURL-UPS
Illustration reprinted with
permission from B. S.
Mohnsen, *Teaching Middle
School Physical Education*
(Champaign, IL: Human
Kinetics), 164. ©1997.

**HANDS BEHIND THE
NECK SIT-UPS**
Illustration courtesy of the
Dover Clip Art Collection.

Sources: Dangerous Exercise Task Cards. Cerritos, CA: Bonnie's Fitware Inc., 2007. Fitness Task Cards. Cerritos, CA: Bonnie's Fitware Inc., 2007.

Contraindicated exercises	Alternative exercises
 **Double leg lift**	 **Curl-ups**
 **Shoulder stand**	**Not needed**
 **The plough**	**Not needed**
 **Standing side bends**	 **Seated side bends**

ILLUSTRATION CREDITS

DOUBLE LEG LIFT
SHOULDER STAND
THE PLOUGH
STANDING SIDE BENDS
SEATED SIDE BENDS
Illustrations reprinted
with permission from
©Bonnie's Fitware, Inc.

CURL-UPS
Illustration reprinted with
permission from B. S.
Mohnsen, *Teaching Middle
School Physical Education*
(Champaign, IL: Human
Kinetics), 164. ©1997.

Contraindicated exercises	Alternative exercises
 Arm circles	 Across-arm stretch
 Windmill	 Back saver sit-and-reach
 Cherry pickers	 Back saver sit-and-reach

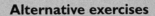

Contraindicated exercises

Alternative exercises

Neck stretch

Neck circles

Butterfly (The Hero) stretch

Lunges

Standing toe touches

Back saver sit-and-reach

ILLUSTRATION CREDITS

NECK CIRCLES
BUTTERFLY STRETCH
STANDING TOE TOUCHES
Illustrations reprinted
with permission from
©Bonnie's Fitware, Inc.

NECK STRETCH
Illustration reprinted
with permission from
C. Hinton, *Fitness for Children*
(Champaign, IL: Human
Kinetics), 51. ©1995.

LUNGES
BACK SAVER SIT-AND-REACH
Illustrations reprinted with
permission from B. S. Mohnsen,
*Teaching Middle School Physical
Education* (Champaign, IL:
Human Kinetics), 164, 318.
©1997.

Contraindicated exercises	Alternative exercises

Hurdler stretch	**Reverse hurdler stretch**

Standing quadriceps stretch	**Lying quadriceps stretch**

Knee pull-down	**Lower back stretch**

ILLUSTRATION CREDITS

**HURDLER STRETCH
STANDING QUADRICEPS
KNEE PULL-DOWN**
Illustrations reprinted
with permission from
©Bonnie's Fitware, Inc

**REVERSE HURDLER STRETCH
LOWER BACK STRETCH**
Illustrations reprinted with
permission from B. S. Mohnsen,
*Teaching Middle School Physical
Education* (Champaign, IL:
Human Kinetics), 317, 318.
©1997.

LYING QUADRICEPS STRETCH
Illustration reprinted with
permission from S. J. Virgilio,
*Fitness Education for Children: A
Team Approach* (Champaign, IL:
Human Kinetics), 162. ©1997.

Appendix G
Standards-Based Report Card, Example #1

The following example is suitable for use in kindergarten through grade eight.

Grade 3 Example

Overarching Physical Education Content Standard	Progress Toward Overarching Standard				Teacher Comments
	1	2	3	4	
Student demonstrates the motor skills and movement patterns needed to perform a variety of physical activities.				X	Jamie performs above standard on the following skills: chasing, fleeing, tripod, forward roll, straddle roll, jumping a rope, balancing, catching, rolling, throwing, kicking, striking, dribbling, foot dribbling, and line dancing.
Student demonstrates knowledge of movement concepts, principles, and strategies that apply to the learning and performance of physical activities.			X		Jamie has met the standard on understanding of game strategies, dance, and critical features for catching, throwing, rolling, and dribbling.
Student assesses and maintains a level of physical fitness to improve health and performance.			X		Jamie has the met the standard for participation in physical activity and improving muscular strength/endurance and flexibility.
Student demonstrates knowledge of physical fitness concepts, principles, and strategies to improve health and performance.		X			Jamie is below the standard in understanding of fitness concepts. Specifically, Jamie needs a better understanding of dangerous exercises, fitness components, benefits of a stronger heart, and name/location of major muscles.
Student demonstrates and utilizes knowledge of psychological and socio-logical concepts, principles, and strategies that apply to the learning and perfor-mance of physical activity.			X		Jamie has met the standard for goal setting and monitoring progress, safety procedures, working with others, respecting individual differences, and using words of encouragement.

4 = Advanced   3 = Proficient   2 = Approaching   1 = Below

Appendix H
Standards-Based Report Card, Example #2

The following example is suitable for kindergarten through grade twelve.

Grade 3 Example

	Specific Standard	Overarching Standard
Standard 1. Students demonstrate the motor skills and movement patterns needed to perform a variety of physical activities.		4
1.1 Identify and demonstrate square dance steps, positions, and patterns set to music.	5	
1.2 Create and perform a square dance.	4	
1.3 Demonstrate basic offensive and defensive skills and strategies in team physical activities.	5	
1.4 Apply locomotor, nonlocomotor, and manipulative skills to team physical activities.	6	
1.5 Demonstrate fundamental gymnastic/tumbling skills	4	
1.6 Create and perform a routine using fundamental gymnastic/tumbling skills, locomotor and nonlocomotor movement patterns, and the elements of speed, direction, and level.	5	
Standard 2. Students demonstrate knowledge of movement concepts, principles, and strategies that apply to the learning and performance of physical activities.		3
2.1 Describe and demonstrate how movement skills learned in one physical activity can be transferred and used to help learn another physical activity.	3	
2.2 Explain the rotation principles used in performing various manipulative skills.	4	
2.3 Explain how growth in height and weight affects performance and influences the selection of developmentally appropriate physical activities.	5	

1 – Initial attempt at the standard
2 – Beginning to move toward standard
3 – Moving toward standard
4 – Meets the standard
5 – Exceeds the standard
6 – Greatly exceeds the standard

	Specific Standard	Overarching Standard
2.4 Identify the characteristics of a highly skilled performance for the purpose of improving one's own performance.	3	
2.5 Diagram, explain, and justify offensive and defensive strategies in modified and team sports, games, and activities.	6	
2.6 Develop and teach a team game that uses elements of spin or rebound, designated offensive and defensive space, a penalty system, and a scoring system.	4	
Standard 3. Students assess and maintain a level of physical fitness to improve health and performance.		4
3.1 Assess the components of health-related physical fitness (muscle strength, muscle endurance, aerobic capacity, flexibility, and body composition) by using a scientifically based health-related physical fitness assessment.	4	
3.2 Refine individual personal physical fitness goals for each of the five components of health-related physical fitness, using research-based criteria.	4	
3.3 Plan and implement a two-week personal physical fitness plan in collaboration with the teacher.	5	
3.4 Participate in moderate to vigorous physical activity a minimum of four days each week.	4	
3.5 Assess periodically the attainment of, or progress toward, personal physical fitness goals and make necessary adjustments to a personal physical fitness program.	4	
3.6 Participate safely in moderate to vigorous physical activity when conditions are atypical (weather, travel, injury).	4	
Standard 4. Students demonstrate knowledge of physical fitness concepts, principles, and strategies to improve health and performance.		5
4.1 Develop a two-week personal physical fitness plan specifying the proper warm-up and cool-down activities and the principles of exercise for each of the five components of health-related physical fitness.	5	
4.2 Identify appropriate physical activities that can be performed if one's physical fitness program is disrupted by inclement weather, travel from home or school, or a minor injury.	5	

	Specific Standard	Overarching Standard
4.3 Identify ways of increasing physical activity in routine daily activities.	6	
4.4 Identify and apply basic principles in weight/resistance training and safety practices.	5	
4.5 Explain the effects of nutrition and participation in physical activity on weight control, self-concept, and physical performance.	5	
4.6 Explain the different types of conditioning for different physical activities.	5	
Standard 5. Students demonstrate and utilize knowledge of psychological and sociological concepts, principles, and strategies that apply to the learning and performance of physical activity.		3
5.1 Abide by the decisions of the officials, accept the outcome of the game, and show appreciation toward participants.	3	
5.2 Organize and work cooperatively with a group to achieve the goals of the group.	4	
5.3 Identify and evaluate three preferences for lifelong physical activity and determine one's responsibility for developing skills, acquiring knowledge of concepts, and achieving fitness.	5	
5.4 Identify the contributions of members of a group or team and reward members for accomplishing a task or goal.	4	
5.5 Accept the roles of group members within the structure of a game or activity.	3	
5.6 Describe leadership roles and responsibilities in the context of team games and activities.	3	
5.7 Model support toward individuals of all ability levels and encourage others to be supportive and inclusive of all individuals.	3	

Appendix I
Adapted Physical Education Pre-referral Checklist

A parent, teacher, nurse, or other concerned school staff member may request observation of the motor skills of a student or consultation with the adapted physical education specialist.

Date of request: _____ Referred by: _____

Student's name: _____ Birth date: _____ Grade: _____

School: _____Teacher:_____Room No.: _____

Parent or legal guardian: _____

Home address:_____

Telephone No.(Home): _____ (Work)_____

Language spoken at home: _____

Recess/lunch times: _____PE days and times:_____

Reason for referral/ specify areas of concern: _____

_____

_____

Pertinent medical information (if any):_____

_____

Does the student receive any other special education services? Yes _____ No _____

What services? _____

Difficulty in performing the various motor skills listed below **MAY** indicate a need for adapted physical education services. Please check all that apply in relation to the grade-level physical education standards and as observed in physical education lessons as well as free-play opportunities (recess).

Skill	Can	Most of the time	Often	Some of the time	Cannot
Balance on one foot (2 seconds)					
Hop					
Jump					
Skip					
Gallop					
Slide					

Skill	Can	Most of the time	Often	Some of the time	Cannot
Run					
Bounce and catch to self					
Dribble a ball with hands					
Catch a ball with hands					
Throw a ball 15 feet					
Kick a stationary ball					
Kick a rolled ball					
Hit a ball off a batting "T"					
Jump rope turned by others					
Turn own jump rope					
Falls excessively					
Awkward and clumsy when moving					

Please return this completed form to the adapted physical education specialist at your school or district office. Receipt of form will be acknowledged through an appropriate line of communication, such as e-mail.

Appendix J
Quality Indicators
Physical Education Standards-Based Instruction

Planning	Warm-up	Instruction	Activity/Practice	Closure	Class Management
Standard is identified.	Type of warm-up matches lesson requirement.	Standard is identified.	There are sufficient opportunities for practice of standards skill.	Standard is revisited.	Roll call is taken efficiently.
Standard is appropriate to the grade level.	Physical warm-up precedes strenuous activity.	There is an accurate explanation or demonstration of standards-related skill.	Activity is well organized for multiple practice opportunities.	Students are attentive to closing words.	Students are on task.
Teacher has background knowledge to teach standard.	There are no contraindicated exercises.	Standard is broken down for less-skilled students.	Teacher circulates through all areas.		Students are active at least 50% of time.
There is a management plan for behavior.	Moderate to vigorous physical activity occurs three to four times a week.	Planned activities are accomplished.	Teacher gives standard-specific feedback to students.		Equipment is collected efficiently.
		Assessment of student learning is accomplished.			Students interact respectfully with peers and teacher.
					There are equal opportunities for both genders.

Highlight the indicators observed. It is not expected that all indicators will be observable during all lessons.

Appendix K
Careers in Physical Education

The following list contains a sample of careers in physical education and related fields.

Adapted Physical Education Teacher

Elementary school, middle school, high school, community college, college, and university; non-profit agencies, therapeutic recreation, community organizations, and social service agencies

Athletic Coach

Elementary school, middle school, high school, community college, college, and university; professional and amateur sports; public park and recreation agencies, community organizations

Athletic Trainer

Elementary school, middle school, high school, community college, college, and university; professional and amateur sports; public park and recreation agencies, community organizations

Chiropractic Services

Professional services, hospitals, clinics, and skilled-nursing facilities

Corporate Fitness

Employee services

Dance Teacher

Elementary school, middle school, high school, community college, college, and university; public park and recreation agencies, nonprofit agencies, therapeutic recreation, and campus recreation

Exercise/Sport Physiologist

Elementary school, middle school, high school, community college, college, and university; nonprofit agencies, therapeutic recreation, community organizations, and social service agencies; professional and amateur sports; and sporting goods firms

Geriatric Fitness

College and university, hospitals, and skilled-nursing facilities

---

Adapted from Charles B. Corbin, *Fitness for Life*, 1990, pp. 226–227, and Daryl Siedentop, ed., *Introduction to Physical Education, Fitness, and Sport* (Seventh edition), 2004, pp. 381–408.

Health Educator

Elementary school, middle school, high school, community college, college, and university; hospitals, clinics, community organizations, nonprofit agencies, employee services, and social service agencies

Leisure Services

Public park and recreation agencies, nonprofit agencies, employee services, private-membership clubs, commercial recreation, therapeutic recreation, and campus recreation

Occupational Therapist

Hospitals, clinics, community organizations, nonprofit agencies, employee services, skilled-nursing facilities, and public and private schools

Physical Education Teacher/Professor

Elementary physical education specialist, middle school, high school, community college, college, and university

Physical Therapist

Hospitals, clinics, community organizations, nonprofit agencies, employee services, skilled-nursing facilities, and public and private schools

Sports Law

Expert witness, lawyer, and college and university

Sports Management

College, professional, and amateur sports; social service agency sports programs, community recreation sports programs; sport marketing, management, and communications firms; and sporting goods firms

Sports Medicine

College, professional, and amateur sports

Sports Psychologist

College, professional, and amateur sports

Appendix L

Online Resources

The following list of resources may assist administrators and teachers with the design, implementation, and evaluation of physical education instruction. Many of the resources are available at no cost on the California Department of Education Web site.

California Department of Education Resources

CDE Home Page
http://www.cde.ca.gov

Curriculum and Instruction: Physical Education
http://www.cde.ca.gov/ci/pe/

Healthy Children Ready to Learn: Facilities Best Practices
http://www.cde.ca.gov/re/pn/fd/documents/hcrtlfacilities.pdf

Physical Education Model Content Standards for California Public Schools
http://www.cde.ca.gov/re/pn/fd/documents/pestandards.pdf

Physical Fitness Testing (PFT)
http://www.cde.ca.gov/ta/tg/pf/

Special Education: Laws, Regulations, & Policies
http://www.cde.ca.gov/sp/se/lr/

Special Education: Services and Resources
http://www.cde.ca.gov/sp/se/sr/

Taking Action for Healthy School Environments: Linking Education, Activity, and Food in California Secondary Schools
http://www.cde.ca.gov/re/pn/fd/documents/takingaction051706.pdf

CDE Facilities Home Page
This site has information to assist school districts and their communities in creating well-planned, K–12 learning environments in safe, clean, and up-to-date schools.
http://www.cde.ca.gov/ls/fa/

Design-Build Projects Guidelines, 2002
http://www.cde.ca.gov/re/pn/fd/documents/dbpguidelines.pdf

Guide to School Site Analysis and Development
http://www.cde.ca.gov/ls/fa/sf/guideschoolsite.asp

Physical Education Guidelines Middle & High School
http://www.cde.ca.gov/ls/fa/sf/peguidemidhi.asp

Physical Education Guidelines - Elementary Schools
http://www.cde.ca.gov/ls/fa/sf/peguideelement.asp

Plan Review Process
http://www.cde.ca.gov/ls/fa/sf/planreview.asp

Small School Site Guidelines
http://www.cde.ca.gov/ls/fa/sf/smallschoolsite.asp

External Resources

American Alliance for Health, Physical Education, Recreation and Dance (AAHPERD)
http://www.aahperd.org

American College of Sports Medicine (ACSM)
http://www.acsm.org/

American Heart Association
http://www.americanheart.org

California Association for Health, Physical Education, Recreation, and Dance (CAHPERD)
http://www.cahperd.org/

California Healthy Kids Resource Center
http://www.californiahealthykids.org/

California Learning Resource Network (CLRN)
http://www.clrn.org

California Playground Safety Regulations
http://www.cdph.ca.gov/healthinfo/injviosaf/pages/californiaplaygroundsafetyregulations.aspx

California Physical Education-Health Project (CPE-HE)
http://csmp.ucop.edu/cpehp/

Centers for Disease Control and Prevention (CDC)
http://www.cdc.gov/

Physical Education Curriculum Analysis Tool (PECAT) http://www.cdc.gov/HealthyYouth/PECAT/index.htm

Overweight & Obesity: Childhood Overweight
http://www.cdc.gov/nccdphp/dnpa/obesity/childhood/index.htm

Healthy Youth! School Health Guidelines & Strategies
http://www.cdc.gov/HealthyYouth/publications/Guidelines.htm

Physical Activity and the Health of Young People
http://www.cdc.gov/HealthyYouth/physicalactivity/pdf/facts.pdf

Body and Mind (BAM)
http://www.bam.gov/

Governor's Council on Physical Fitness & Sports
http://www.activeca.org/

MyPyramid (Food Pyramid)
http://www.mypyramid.gov/

National Association for Sport & Physical Education (NASPE)
http://www.aahperd.org/naspe/

National Athletic Trainers' Association (NATA)
http://www.nata.org

National Board for Professional Teaching Standards
http://www.nbpts.org

National Center for Education Statistics (NCES)
http://nces.ed.gov/

   Calories In, Calories Out: Food and Exercise in Public Elementary
   Schools, 2005
      http://nces.ed.gov/pubsearch/pubsinfo.asp?pubid=2006057

National Dance Association (NDA)
http://www.aahperd.org/nda/

National Marfan Foundation (NFM)
http://www.marfan.org

   Physical Activity and Exercise for People with Marfan Syndrome
   http://www.marfan.org/nmf/GetSubContentRequestHandler.do?sub_menu_
   item_content_id=43&menu_item_id=7

State Council on Adapted Physical Education (SCAPE)
http://www.cahperd.org/sections/scape/

Tolerance.org
http://www.tolerance.org/

   Bullying: Guidelines for Teachers
   http://www.tolerance.org/teach/activities/activity.jsp?ar=768

U.S. Consumer Product Safety Commission
http://www.cpsc.gov/

   Handbook for Public Playground Safety
   http://www.cpsc.gov/cpscpub/pubs/325.pdf

U.S. Department of Agriculture: MyPyramid
http://www.mypyramid.gov

Appendix M
Guidelines for Facilities

The guidelines are intended to provide district and school personnel with suggestions for the evaluation of current facilities and a beginning checklist for the design, renovation, reconfiguration, and remodel of facilities. The guidelines are not a comprehensive list and will not apply in all circumstances.

Special guidelines for dance studios:

- A resilient wood floor (Injuries commonly occur on hard surfaces.)
- A ceiling high enough to allow for one partner lifting another overhead
- A well-ventilated room equipped with adjustable heating and cooling
- Storage space for materials and equipment
- Theatrical lighting
- Stagecraft areas
- Sound systems
- Adequate drinking water

Special guidelines for fitness labs:

- Wiring for technology equipment use, including multiple electrical outlets, interior wiring, and wiring to meet the requirements of fitness equipment
- A plan for future technology needs
- Internet access, hard wired or wireless
- Water fountains
- Adequate drinking water
- Adequate station numbers
- Audiovisual and sound system
- Display space for posters
- Air conditioning, fans, and adequate ventilation
- Padding, where appropriate
- Large enough space to move safely and to have safety zones, especially around treadmills
- Proper flooring for weights and weight machines
- Adequate storage for loose equipment, including aerobic steps, weights, physio-balls, etc., both to maintain the equipment and provide for the safety of those using the facility

Special guidelines for gymnasiums:

- Provide lighting systems that allow for darkness and return to full power with minimal wait time, sectional lighting patterns that allow for lights to be dimmed in the area of the instructional facilities using technology, and adjustable window coverings to lower natural light

- Provide wiring for technology equipment use (e.g., multiple electrical outlets, interior wiring, and wiring to meet the electrical needs of fitness equipment) and to allow for future needs
- Internet access, hard wired or wireless
- Audiovisual systems
- Whiteboards, interactive whiteboards, document camera projectors, or other display devices for academic instruction
- Adequate drinking water
- Adequate restroom facilities
- Appropriate padding for walls and equipment
- Adequate storage of equipment
- Adequate space for instruction
- Facility can be used for a variety of standards-aligned physical education activities (e.g., floor/wall markings)

Special guidelines for field space:

- Regularly watered and maintained
- Marked with boundary and field lines
- Free of holes and level
- Consider artificial turf
- Backstops placed appropriately
- Pop-up sprinklers
- Free of standing water

Special guidelines for computer lab:

- Mobile laptop carts
- Sufficient wiring and outlets

Special guidelines for locker rooms:

- A floor plan that allows for adequate supervision
- Space for storage of personal belongings
- Adequate number of changing rooms
- Determine whether to install showers

Special guidelines for climbing wall/challenge course/adventure course:

- Courses are designed and built by a recognized challenge course program. Courses built in living trees or from wood may require more maintenance.
- Secure fencing and storage should be provided for challenge course equipment. Tightly controlled access is necessary for high elements, especially when ropes are in place.
- Ground surface under the challenge course is wood chips or well-irrigated grass. Sand or dirt is not appropriate because the particles can get into the rope fibers and weaken the rope. Mats are not recommended under high elements because they may cause the belayer to trip. Mats may be used under low horizontal climbing walls.

- Physical education teachers should receive extensive training from a recognized challenge course program before conducting challenge course activities.
- Safety equipment (ropes, harnesses, helmets, carabineers, belay devices, and any other equipment used in the belay process) is maintained.
- Challenge course equipment is inspected regularly. The teacher inspects each element of the course and all safety equipment daily. The structure of the course and all safety equipment are inspected annually by a certified challenge course inspector.

Glossary

academic content knowledge—The knowledge of the physical education discipline; concepts and principles related to motor development, motor learning, biomechanics, exercise physiology, sport psychology, sport sociology, sport history, and sport philosophy. The content standards for all subjects, including physical education, are based on the disciplinary knowledge of the field.

academic learning time (ALT)—A unit of time during which students are engaged in learning content at an appropriate level of difficulty and in such a way that they have a chance to be successful (Rink 1998; Siedentop 1991).

accommodations—Adaptations that address the needs of the student by removing the effects of the disability but not altering the performance outcome.

accumulated physical activity—The total number of minutes of physical activity performed during a 24-hour period of time. Includes minutes from short periods of activity performed during the day and the physical activity done in "bouts" (longer periods of time).

adapted physical education—A physical education program designed to meet the unique needs of an individual with a disability who is unable to fully participate in the general physical education program.

adventure/outdoor activities—Physical activities centered in natural settings. Examples include orienteering, backpacking, hiking, rope activities, canoeing, cycling, skating, and rock climbing.

aesthetic dimension—Refers to space, time, energy, and flow.

aesthetics—The understanding and appreciation of beauty in human movement.

aerobic activity—Exercise that can be performed for a long duration because the energy required can be provided by the burning of fuel, which normally occurs in muscle cells in the presence of oxygen. Aerobic activity may help control body weight, reduce the percentage of body fat, improve the circulatory function and respiratory functions, and reduce blood pressure. Examples include aerobic dance, cycling, jogging, power walking, in-line skating, step aerobics, kickboxing, and super circuit.

agility—A skill-related component of fitness that describes the ability to rapidly change the position of the entire body.

alignment—Clear and direct relationship among standards, curricula, instructional materials, instructional methods, and assessments.

anaerobic activity—Exercise of short duration that is performed at a more strenuous level, so increased respiration and heart rate cannot provide sufficient oxygen to the muscle cells. Examples of anaerobic activity include sprinting, weight training, curl-ups, gymnastics, and some team activities, such as softball and football.

assessment—The process of gathering evidence about a student's level of achievement.

balance—A skill-related component of fitness that relates to the maintenance of equilibrium while stationary or moving.

base of support—The area of the base or foundation that supports the body. The base of support may include one or more body parts and the distance between them. The ability to stabilize the body is directly proportional to the area of the base of support. For example, if two feet are close together, the base of support is narrow and stability is limited. If the two feet are separated by some distance, the base of support is larger and provides more stability.

basic resistance principles—Resistance is the weight or force that is used to oppose a motion. Resistance training increases muscle strength by pitting the muscles against a weight, such as a dumbbell or barbell. The type of lift; intensity, volume, and variety of training; progressive overload; rest; and recovery constitute the basic principles of resistance training.

biomechanics—The study of human movement and how such movement is influenced by gravity, friction, and the laws of motion. It involves the analysis of force, including muscle force that produces movements and impact force that may cause injuries. It explains why motor skills are performed in explicit ways in order to improve efficiency and effectiveness.

body composition—The proportion of fat-free mass (e.g., muscle, bone, vital organs, and tissues) to fat mass in the body.

body management—Basic skills focusing on the ability to control the body and body parts in actions such as those involving traveling, balancing, rolling, and supporting body weight.

body mass index (BMI)—A formula used to assess body fat based on a ratio between height and weight.

body orientation—The direction that the body is facing.

cardiovascular endurance—A component of health-related fitness that describes the ability of the heart, blood vessels, and respiratory system to supply oxygen and nutrients to the muscles during exercise.

circle dance—A dance performed in a circle.

closed skill—Motor skills that are performed in an environment that is stable and predictable.

cognate—A word related to one in another language; a word sharing an ancestral root with another word.

collaborative consultation—A process for providing services to special education students in which adapted physical education specialists collaborate with regular education staff, general classroom teachers, teachers of special education, and other school professionals and/or paraprofessionals and parents to plan, implement and evaluate interventions carried out in the adapted, regular, modified or specially designed physical education program for the purpose of ensuring each student's success in the educational system.

combative activities—A group of physical activities that utilize basic combatives— pulling, pushing, stands, and guards. Some examples include wrestling, fencing, kickboxing, martial arts, and self-defense.

competence—Sufficient ability, skill, and knowledge to meet the demands of a particular task.

complex skills—Skills that combine two or more locomotor and/or manipulative fundamental movements (for example, catching and throwing or trapping and passing).

components of health-related physical fitness—Muscle strength, muscle endurance, aerobic capacity, flexibility, and body composition.

content standards—What students should know and be able to do at the end of every grade level. Content standards represent the academic content of the discipline of kinesiology.

content standards matrix—A holistic view of all standards across all grade levels.

contraindicated—Is not advisable, should not be done.

contraindicated exercises—Exercises that are dangerous and should not be done.

cool-down exercises—Five to ten minutes of light to moderate physical activity. Cool-down exercises help the body recover from exercise. This process maintains blood pressure, helps enhance venous return, and prevents blood from pooling in the muscles.

coordination—A skill-related component of fitness that relates to the ability to perform tasks smoothly and accurately.

core muscles—The abdominal, back, hip, and pelvic floor muscles.

critical elements—Those elements of performing a skill deemed necessary for its correct execution. Also referred to as critical features.

criterion-referenced assessment—Describes how well a student performs compared with a predetermined and specified standard of performance, as opposed to a norm-referenced assessment where a student's performance is compared with a normative sample of other students.

cues—Short phrases that describe the correct technique for performing a skill.

dehydration—The loss of water and important blood salts, such as potassium and sodium, that are essential for vital organ functions.

developmental stages—Children pass through three stages before they can demonstrate the mature form for a movement or motor skill: initial stage, elementary stage, and mature stage.

disability—The term "child with a disability" means a child with mental retardation, a hearing impairment (including deafness), speech or language impairment, a visual impairment (including blindness), a serious emotional disturbance (referred to as "emotional disturbance"), an orthopedic impairment, autism, traumatic brain injury, an other health impairment, a specific learning disability, deaf-blindness, or multiple disabilities; and who by reason thereof, needs special education and related services.

distributed practice—Spreading practice time across several shorter practice sessions.

dual activities—Physical activities that require two participants. Examples include tennis, racquetball, and badminton.

egg roll—A roll toward the right and then toward the left while in a tucked position.

elementary stage of development—The stage of skill development during which coordination and rhythmical performance improve and the performer gains greater control over their movement. The performance, however, is still somewhat awkward and lacking in fluidity.

embedded assessment—Assessment that occurs simultaneously with instruction.

equipment—Refers to those items that are not considered expendable but are used for a period of years, such as fitness and gymnastics equipment.

ergogenic aids—Substances, devices, or practices that enhance an individual's energy use, production, or recovery.

evaluation—Judging the quality of a performance.

even-beat locomotor skills—Skills performed to a regular beat (for example, walking, running, hopping, and jumping).

exercise—Physical activity conducted with the intention of developing physical fitness.

feedback—Information that is given to the learner about performance (internal or external); this can be knowledge of performance or knowledge of results. See also specific feedback, specific corrective feedback, and specific positive feedback.

F.I.T.T. principles/concepts—An acronym for the exercise variables necessary for gaining and maintaining physical fitness: frequency, intensity, time, and type of physical activities.

flexibility—A component of health-related fitness that describes the range of motion at a joint. The ability to move joints of the body through a normal range of motion.

folk dance—A dance that has been developed through the traditions of culture and has been passed down from generation to generation.

frequency—A principle of training that establishes how often to exercise.

fundamental movement skills—Basic movements that involve the combination of movement patterns of two or more body segments. Locomotor, nonlocomotor, and manipulative skills are all considered fundamental, as they form the basis of numerous forms of specialized movement and manipulative skills.

gallop—A step together step in a forward direction with the same foot always leading.

general space—Refers to the area surrounding personal space.

graphic organizer—A visual representation of information, with the purpose of organizing the material into a usable format.

group dynamics—The interactions and interrelationships of people in a group.

health—Optimal well-being that contributes to the quality of life. It is more than freedom from disease and illness. Optimal health includes high-level mental, social, emotional, spiritual, and physical wellness within the limits of one's heredity and personal abilities.

health-related physical fitness—Consists of those components of physical fitness that have a relationship to good health: body composition, aerobic capacity, flexibility, muscle endurance, and muscle strength.

hip abductors—Muscles that move the leg away from the midline of the body.

hip adductors—Muscles that move the leg toward the midline of the body.

hop—To take off and land on the same foot.

horizontal slice—An informal way to describe sequence. A way to use/see the content standards that represents one content standard across all grade levels.

hyperextension—Greater-than-normal stretching or straightening of an extended limb.

hyperflexion—Bending a joint beyond its normal range of motion.

hypokinetic—Lack of exercise or physical activity.

hypokinetic diseases—Diseases that develop through poor diet, lack of exercise, and a sedentary lifestyle. Examples include heart disease, high blood pressure, obesity, diabetes, and osteoporosis (Sidentop 2004, 168).

impact force—The slap or jolt a person senses when contact sharply changes the motion of an object, as when a ball is caught, or contact sharply changes the motion of the person, as when a jumper strikes the ground. Impact force is related to the pressure, the force per unit area (in Newtons per square meter) sustained by the part of the body in contact. For a given change of motion, the product of the force (in Newtons) required and the time over which the change occurs is a constant. To reduce the impact force when a ball is caught, one can either take longer to slow the ball, which reduces the force required and therefore the pressure; or one can increase the area of one's body in contact with the ball (two hands are better than one). To reduce the impact force when a jumper lands, the jumper cannot lock knees but must bend them; bending the knees increases the time over which the body is brought to rest, and reduces the force the ground has to apply to the soles of the feet, and the force that is thus transmitted through the ankles, knees, and hips.

indicators of increased capacity—Responses of the body due to changes in the intensity of, duration of, frequency of, or time spent participating in physical activity. Indicators may consist of changes in muscle fatigue, breathing, and heart rate.

individual activity—Physical activities that require only one participant. Examples include weight training, yoga, archery, and jogging.

individuality—A principle of training that takes into account the particular needs and abilities of the individual for whom it is designed.

initial stage of development—The stage of development during which the first observable and purposeful attempts at performing a skill are made.

intensity—A principle of training that establishes how hard to exercise.

interpersonal communication skills—Verbal or nonverbal abilities that allow the sharing of feelings, thoughts, and information with another person in a positive manner.

interpersonal social skills—Skills that enhance the ability to work together, including cooperation, respect, and encouragement.

jump—To take off from both feet and land on one or both feet.

large-muscle groups—Muscles that work together and have a large mass relative to other muscle groups in the body. Examples of large-muscle groups are the muscles in the arms, back, and legs.

lead-up game—A game that involves one or more skills or strategies of a sport.

leap—A light transfer of weight from one foot to the other foot. To spring through the air from one point to another.

level—The position of the body or an apparatus relative to the floor.

line dance—A dance in which individuals line up without partners and follow a choreographed pattern of steps, usually performed to country music.

locomotor skills—Basic motor skills involving a change of position of the feet and/or a change of direction of the body. Locomotor skills include walking, running, hopping, skipping, jumping, leaping, sliding, and galloping.

log roll—A side roll in which the performer is in an extended position.

long-handled implement—A piece of equipment used in performing motor skills. The long handle positions the hand some distance away from the surface of the implement that comes in contact with the ball. Some examples include a hockey stick, softball bat, tennis racquet, and lacrosse stick.

low organized games—Activities that have a few simple rules and that require little or no equipment.

manipulative movements—Basic motor skills involving handling an object. Examples include throwing, catching, kicking, trapping, rolling, dribbling, striking, and volleying.

massed practice—The continuous practice of a skill for a long period of time.

mature form—The critical elements of a skill, performed in a smooth and continuous motion.

mature stage—The stage of development characterized by the integration of all component parts of a pattern of movement into a well-coordinated, technically correct form.

moderate physical activity—Moderate-intensity physical activity generally requires sustained rhythmic movements and refers to a level of effort a healthy individual might expend while, for example, walking briskly, dancing, swimming, or bicycling on level terrain. A person should feel some exertion but should be able to carry on a conversation comfortably during the activity.

modification—Adaptations that address the needs of the student by fundamentally altering the performance outcome.

modified/lead-up game—Active games that involve the use of two or more of the sport skills, rules, or procedures used in playing the official sport.

motor development—The study of change in movement behaviors and motor skills across the life span.

motor learning—The study of change in a person's ability to perform a motor skill.

motor skills—A skill that requires voluntary body and/or limb movement to achieve its goal. A skill where the primary determinant of success is the movement component itself. Physical activity that is directed toward a specific function or goal. The term may be used to refer to one discrete skill (e.g., throwing) or a more general ability to perform physical skills competently (e.g., as in "The student has the motor skill needed to perform that sport") (NASPE 2004).

movement concepts—The ideas used to modify or enrich the range and effectiveness of the skills employed. They involve learning how, where, and with what the body moves.

movement patterns—An organized series of related movements.

multicultural dance—A dance that originated from cultural or ethnic traditions. Typically refers to an instructional unit that includes dances that originated from two or more cultural or ethnic groups.

muscle endurance—The ability to contract the muscles many times without tiring or the ability to hold one contraction for an extended period.

muscle strength—The ability of a muscle to exert force against a resistance one time. Strength is measured as the amount of force a muscle can produce.

nonlocomotor movements—Movement of the body performed from a relatively stable base of support. Examples include bending, stretching, twisting, turning, leaning, swaying, and swinging.

open skills—Motor skills that are performed in a changing environment.

overload—A principle of training that establishes a minimum threshold and requires one to exceed that threshold to benefit from the chosen physical activity.

perceived exertion index—A way of rating how hard one feels the body is working during physical activity. It is based on physical sensations experienced, including increased heart rate, increased respiration or breathing rate, increased sweating, and muscle fatigue.

performance standard—Answers the question "How good is good enough?"

personal space—Space that extends outward to the farthest reach of all body parts.

physical activity—Bodily movement that is produced by the contraction of skeletal muscle and that substantially increases energy expenditure, including exercise, sport, dance, and other movement forms.

physical education—The sequential educational program that teaches students to:
- Understand and participate in regular physical activity that assists in developing and maintaining physical fitness throughout their lifetimes.
- Understand and improve their motor skills.
- Enjoy using their skills and knowledge to establish a healthy lifestyle.
- Understand how their bodies work.

physical fitness—A positive state of well-being with a low risk of premature health problems and with the energy to participate in a variety of physical activities. It is influenced by regular, vigorous physical activity, genetic makeup, and nutritional adequacy.

pickleball—A mini-tennis game played by two or four people on a badminton-sized court using wood paddle racquets and a plastic baseball with holes.

plyometric exercise—A muscular activity that involves an eccentric contraction (muscle is lengthened) of a muscle, followed immediately by a concentric contraction (muscle is shortened) of the same muscle. Plyometric exercises are often used to increase power.

power—A skill-related component of fitness that relates to the rate at which one can perform work.

principle of individual differences—Each individual is different and will require a somewhat unique fitness plan.

principle of overload—Increasing the work and stress that are normally experienced will improve one's fitness.

principle of progression—A progressive increase in the level of exercise is more effective.

principle of regularity—Exercise must be performed on an ongoing basis to be effective.

principle of specificity—Specific exercises must be performed to improve each component of health-related fitness.

principles of training/principles of exercise—Principles to follow in planning an exercise program to effect physiological changes in the human body related to health and performance: individual differences, overload, progression, regularity, and specificity.

progression—A principle of training that establishes increases in the amount and intensity of physical activity needed to provide improvement over periods of time.

proprioception—The ability to sense the position, location, and orientation of the body.

rating of perceived exertion (RPE)—The Borg Rating of Perceived Exertion (RPE), or Borg Scale, is a measure from 6 to 20 that a person can use to describe how hard one feels the body is working. Practitioners generally agree that moderate physical activity has a perceived exertion rating of 12 to 14 on the Borg Scale. http://sportsmedicine.about.com/cs/strengthening/a/030904.htm

reaction time—A component of skill-related fitness that describes the interval of time from a suddenly presented stimulus until the beginning of the response.

rebound principles—Newton's Third Law: An object, when struck, will rebound in the opposite direction with the same amount of force with which it was hit.

recovery rate—The time necessary for an exercise-induced elevated heart rate to return to a normal resting heart rate.

regularity—A principle of training that establishes exercise on a regular schedule. A pattern of physical activity is regular if activities are performed most days of the week, preferably daily; if moderate-intensity activities are performed five or more days of the week; or if vigorous-intensity activities are performed three or more days of the week.

relationship—The position of the body in relation to the floor, apparatus, or other performers.

reliable assessment—An assessment for which the results are consistent when administered to the same individual on different occasions.

resistance principle—The principle that the use of an implement, a device, or the body weight as a resistance can enhance some physical characteristic, such as strength or muscular endurance.

rhythmic skills—Skills that develop an understanding of and a feeling for the elements of rhythm. Examples of physical activities that allow students to express themselves rhythmically include creative movement, folk dance, square dance, and interpretive dance.

short-handled implement—A piece of equipment used in performing motor skills. The short handle allows the hand to be close to the surface of the implement that comes in contact with the ball. Some examples include a racquetball racket, a paddle used in paddle games, and a modified lacrosse stick.

simple skills—Skills that have only one or two parts (for example, running or skipping).

skill-related physical fitness—Those components of physical fitness that relate to an enhanced performance in sports: agility, balance, coordination, power, speed, and reaction time.

skip—A step-hop on one foot and then the other.

slide—A step-together-step in a sideward direction with the same foot always leading.

special education—"Special education means specially designed instruction, at no cost to the parent, to meet the unique needs of a child with a disability, including instruction conducted in the classroom, in the home, in hospitals, and institutions, and in other settings; and instruction in physical education" (U.S. Department of Education 2006. Assistance to states for the education of children with disabilities program and preschool grants for children with disabilities; final rules. *Federal Register, 71,* 34 CFR Parts 300 and 301).

specialized manipulative skills—Fundamental skills that have been adapted to the special requirements of a particular sport, game, or physical activity (e.g., volleyball serve, tennis forearm stroke, badminton clear, basketball layup, soccer trap, softball pitch, golf swing).

specialized movement skills—Fundamental skills that have been adapted to the special requirements of a particular sport, game, or physical activity (e.g., grapevine step, high jump, long jump, hurdles).

specific corrective feedback—Feedback that provides the performer with specific information on how to perform the skill correctly ("You need to step forward on your left foot").

specific feedback—Feedback that provides the performer with specific recommendations on how to perform the skill correctly.

specific positive feedback—Feedback that is positive ("Good job!") and specific ("You stepped forward on the left foot").

specificity—A principle of training that establishes a particular kind of activity for each component of physical fitness.

speed—A skill-related fitness component related to performing movement in a short period of time.

squat—A lower body exercise performed by bending the knees (no lower than a 90-degree angle), lowering the torso, and then rising to a standing position.

stability movements—Stability reflects balance and equilibrium, which are important components in performing many motor skills. Stability movements include those that are vital for the body to maintain balance while moving. Examples include moving the arms while walking or running and lowering one's center of gravity when stopping quickly.

stages of learning—Individuals pass through three stages to become proficient at a motor skill (Fitts and Posner 1967):

- Stage 1 (verbal-cognitive stage): initial stage of learning, in which verbal and cognitive processes predominate.
- Stage 2 (associative or motor stage): stage of learning in which motor programs are developed and the performance becomes increasingly consistent.
- Stage 3 (autonomous stage): an advanced stage of learning in which the learner develops automaticity in action and information processing.

static—A stationary condition. For example, static stretching or static balance.

station teaching—The creation of discrete learning areas where students perform a movement at a station for a designated period of time and then move on to the next station.

strategies—Decisions made by individuals or a team about the overall play of the game.

striking pattern—A fundamental motor skill in which an object is hit with or without an implement.

student discipline plan—Guides student behavior, outlines consequences for inappropriate behavior, and sets goals for student improvement in behavior.

students with special needs—Refers to students who are marginalized in physical education, students whose cultural and religious practices require special consideration, English learners, students with long-term and short-term medical needs, at-risk learners, advanced learners, and students with disabilities.

stunts—Activities that require balance, agility, coordination, weight transfer, and strength. Typically referred to as activities that lead up to tumbling and gymnastics.

supplies—Refers to those materials that are expendable and that need to be replaced at frequent intervals, usually annually, such as basketballs and playground balls.

tactics—Individual movement of players or teams to accomplish an immediate goal or accommodate a situation. Tactics take place within the game as an ongoing part of game play and include decisions an individual makes about when, why, and how to respond to a particular situation.

target heart-rate zone—A safe range of activity intensity that can be used to enhance the level of aerobic capacity.

time—A principle of training that establishes the amount of time for each exercise period.

transitional strategy—Game strategy that occurs during the change of ball possession. It refers to the process or plan used when going from offense to defense or defense to offense.

travel—Movement of the body from one point to another.

triceps push-ups—A reverse push-up performed with the belly up and hands on the floor or on a chair or bench (younger students) or a push-up performed with hands parallel to chest and spaced shoulder-width apart, with elbows tight to the body (older students). A push-up that isolates the triceps.

tripod—A balanced position in which the hands and head are on a floor mat, forming a triangular base of support, and bent knees rest on the elbows.

trunk lift—An exercise performed while lying facedown with hands at sides and toes pointed. The upper body is lifted off the floor slowly keeping the head straight. The head is raised no more than 12 inches off the ground.

type—A principle of training that establishes the specific activity to use or the muscles to target during an exercise period.

uneven-beat locomotor skill—Skills performed to an uneven beat. Examples include galloping, sliding, and skipping.

unpacking a content standard—The process of revealing the content and prerequisite skills needed to learn a content standard. Unpacking reveals the level of performance that is necessary. The verbs in the content standards assist teachers in developing appropriate assessments. Unpacking a standard is similar to backward planning and deconstructing the standards.

Ultimate—A soccer/football-type game played by teams of seven using a flying disc. The goal is to pass the disc to a player in the opposing end zone.

valid assessment—An assessment that measures what it is intended to measure.

variable—Something that can change.

vertical slice—An informal way to describe scope. A way to use or see the content standards that represent all content standards across one grade level.

vigorous physical activity—Vigorous-intensity physical activity generally requires sustained, rhythmic movements and refers to a level of effort a healthy individual might expend while, for example, jogging, participating in high-impact aerobic dancing, swimming continuous laps, or bicycling uphill. Vigorous-intensity physical activity may be intense enough to result in a significant increase in heart and respiration rate.

volley—To strike a ball upward.

warm-up exercises—Low-intensity exercises that prepare the muscular/skeletal system and heart and lungs (cardiorespiratory system) for high-intensity physical activity.

weight-bearing activities—Any activity in which one's feet and legs carry one's own weight. Examples include walking, running, tennis, and aerobic dancing.

Works Cited

American Academy of Pediatrics. 2000. "Physical Fitness and Activity in Schools," *Pediatrics,* Vol. 105, No. 5 (May), 1156–57.

American Academy of Pediatrics. 2003. "Policy Statement: Prevention of Pediatric Overweight and Obesity," *Pediatrics*, Vol. 112, No. 2 (August), 424–30.

Assistance to States for the Education of Children with Disabilities and Preschool Grants for Children with Disabilities: Final Rule. 34 Code of Federal Regulations, Parts 300 and 301. *Federal Register,* Vol. 71, No. 156, Monday, August 14, 2006.

Bassett, David R., et al. 2000. "Validity of Four Motion Sensors in Measuring Moderate Intensity Physical Activity," *Medicine and Science in Sports and Exercise,* Vol. 32, S471–80.

Before It's Too Late: A Report to the Nation from the National Commission on Mathematics and Science Teaching for the 21st Century. 2000. Washington, DC: U.S. Department of Education.

Benbow, Camilla Persson, and Julian C. Stanley. 1996. "Inequity in Equity: How 'Equity' Can Lead to Inequity in High-Potential Students," *Psychology, Public Policy, and Law,* Vol. 2, No. 2, 249–92.

Bonnie's Fitware Inc. 2007. Dangerous Exercise Task Cards. Cerritos, CA.

Bonnie's Fitware Inc. 2007. Fitness Task Cards. Cerritos, CA.

Booth, Frank W., and Manu V. Chakravarthy. 2002. "Cost and Consequences of Sedentary Living: New Battleground for an Old Enemy," *President's Council on Physical Fitness and Sports Research Digest,* Series 3, No. 16 (March), 1–8.

Bouten, Carlijn V., et al. 1997. "Effects of Placement and Orientation of Body-Fixed Accelerometers on the Assessment of Energy Expenditure During Walking," *Medical and Biological Engineering and Computing,* Vol. 35 (January), 50–56.

Brustad, Robert J. 1993. "Who Will Go Out and Play? Parental and Psychological Influences on Children's Attraction to Physical Activity," *Pediatric Exercise Science*, Vol. 5, No. 3, 210–23.

Brustad, Robert J. 1996. "Attraction to Physical Activity in Urban School-children: Parental Socialization and Gender Influences," *Research Quarterly for Exercise and Sport.* Vol. 67, No. 3 (September 1), 316–23.

California School Boards Association. 2006. *Student Wellness: A Healthy Food and Physical Activity Policy Resource Guide.* http://www.csba.org/education issues/educationissues/wellness/wellnesspolicyrequirements.aspx (accessed February 18, 2009).

Corbin, Charles B. 2003. Fitness for Life Physical Activity Pyramid for Children Poster. Champaign, IL: Human Kinetics.

Corbin, Charles B., et al. 2008. *Concepts of Fitness and Wellness: A Comprehensive Lifestyle Approach (*Seventh edition*).* New York: McGraw-Hill.

Corbin, Charles B., and Ruth Lindsey. 1990. *Fitness for Life* (Third Edition). Glenview, IL: Scott, Foresman, and Company

Crouter, Scott E., et al. 2003. "Validity of 10 Electronic Pedometers for Measuring Steps, Distance, and Energy Cost," *Medicine and Science in Sports and Exercise*, Vol. 35, No. 8, 1455–60.

Darling-Hammond, Linda. 1997. *The Right to Learn: A Blueprint for Creating Schools That Work*. San Francisco: Jossey-Bass Publishers.

Echevarria, Jana; Mary Ellen Vogt; and Deborah Short. 2000. *Making Content Comprehensible for English Learners: The SIOP Model*. Boston: Allyn & Bacon.

Etnier, Jennifer L., and Benjamin A. Sibley. 2003. "Exercise and Cognitive Functioning in Humans," *Research Quarterly for Exercise and Sport*.

Etnier, Jennifer L., et al. 1997. "The Influence of Physical Fitness and Exercise upon Cognitive Functioning: A Meta-Analysis," *Journal of Sport and Exercise Physiology*, Vol. 9, No. 3, 249–77.

Evaul, Tom. 2007. Personal Communication to Bonnie Mohnsen, October 2, 2007.

Gallahue, David L. and John C. Ozmun. 2006. *Understanding Motor Development: Infants, Children, Adolescents, Adults* (Sixth edition). Columbus, OH: McGraw-Hill.

Getting Results: Developing Safe and Healthy Kids Update 5: Student Health, Supportive Schools, and Academic Success. 2005. Sacramento: California Department of Education.

Guarino, A. J., et al. 2001. "The Sheltered Instruction Observation Protocol," *Journal of Research in Education*, Vol. 11, No. 1 (Fall), 138–40.

Guide to School Site Analysis and Development. 2000. Sacramento: California Department of Education. http://www.cde.ca.gov/ls/fa/sf/schoolsiteguide.asp (accessed October 12, 2007)

Hager, Ron, and Pat Vehrs. 2006. "Assessment and Interpretation of Body Composition in Physical Education: Should You Use Skinfolds, Bio-Electrical Impedence, or BMI?" *Journal of Physical Education, Recreation and Dance*, Vol. 77, No. 7 (September), 46–51.

Harrison, Joyce M.; Connie L. Blakemore; and Marilyn M. Buck. 2001. *Instructional Strategies for Secondary School Physical Education* (Fifth edition). Boston: McGraw-Hill.

Health, United States, 2005 with Chartbook on Trends in the Health of Americans. 2005. Hyattsville, MD: U.S. Department of Health and Human Services.

Healthy Children Ready to Learn: Facilities Best Practices. 2007. Sacramento: California Department of Education.

Healthy People 2010, "Chapter 22, Physical Activity and Fitness." Centers for Disease Control and Prevention and President's Council on Physical Fitness and Sports. http://www.healthypeople.gov/document/pdf/volume2/22physical.pdf (accessed November 24, 2007).

Jarrett, Olga S., et al. 1998. "Impact of Recess on Classroom Behavior: Group Effects and Individual Differences," *The Journal of Educational Research*, Vol. 92, No. 2 (November 1), 121–26.

Works Cited

Kalakanis, Lisa E., and others. 2001. "Parental Activity as a Determinant of Activity Level and Patterns of Activity in Obese Children," *Research Quarterly for Exercise and Sport,* Vol. 72, No. 3 (September 1, 2001), 202–9.

Langton, Terence W. 2007. "Applying Laban's Movement Framework in Elementary Physical Education," *Journal of Physical Education, Recreation and Dance,* Vol. 78, No. 1 (January), 17–24, 39, 53.

Los Angeles County Office of Education. 1993. *Teacher Expectations and Student Achievement.* Downey, CA: Los Angeles County Office of Education.

Magill, Richard A. 2001. *Motor Learning: Concepts and Applications* (Sixth edition). Boston: McGraw-Hill.

Mei, Zugu, et al. 1998. "Increasing Prevalence of Overweight among US Low-Income Preschool Children: The Centers for Disease Control and Prevention Pediatric Nutrition Surveillance, 1983 to 1995, *Pediatrics,* Vol. 101, No. 1 (January), e12.

Metcalf, B. S., et al. 2002. "Technical Reliability of the CSA Activity Monitor: The Earlybird Study," *Medicine and Science in Sports and Exercise,* Vol. 34, No. 9, 1533–37.

Mohnsen, Bonnie S. 2003. *Teaching Middle School Physical Education* (Second edition). Champaign, IL: Human Kinetics.

Mohnsen, Bonnie S. 2008. *Teaching Middle School Physical Education* (Third edition). Champaign, IL: Human Kinetics.

Morrow, Ronald G., and Diane L. Gill. 2003. "Perceptions of Homophobia and Heterosexism in Physical Education," *Research Quarterly for Exercise and Sport,* Vol. 74, No. 2, 205–14.

NASPE/STARS Criteria for Recognition. 2006. Reston, VA: National Association for Sport and Physical Education.

A Nation at Risk: Obesity in the United States. 2005. Dallas, TX: The Robert Wood Johnson Foundation.

National Association of State Boards of Education. *Fit, Healthy, and Ready to Learn: A School Health Policy Guide.* http://www.nasbe.org/index.php/shs/53-shs-resources/396-fit-healthy-and-ready-to-learn-a-school-health-policy-guide.htm (accessed February 18, 2009).

Ogden Cynthia L., et al. 1997. "Prevalence of Overweight Among Preschool Children in the United States, 1971 through 1994," *Pediatrics,* Vol. 99, No. 4 (April), e1.

Pate, Russell R., et al. 2006. *Promoting Physical Activity in Children and Youth: A Leadership Role for Schools: A Scientific Statement From the American Heart Association Council on Nutrition, Physical Activity, and Metabolism (Physical Activity Committee) in Collaboration With the Councils on Cardiovascular Disease in the Young and Cardiovascular Nursing.* Dallas, TX: American Heart Association.

Payne, V. Gregory, and Larry D. Isaacs. 1995. *Human Motor Development: A Lifespan Approach* (Third edition). Mountain View, CA: Mayfield Publishing Company.

Physical Activity for Everyone: Glossary of Terms. Centers for Disease Control and Prevention. http://www.cdc.gov/physicalactivity/everyone/glossary/index.html (accessed February 18, 2009).

Physical Education for Lifelong Fitness: The Physical Best Teacher's Guide (Second edition). 2005. Champaign, IL: Human Kinetics and National Association for Sport and Physical Education.

Public Playground Safety Handbook. 2008. Publication No. 325. Washington, DC: U.S. Consumer Product Safety Commission.

Rating of Perceived Exertion Scale. http://sportsmedicine.about.com/cs/strengthening/a/030904.htm (accessed November 12, 2008).

Rink, Judith E. 1998. *Teaching Physical Education for Learning* (Third edition). Boston: McGraw-Hill.

Sallis, James F., et al. 1999. "Effects of Health-Related Physical Education on Academic Achievement: Project SPARK," *Research Quarterly for Exercise and Sport*, Vol. 70, No. 2 (June), 127–34.

Schmidt, Richard A., and Craig A. Wrisberg. 2000. *Motor Learning and Performance* (Second edition). Champaign, IL: Human Kinetics.

Schneider, Patrick L., et al. 2003. "Accuracy and Reliability of 10 Pedometers for Measuring Steps Over a 400-m Walk," *Medicine and Science in Sports and Exercise,* Vol. 35, No. 10, 1779–84.

Seaman, Janet, et al. 2007. *Making Connections from Theory to Practice in Adapted Physical Education* (Second edition). Scottsdale, AZ: Holcomb Hathaway.

Siedentop, Daryl, and Deborah Tannehill. 2000. *Developing Teaching Skills in Physical Education* (Fourth edition). Mountain View, CA: Mayfield Publishing Company.

Siedentop, Daryl, ed. 1991. *Developing Teaching Skills in Physical Education* (Third edition). Mountain View, CA: Mayfield Publishing Company.

Siedentop, Daryl, ed. 2004. *Introduction to Physical Education, Fitness, and Sport* (Fifth edition). Boston: McGraw-Hill Publishing Company.

Single-Sex Versus Coeducational School: A Systematic Review. 2005. Washington, DC: Office of Planning, Evaluation, and Policy Development, Policy and Program Studies Service, U.S. Department of Education.

Standards for Evaluating Instructional Materials for Social Content. 2000. Sacramento: California Department of Education.

State Council on Adapted Physical Education. 2003. *Adapted Physical Education Guidelines in California Schools.* http://www.sc-ape.org/Guidelines-Index.htm (accessed February 18, 2009).

State Council on Adapted Physical Education. N.d. *Position Paper on Physical Education Content Standards for Students with a Disability.* Sacramento: California Alliance for Health, Physical Education, Recreation, and Dance. http://sc-ape.org/Practices.htm (accessed October 12, 2007).

A Study of the Relationship Between Physical Fitness and Academic Achievement in California Using 2004 Test Results. 2005. Sacramento: California Department of Education.

The *Superintendent's Task Force on Obesity, Type 2 Diabetes, and Cardiovascular Disease: Final Report.* 2006. Sacramento: California Department of Education. http://www.cde.ca.gov/ls/he/cd

The Surgeon General's Call to Action to Prevent and Decrease Overweight and Obesity. 2001. Rockville, MD. Public Health Service, Office of the Surgeon General, Department of Health and Human Services.

Teaching Large Class Sizes in Physical Education: Guidelines and Strategies. 2006. Reston, VA: National Association for Sport and Physical Education.

Thompson, Donna; Susan Hudson; and Heather Olsen. 2007. *S.A.F.E. Play Areas.* Champaign, IL: Human Kinetics.

United States Department of Health and Human Services. 1996. *Physical Activity and Health: A Report of the Surgeon General.* Atlanta, GA: Centers for Disease Control and Prevention.

United States Department of Health and Human Services. 2000. *Healthy People 2010: Understanding and Improving Health* (Second edition). Washington, DC: U.S. Government Printing Office.

Weiss, Maureen R. 2000. "Motivating Kids in Physical Activity," *President's Council on Physical Fitness and Sports Research Digest,* Series 3, No. 11 (September).

Welk, Greg J. 2002. *Physical Activity Assessments for Health-Related Research.* Champaign, IL: Human Kinetics.

Whitehead, James R. 1993. "Physical Activity and Intrinsic Motivation," *President's Council on Physical Fitness and Sports Research Digest,* Series 1, No. 2.

Wright, W., and Grace G. Karp. 2006. "The Effect of Four Instructional Formats on Aerobic Fitness of Junior-High School Students," *The Physical Educator* (Fall), 143–53.

Additional References

Appropriate Practices for Elementary School Physical Education. 2000. Reston, VA: National Association for Sport and Physical Education.

Appropriate Practices for High School Physical Education. 2004. Reston, VA: National Association for Sport and Physical Education.

Appropriate Practices for Middle School Physical Education. 2001. Reston, VA: National Association for Sport and Physical Education.

Asthana, Anushka. 2006. *Single-sex Schools No Benefit for Girls.* http://www.guardian.co.uk/uk/2006/jun/25/schools.gender (accessed October 6, 2008).

Belben, Cathy. 2002. "How Library Media Specialists Can Promote Physical Fitness and Why They Should," *The Book Report* (November/December), 28–30.

Clark, Jane E., et al. 2005. "Developmental Coordination Disorder: Issues, Identification, and Intervention," *Journal of Physical Education, Recreation and Dance*, Vol. 76, No. 4 (April), 49–53.

Co-curricular Physical Activity and Sport Programs for Middle School Students. 2002. Reston, VA: National Association for Sport and Physical Education.

Datnow, Amanda; Lea Hubbard; and Elisabeth Woody. 2001. *Is Single Gender Schooling Viable in the Public Sector? Lessons from California's Pilot Program. Final Report.* New York: Ford Foundation; Chicago, IL: Spencer Foundation.

Johnson, Lynn V. 2005. "Choosing Appropriate Assessments," *Journal of Physical Education, Recreation and Dance*, Vol. 76, No. 8 (October), 46–47, 56.

Lieberman, Lauren J.; Alisa R. James; and Nicole Ludwa. 2004. "The Impact of Inclusion in General Physical Education for All Students," *Journal of Physical Education, Recreation and Dance*, Vol. 76, No. 5 (May 2004), 37–41, 55.

Mohnsen, Bonnie, ed. 2003 *Concepts and Principles of Physical Education: What Every Student Needs to Know.* Reston, VA: National Association for Sports and Physical Education.

Physical Education and Activity Guidelines. 1999. Port Washington, NY: National Marfan Foundation.

Smith, Shelley Paul. 2005. "Beyond Games, Gadgets and Gimmicks: Differentiating Instruction Across Domains in Physical Education," *Journal of Physical Education, Recreation and Dance*, Vol. 76, No. 8 (October 2005), 38–45.

Smithers, Alan, and Pamela Robinson. 2006. *The Paradox of Single-Sex and Co-Educational Schooling.* Centre for Education and Employment Research, University of Buckingham, England.

Taking Action for Healthy School Environments: Linking Education, Activity, and Food in California Secondary Schools. 2006. Sacramento: California Department of Education.

Understanding the Difference: Is It Physical Education or Physical Activity? N.d. Reston, VA: National Association for Sport and Physical Education. http://www.aahperd.org/naspe/template.cfm?template=difference.html (accessed January 21, 2009).

**Additional
References**

United States Department of Health and Human Services. 2007. *The Surgeon General's Call to Action to Prevent and Decrease Overweight and Obesity Fact Sheet: Overweight in Children and Adolescents.* http://www.surgeongeneral.gov/topics/obesity/calltoaction/fact_adolescents.htm (accessed February 18, 2009).

Wegis, Heidi, and Hans Van Der Mars. 2006. "Integrating Assessment and Instruction: Easing the Process with PDAs," *Journal of Physical Education, Recreation and Dance,* Vol. 7, No. 1 (January 2006), 27–34, 52.

08-008 PR080020-00 5-09 20M

OSP 09 114452